The Interactional Instinct

To Alison,
With warmest
regards,

The Interactional Instinct

The Evolution and Acquisition of Language

Namhee Lee
Lisa Mikesell
Anna Dina L. Joaquin
Andrea W. Mates
John H. Schumann

UNIVERSITY PRESS

2009

OXFORD
UNIVERSITY PRESS

Oxford University Press, Inc., publishes works that further
Oxford University's objective of excellence
in research, scholarship, and education.

Oxford   New York
Auckland   Cape Town   Dar es Salaam   Hong Kong   Karachi
Kuala Lumpur   Madrid   Melbourne   Mexico City   Nairobi
New Delhi   Shanghai   Taipei   Toronto

With offices in
Argentina   Austria   Brazil   Chile   Czech Republic   France   Greece
Guatemala   Hungary   Italy   Japan   Poland   Portugal   Singapore
South Korea   Switzerland   Thailand   Turkey   Ukraine   Vietnam

Copyright © 2009 by Oxford University Press, Inc.

Published by Oxford University Press, Inc.
198 Madison Avenue, New York, New York 10016

www.oup.com

Library of Congress Cataloging-in-Publication Data
The interactional instinct : the evolution and acquisition
of language / Namhee Lee . . . [et al.].
p.   cm.
Includes bibliographical references.
ISBN 978-0-19-538424-6; 978-0-19-538423-9 (pbk.)
1. Language acquisition.   2. Language and languages—Origin.
3. Social interaction.   I. Lee, Namhee, 1961–
P118.I493   2009
401'.93—dc22   2008036807

1 3 5 7 9 8 6 4 2

Printed in the United States of America
on acid-free paper

Preface

This book is the product of an ongoing research program conducted by the Neurobiology of Language Research Group (NLRG), which is part of the graduate program in applied linguistics at the University of California, Los Angeles. Students in this group are trained in linguistics, conversational analysis, neurobiology, evolution, language acquisition, and complex adaptive systems theory. Each master's degree student completes a thesis, and in the doctoral program, students write two qualifying papers that must be judged by two faculty advisers to be of publishable quality; additionally, of course, the PhD students write doctoral dissertations. The NLRG has been able to organize these academic projects into coauthored books. The first volume in the series, *The Neurobiology of Learning: Perspectives from Second Language Acquisition*, by John H. Schumann, Scheila E. Crowell, Nancy E. Jones, Namhee Lee, Sara Ann Schuchert, and Lee Alexandra Wood, was published in 2004. *The Interactional Instinct* is the series' second volume. Its first two chapters are based on Namhee Lee's doctoral dissertation, and chapters 3, 4, and 5 are based on qualifying papers written by Lisa Mikesell, Anna Dina L. Joaquin, and Andrea W. Mates. Chapter 6 was prepared by Andrea W. Mates and Namhee Lee, and the concluding chapter was written by John H. Schumann.

A framework for the book emerged from courses taught by Schumann on the neurobiology of language, the evolution of language, and the acquisition of language between 2003 and 2006. The material in the book, beyond being vetted for academic requirements, was also taught by the authors as an interdisciplinary course for the Center for Culture, Brain, and Development at UCLA and was presented as a colloquium at the 2007 conference of the American Association for Applied Linguistics. We have incorporated into the text the very valuable feedback we received from participants in these venues.

The long-term goal of the NLRG is to understand how brains interact. Cognitive science in its various manifestations—the study of linguistics, psychology, and the brain—has traditionally operated under a deficit of perspective. Each of these subfields has had as its focus the isolated language user, the isolated learner, and the isolated brain. Throughout evolution, though, the greatest selective pressure on brains has likely been other brains. Human brains are equipped to interact with other brains, and it is in this interaction that mental capacities are revealed. But such interaction has been largely ignored in all sciences of the mind.

One area of linguistics in which the isolated speaker/hearer has not been the focus of study has been conversational analysis. Here, multiperson interaction has been studied in minute detail. And recently, in neuroscience, the discovery of mirror neurons has allowed brain scientists to begin to understand how individuals resonate with each other biologically. Certain neurons become active when an individual performs an action and when he or she observes that action performed by another person. When subjects observe actions performed by others, motor programs in their brains that correspond to those movements are activated. Indeed, when one listens to someone else speaking, activations are generated in the listener's tongue and lips in response to the mouth movements and sounds produced by the speaker. Thus, there is a biology-subserving resonance between individuals as they interact.

Such interaction is the focus of this book. We explore how interaction produces grammatical structure in evolutionary time and how innate mechanisms for bonding, attachment, and affiliation ensure that children engage in sufficient and appropriate interactions to guarantee language acquisition.

Acknowledgments

We want to express our appreciation to the scholars who gave us guidance as we wrote this book: Lyle Bachman, Charles Goodwin, Patricia Greenfield, Robert Kersner, Diane Larsen-Freeman, Arnold Scheibel, Dan Seigel, Michael Smith, and Hongyin Tao. In addition, we want to thank the members of the Westside Neuroscience Study Group—Harvey Karp, Valery Krupnik, Hans Miller, Regina Pally, Sara Ann Schuchert, and Leon Sones—who commented on the whole book.

We would also like to acknowledge the support of the Foundation for Psycho-Cultural Research and the UCLA Center for Culture, Brain, and Development for the opportunity to teach this material during an interdisciplinary seminar in the spring of 2006.

Finally, we would like to thank Elinor Ochs for suggesting the term "interactional instinct" in discussions of language and language acquisition in the mid-1990s.

Contents

Introduction: Overview, *3*

1. Grammar as a Complex Adaptive System, *11*

2. Evidence for Language Emergence, *29*

3. The Implications of Interaction for the Nature of Language, *55*

4. Interactional Readiness: Infant-Caregiver Interaction and the Ubiquity of Language Acquisition, *108*

5. A Neurobiology for the Interactional Instinct, *151*

6. The Interactional Instinct in Primary- and Second-Language Acquisition, *167*

Conclusion: Broader Implications of the Interactional Instinct, *187*

References, *195*
Index, *223*

The Interactional Instinct

Introduction:
Overview

This book offers a perspective on language acquisition based on evolutionary biology and neurobiology. We argue here that language is a cultural artifact that emerges as a complex adaptive system from the verbal interaction among humans. We see the ubiquity of language acquisition among children generation after generation as the product of an interactional instinct that, as Tomasello (2003) indicates, is based on an innate drive to communicate with and become like conspecifics.

Almost 50 years ago, generative linguistics offered an evolutionary biological and neurobiological account of language: A mutation in hominid DNA led to the neural instantiation of "universal grammar" (UG), which provided humans with an a priori knowledge of the structure of language. In the early 1960s, when generative linguistics was developing, we did not know enough about genes, evolution, or the brain to think about language in biological terms. So the theory held. However, in the last 20 years, beginning in the mid-1980s, our knowledge of genetics, evolutionary biology, and neurobiology has exploded. In biological investigations of language during this period, we have had no success in finding a neural substrate that would instantiate UG. Nor has it been possible to conceive of a credible evolutionary scenario for the genetic basis of UG. Therefore, it may be time to consider other views of language. In this book, we use complex adaptive systems theory and the neurobiology of affiliation to understand how language evolved and how it is acquired without postulating innate knowledge of grammar.

Language as a Cultural Artifact

Following work by Deacon (1997), Batali (1998), Kirby (1998), Steels (1998), MacNeilage and Davis (2000), and DeBoer (2000), we argue for a view of language evolution in which a group of hominids has acquired the ability to make particulate sounds and to use them to form words, eventually producing a substantial lexicon. We suggest that further developments in the structure of this oral language emerge through the conversational interaction among the hominids as they attempt to express meanings with consistent form over time. This position follows from the principles of complexity theory, in which complex adaptive systems are seen to emerge spontaneously from the interaction of a large number of agents and/or large number of items. Such structure is seen in the large-scale flight formation of flocks of birds, where each individual bird interacts on the basis of certain principles with its local neighbors. Traffic jams have also been explained in terms of complex adaptive systems, where the accrual of a sufficiently large number of automobiles requires that the drivers focus not merely on their goals but also on interaction with the cars immediately in front of them, behind them, and on their sides. This interaction results in the cars moving as a single unit until their numbers fall or until the distance between them reduces the need for local interaction. Ant colonies are also characterized as complex adaptive systems in which individual ants behave according to local rules without any awareness of the total state of the colony. These local interactions ultimately produce elaborate anthills with intricate structure. Slime molds are amoebas that operate in the environment as individuals, but when supplies of nutrients become depleted, the cells spontaneously organize into large configurations, which move across the forest floor as single structures. When sources of food again become plentiful, the amoebas individuate and operate on their own (Prigogine, 1988; Briggs and Peat, 1989; Holland, 1995; Larsen-Freeman, 1997; Weber and Deacon, 2000; Johnson, 2001).

From our perspective, linguistic structure emerges as a complex adaptive system from the verbal interaction of hominids attempting to communicate with one another. Individuals organize lexical items into structures, and if the structures are efficiently producible, comprehensible, and learnable, then their use will spread throughout the community and become part of the "grammar" of the language. The conversational interaction ensures that the forms that ultimately become part of the grammar are those that fit the cognitive and motor capacities of the brain (Kirby, 1998). The vetting process inherent in the interaction modifies the grammatical structures to fit the brain rather than requiring the brain to evolve a genetically based mechanism designed to specify the form of the language. The resulting language is a technology that is passed on to succeeding generations as a cultural artifact.

But in order for this technological inheritance to take place, some genetic assimilation may be required. However, we see such selection taking place not based on the principles of universal grammar but rather through more abstract processes. In other words, we would see genetic assimilation producing capacities for joint attention, for understanding communicative intentions, and for cultural learning (Tomasello, 1999, 2003). Children would be born with the innate capacity to identify with conspecifics and to imitate both the results and the intentions of conspecifics' actions and with a powerful drive to pay attention to faces, voices, and body movements of conspecifics. The ontogenesis of language would then result from these powerful preadaptations. Children have the aptitude for language acquisition because interaction has molded the language to fit their learning capacities. What is innate is the child's appetite for language learning.

Language as Dependent on the Earlier Evolution of Pattern-Finding Capacities

Tomasello (2003) points out that another crucial prerequisite for language acquisition is the ability of children to detect patterns in their environments. He reports research that has demonstrated that infants can detect artificial nonsense words made up of three-syllable sequences. Later, the infants respond to those words, but they do not respond to the syllables presented in a different order (Saffran, Aslin, and Newport, 1996). Marcus, Vijayan, Bandi Rao, and Vishton (1999) briefly trained seven-month-olds on three-syllable sequences of the form ABB. Later, the infants responded to this pattern even when the syllables were different (e.g., XYY). Tomasello notes that this ability to detect abstract patterns in auditory and visual input is not unique to humans. Other primates, such as tamarin monkeys, also have this skill. Therefore, pattern finding is a cognitive capacity that has a deep evolutionary history and certainly cannot be seen as a specific adaptation for language.

The Innate "Interactional Instinct"

We argue that language is a culturally transmitted artifact or technology that requires no innate a priori linguistic representations. We also argue that a major mechanism in language acquisition is a domain-general system for tracking input frequencies and for discovering patterns in the input. Crucial for language acquisition is what we call an "interactional instinct." This instinct is an innate drive among human infants to interact with conspecific caregivers. While such an instinct may exist in other social animals, we contend that it has become much more powerful in humans.

The human brain may be seen as composed of systems performing three major functions: posterior sensory systems (touch, hearing, vision), anterior motor systems, and a more or less ventral and mesial appraisal system (Schumann, 1997). The appraisal mechanism determines the emotional relevance and motivational significance of stimuli received by the sensory systems, and it directs appropriate action by motor systems vis-à-vis those stimuli. The appraisal system determines three kinds of value: homeostatic, sociostatic, and somatic. Homeostatic value is centered on the autonomic nervous system and involves heart rate, body temperature, hunger, thirst, sexual drives, and so on. An organism strives for homeostasis and undertakes motor activity in the world in order to maintain appropriate balance among bodily states. Sociostatic value is essentially what underlies the interactional instinct. It motivates the organism to take action to achieve attachment and social affiliation with conspecifics who are initially caregivers and who are later members of the community at large. Somatic value involves the preferences and aversions that are acquired in a lifetime. They are not innate but instead are the products of our experiences with stimuli we encounter in the world.

Evidence for sociostatic value and an interactional instinct comes from observations of human neonate behavior. Infants from shortly after birth seek out the faces and voices of their mothers. They can distinguish happy, sad, and surprised facial expressions within hours of birth. Very early, they vocalize to get caregivers' attention, and they coordinate their vocalizations with caregiver speech in a manner similar to conversational turn taking (Schumann, 1997). Schore (1994) presents arguments that this interaction actually builds a postnatal brain by stimulating axonal extension from the brain stem to the prefrontal cortex. It would appear that the interactional instinct exists because human infants are born before their brains are fully developed, with the result that substantial neural development takes place postnatally. The emotional entrainment of the child on caregiver conspecifics may be evolutionarily designed to provide appropriate brain development and hence socialization during the extended human infant and juvenile periods.

A question that is very relevant for our research concerns the neurobiology that might serve as emotional basis for the interactional instinct and ultimately language. Research by Depue and Morrone-Strupinsky (2005) has generated a model for the neurobiology of social affiliation. It is divided into two parts: an appetitive component and a consummatory phase. Luciana (2001) suggests that the biology underlying consummation develops first and involves the expression of endogenous opiates during child-caregiver interaction. These opiates provide the child and the adult with feelings of calmness, and attachment and affiliation with each other. The opiates are modulated by neuropeptides, such as vasopressin and oxytocin. They are secreted from the arcuate nucleus in the hypothalamus and project to the central nucleus of the extended amygdala and the bed nucleus of the stria terminalis, where they encode general, nonexplicit features of the context in which attachment/affiliation takes place. They also project to the lateral nuclei of the basolateral amygdala and encode the discrete, explicit stimuli related to the affiliative interaction. As children first develop attachment relations with persons and environmental settings, endogenous opiates, similar to morphine and heroin, induce reward in the form of comfort and pleasantness. The process, we would argue, entrains the child's attentional mechanisms on the caregivers and serves as a hardwired motivational mechanism that ensures social-ization in general and language acquisition in particular.

These intensely rewarding aspects of the attachment bond become part of the child's sociostatic memory and serve as a template for subsequent affiliative relationships. As the infant grows and becomes capable of self-generated action in the world (e.g., moving, walking), the appetitive aspects of affiliative process develop. Now the child will seek other conspecifics with whom attachments can be made. The neurobiology supporting this appetitive phase involves the ventral tegmental dopamine interactions with the nucleus accumbens shell, the hippo-campus, the medial orbital area (area 13), and, as mentioned earlier, the extended amygdala and the basolateral amygdala. The last two regions provide incentive information concerning nonexplicit and explicit context reinforcement to the nucleus accumbens shell, where it is associated with contextual information (spatial, temporal) from the hippocampus and with appraisal information from the medial orbital cortex.

This neural mechanism corresponds to the mechanism described in Schu-mann et al. (2004) that subserves foraging and learning. In encountering conspe-cifics more distal than immediate caregivers, the child responds to affiliative stimuli such as friendly vocalizations, gestures, smiles, and touch with positive appraisals and a desire to approach. The appraisals are communicated by the medial orbital cortex with contextual information related to the affiliative stimuli coming from the hippocampus and the basolateral and extended amygdala (Depue and Morrone-Strupinsky, 2005). Dopaminergic innervation of the nucleus accumbens facilitates the integration of these various inputs and provides a "go" signal for motoric and cognitive approach and exploration of the affiliative target and its context. This transformation of motivational information into motor activ-ity involves projections from the nucleus accumbens shell to the ventromedial ventral pallidum, to the medial dorsal thalamus, to area 32 of the prefrontal cortex, and from there back to the nucleus accumbens core and the ventrolateral ventral pallidum and on to the pedunculopontine nucleus, the brain-stem motor nuclei, and finally the spinal cord. The dopamine in this system operates to encode stimuli that are predictive of reward (Schultz, 1997), which in this case would be affiliative interaction with the conspecific. The dopamine provides reward corresponding to that generated by the exogenous ingestion of drugs such as nicotine, caffeine, cocaine, amphetamines, and alcohol.

The Maturation Effects of This Mechanism

We argue here that children are advantaged at language learning because their brains are more suitable for this task. As individuals mature, their brains change in ways that may alter these advantages. Maturational modifications in neural architecture involving dendritic arborization, synaptogenesis, and pruning; com-petition between the declarative learning system and the procedural learning system (Poldrack et al., 2001; Poldrack and Packard, 2003); and declines in dopaminergic and opiate levels may attenuate the interactional instinct, making successful second-language acquisition by older learners much more variable. However, under conditions where social and emotional affiliation with target language speakers is sufficiently strong, aspects of the mechanisms underlying the interactional instinct may be activated in ways that facilitate second-language learning.

In sum, we believe that there is a neurobiology that subserves an emotional basis for language acquisition. This biological substrate guarantees successful language acquisition in all normal children, and developmental changes in the system may cause difficulties that older learners experience in second-language acquisition (SLA).

Chapter 1 presents the theory of complex adaptive systems (CASs) as a basis for the evolution of grammar. From this perspective, grammatical structure and language in general exist as an invisible nonmaterial cultural artifact or technology. Language structure emerges from the interaction of speakers using sounds and words to communicate meanings. This emergent structure obviates the need to postulate an innate UG to establish structure or to guarantee the ubiquity of language acquisition by children.

Chapter 2 offers evidence for language as a CAS. This empirical support is drawn from computer simulations of language evolution, the development of pidgin and creole languages, Nicaraguan Sign Language, and historical linguistics.

Chapter 3 offers something rare in mainstream linguistics. It uses audio and visual technology and precise microtranscription to capture authentic language. It provides an indexicalization of the current state of English by representing, as accurately as possible, language as people actually use it. Because generative linguists rely on self-created sentences and self-generated grammaticality judgments as their data, they are unfamiliar with the structure of language in use.

Language and grammatical patterns emerge out of interaction, making conversation the primordial form of language. Therefore, from a neurobiological and evolutionary perspective, it is oral language, specifically naturally occurring and spontaneous spoken language such as that seen in ordinary conversation, that must be explained. To put it plainly, performance is competence. Thus, context is crucial; the brain evolved and language emerged through reliance on context in order to make meaning of the linguistic signal. This presents linguists with language that is distinctly different from the written variety, which may have its own distinct attributes (of which the structural ones have been the focus). Several interesting features of naturally occurring spoken language have been discovered: conversation (or talk in interaction) has universal properties (Sacks, Schegloff, and Jefferson 1974; Schegloff, 1996a, 1996c), it is designed for one's interlocutors, context is important (Goodwin, 1979), its grammatical properties are often simple or seemingly "incomplete" (Chafe, 1985; Thompson and Hopper, 2001; Mikesell, 2004a; Schumann et al., 2006), and its structural characteristics, which are often described as complex, are not complex in the way that formal linguists have proposed (Deacon, 1997, 2003). In fact, much of the structural character of spoken language can be explained by rather simple properties, which do not require an adaptation of the brain to language.

Chapter 4 provides behavioral evidence that human infants have an innate drive to attune to, imitate, and interact with conspecifics. This bias is a powerful developmental precursor to the ontogeny of symbolic formation and referencing in humans and, therefore, for the acquisition of language. The interactional drive essentially motivates infants to achieve attachment and social affiliation with their caregivers. Once this bonding is accomplished, the infant will continue to engage in "reciprocal co-regulated emotional interactions" (Greenspan and Shanker, 2004) with the adult, leading to the emotional entrainment in the ambient language and guaranteeing the child's acquisition of language.

Chapter 5 reports research by Depue and colleagues that has generated a model of social affiliation that may subserve the interactional instinct. It is divided into two parts: an appetitive component and a consummatory phase. The biology underlying consummation develops first and involves the expression of endogenous opiates during child-caregiver interaction. These opiates provide the child and the adult with feelings of calmness, attachment, and affiliation. This process, we argue, entrains the child's attentional mechanisms on the caregiver and serves as a hardwired motivational mechanism that ensures socialization in general and language acquisition in particular.

The intensely rewarding aspects of the attachment bond become part of the child's memory and serve as a template for subsequent affiliative relationships. The child, in encountering conspecifics more distal than immediate caregivers, responds to affiliative stimuli such as friendly vocalizations, gestures, smiles, and touch with positive appraisals and a desire to approach. The appraisals are communicated via the medial orbital cortex, with contextual information relating to the affiliative stimuli coming from the hippocampus and the basolateral and extended amygdala. Dopaminergic innervation of the nucleus accumbens facilitates the integration of these various inputs and provides a "go" signal for motoric and cognitive approach and exploration of the affiliative target and its context.

Chapter 6 argues that in SLA, the affiliative phase comes first. The learner positively appraises one or more speakers of the target language and makes efforts in this phase to affiliate with them. If the efforts are successful, the learner will experience a consummatory reward generated by the opiate system. This reward promotes learning. However, postchildhood successful affiliation is not guaranteed, and, therefore, we see a great deal of variation in the degree to which affiliative motivation supports SLA.

As the child passes into adolescence and adulthood, changes take place in the hormone, peptide, and neurotransmitter systems that support affiliation in primary-language acquisition. Dopamine levels increase until the onset of puberty and then gradually decrease throughout life. The opiate system is modulated by oxytocin and vasopressin. These neuromodulators are also found at high levels in the child and become lower as the individual ages. The abundance of dopamine, opiates, oxytocin, and vasopressin in the child's brain supports interaction with conspecifics and guarantees primary-language acquisition. The reduction of these substances in the mature brain may contribute to the difficulties in SLA experienced by older learners.

The book's conclusion examines the interactional instinct in relation to several additional issues in linguistics, psychology, and biology: Chomsky's notion of autonomous grammar, Williams syndrome, mental retardation, socialization in diverse cultures, the extension of the interactional instinct to pedagogy, and the interactional instinct in other animals.

ONE

Grammar as a Complex Adaptive System

One of the most fundamental questions that linguistics faces is this: Where does grammar come from? Since 1965, when Chomsky's seminal book *Aspects of the Theory of Syntax* was published, the dominant position on this question has been "innatism," a theory that maintains that grammar is a genetically encoded and neurobiologically instantiated entity that develops biologically as other organs, such as eyes and bird wings, do. However, this position—once referred to as "Chomsky's Revolution" (Searle, 1972)—does not seem to be holding up under the scrutiny of neuroscience and genetics (Deacon, 1997) and linguistics (Sampson, 1997, 2005; Schumann et al., 2004) and may, in fact, be edging toward its demise.

Debates on the pages of the *New York Review of Books* (Bromberger, 2002; Chomsky, 2002; Pinker, 2002; Searle, 2002) show how far Chomsky retreated from his initial position. One could argue that he abandoned his previous theory in a landmark paper coauthored with two prominent researchers (Houser, Chomsky, and Fitch, 2002). The paper provoked a fierce debate among some of the foremost theoreticians (Fitch, Houser, and Chomsky, 2005; Jackendoff and Pinker, 2005; Pinker and Jackendoff, 2005). Although this debate is ongoing, the innatist position is losing ground.

Innatists think that grammar must be determined by and reduced to neural modules, which, in turn, must be determined by and reduced to genes. However, with new technologies of modern mathematics and powerful high-speed computers in the late 20th century, a new science was born that investigates complex phenomena in nature. This new science found that unpredictable patterns spontaneously emerge in nature through interactions among agents/items without preordained design or top-down control. Theories following this science include chaos theory, complexity theory, and the like.

This chapter investigates whether complexity theory, though applied so far only to physical phenomena, can also explain a nonphysical phenomenon such as the origin of grammar. If we conclude that grammar is compatible with the principles of complexity theory, the field of linguistics will gain a new tool with which to pursue an answer to the most fundamental question of the field: Where does grammar come from?

Discovery of Chaos

In the 1970s, scientists heralded a new era of science ("new science"), in which simulation experiments began to challenge long-held views of the universe. Influenced by Newton's laws of celestial mechanics and Descartes's coordinates, classical dynamics proceeded on a number of critical assumptions: (a) nature is determined by and reducible to mathematical formulas (determinism and reductionism); (b) nature is a hierarchical structure with smaller components constituting ever increasing levels of structure and with the sum of participating parts always amounting to the whole, because small changes result in small effects and large effects stem from summing small effects (analytic view of the world and linearity); (c) the universe can be perceived as a closed system where external influences, random and minimal, can be disregarded through approximation (closed system and equilibrium); and (d) the universe is static where time is reversible and no spontaneous self-organization is recognized (static view of the world, time reversibility, and no self-organization) (Briggs and Peat, 1989).

The End of Determinism

Newton claimed that mathematical calculations can represent with exact precision the motion of a planet around the sun or of the moon around the earth. Classical dynamics further argued that if the position and momentum of all particles of the universe at a given moment are ascertained, it would then be possible to calculate exactly, through chains of causality, the state of the universe from its birth to infinity. The first person who raised doubts about the ultimate determinism and reductionism of Newtonian mechanics was French physicist Henri Poincaré at the end of the 19th century (Briggs and Peat, 1989). Poincaré noted that Newton's dynamics was based on a two-body system and did not consider any influence from a third source. For example, the movement of the sun and a planet or of the earth and the moon can be mathematically calculated and predicted when there is no intervention of any other external object. Poincaré discovered, however, that in an open system, which is open to external energy input, even the smallest disturbance that increased the nonlinear complexity of those orbits could cause the movements of the bodies to behave erratically to the extent that they could fly out of the solar system altogether. In short, Newton's equations were found to be inapplicable to open systems.

Newton's deterministic reductionism and linear equations came under further attack with Heisenberg's "uncertainty principle," which maintained that at the subatomic level, it is not possible to determine both the position and the momentum of a particle at a given moment. The universe was not characterized by the kind of certainty Newton had described. In an even more decisive fashion, German physicist Max Planck's quantum theory undermined Newton's laws of celestial mechanics. Planck showed that at the quantum level, an elementary unit of light behaves indeterminately, taking on characteristics of a wave at one moment and those of a particle the next (Briggs and Peat, 1989). Introducing indeterminacy into the universe at the most fundamental level of its constitution, quantum theory challenged Newton's optimistic view of the world as an entity determinable by and reducible to linear mathematical formulas.

Furthermore, quantum mechanics found that two geographically separated quanta remained correlated even though there was no mechanism for communication between them. A measurement on one particle was found to be correlated with that of its distant partner instantly. This demonstration cast a serious doubt on the view held by classical dynamics that the whole was the sum of its discrete parts. The boundary between the parts themselves was no longer clear.

Another challenge to the Newtonian view of the world as orderly and eternal was presented by the German scientist Clausius in 1865 (see Prigogine, 1988). Clausius introduced a new concept, entropy, and formulated the second law of thermodynamics. A measure of disorder in a system, entropy is also a measure of how close a system is to equilibrium. The second law of thermodynamics states that the entropy of a system always increases in a closed system and that at the point of maximum entropy (ultimate disorder), the system obtains equilibrium in an undifferentiated murk, where there is neither form nor pattern nor movement. According to Prigogine, "as a result of irreversible, time-oriented process, the entropy of our universe (considered as an isolated system) is increasing" (Prigogine, 1988, p. 70). That is, the universe is moving toward the equilibrium of maximum entropy and will eventually succumb to a heat death, as atoms try to randomize themselves (Briggs and Peat, 1989; Waldrop, 1992). Describing the universe as chaotic and time-irreversible, Murray Gell-Mann, a Nobel laureate in physics, ponders a very different future from the one Newtonian science was able to anticipate: "The era may not last forever in which more and more complex forms appear as time goes on. If, in the very distant future, virtually all nuclei in the universe decay into electrons and positrons, neutrinos and antineutrinos, and photons, then the era characterized by fairly well-defined individual objects may draw to an end" (1995, p. 19).

Chaos and Pattern Emergence

When powerful computers became available, scientists were able to model and simulate diverse systems, and what they found was that there are numerous systems of inherent unpredictability even when no random external influence exists. These systems range from the relative simplicity of pendulum swings and dripping water faucets to the greater complexity of weather conditions, biological organisms, brain waves, heart rhythms, animal populations, lasers, economic trends, and so on. Systems with inherent unpredictability are called chaotic (Briggs and Peat, 1989).

It is in this chaos where patterns emerge through self-organization. Prigogine (1988), a Nobel laureate in chemistry, gives a more detailed description of the concept of chaos and pattern emergence in it. According to him, there are two kinds of chaos: passive chaos and active chaos. He classifies states of a system into three categories based on how much a system is submitted to external constraints such as energy input from the outside. The first is the equilibrium state, in which there is no environmental influence on the state and little or no effect of time. Entropy of the system is stable or increasing. In this state, the molecules either are paralyzed or move around randomly. This is the passive chaos in which the elements are so intricately intermingled that no organization exists. This is also the state of the eventual lukewarm universe predicted by Clausius (Briggs and Peat, 1989) and described by Gell-Mann (1995).

The second state is the near-equilibrium state, in which the system is subject to weak external constraints and responds to the constraints linearly. That is, the system loses energy such as heat as fast as it takes it in. This stage still doesn't produce patterns, and it maintains the initial state of the system.

Finally, there is the nonequilibrium (or far-from-equilibrium) state. In this state, referred to as active chaos, the system is under the control of strong influences from outside, such as a great deal of energy input, and responds to these influences nonlinearly. It is in this last stage that patterns emerge out of chaos through self-organization and systems continuously renew themselves (Prigogine, 1988).

Prigogine (1988) demonstrates his classificatory scheme through such diverse systems as a chemical clock, a pipe pouring oil into a pool, and a phenomenon known as Bernard instability. The last provides a particularly instructive example of Prigogine's three stages. It can be illustrated by the following procedure. First, pour a small amount of liquid, such as water or oil, into a pan so that the liquid forms a thin layer. In this state, the molecules of the liquid maintain maximum entropy, and no orderly movement of the molecules is observed. The state is stable; thus, it is in equilibrium and a passive chaos state. If you start to heat the pan, the bottom of the liquid layer becomes hotter than the upper face. As a result of this boundary condition, the heat travels from the bottom to the top and dissipates into the air by conduction, but the system still remains stable. This is a near-equilibrium state, in which external influence is present but induces only linear response from the system. Still, no spontaneous patterns emerge.

However, when the pan and the liquid in it are heated more, the difference in temperature between the bottom and the top increases, so that convection is created in accordance with the water molecules' coherent movements from the bottom to the top, increasing heat transfer. This is the far-from-equilibrium stage, also called active chaos by Prigogine. In this state, gravity pulls more strongly on the upper layer because it is cooler and therefore denser, whorls and eddies start to appear throughout the liquid, and the system becomes increasingly turbulent and chaotic. However, when the liquid is heated even further, the system finally reaches a threshold at which the heat cannot dissipate fast enough without the aid of large-scale convection currents. At this critical point, the previously chaotic whorls and eddies turn into a lattice of hexagonal currents, which are called Bernard cells. Finally, spontaneous self-organizing patterns emerge (shown in fig. 1.1), as billions of molecules of the liquid suddenly move coherently.

In this far-from-equilibrium state, a system is more sensitive to external influences. A small change in the influence can result in the reorganization of the system nonlinearly, and new patterns emerge and disappear over and over again.

Regarding pattern emergence in chaotic systems, there is also the question of how patterns, which are orderly rather than disorderly, can emerge if the entropy of the universe increases. The second law of thermodynamics and spontaneous pattern emergence in chaos do appear contradictory, but they actually are not. Even though entropy generally increases in the universe, temporary ordering can appear in the process. Gell-Mann (1995) states that "the second law of thermodynamics, which requires average entropy (or disorder) to increase, does not in any way forbid local order from arising through various mechanisms of self-organization, which can turn accidents into frozen ones producing extensive regularities" (p. 19). The emergence of patterns through self-organization in dynamic systems, the focus of

Figure 1.1. Bernard convection. When a thin layer of liquid on a pan is heated to a certain extent, a grid of hexagons appears spontaneously (http://www.meta-synthesis.com/webbook/24_complexity/BenardConvection.gif).

the theory of chaos, has also triggered the formulation of dynamic systems theory, developmental systems theory, success-driven learning theory, complexity theory, and emergence theory.

Nonlinearity

In linear equations, the value for the whole is the sum of the values of its parts. Holland (1995) defines a linear equation as follows: "A function is linear if the value of the function, for any set of value assigned to its arguments, is simply a weighted sum of those values. The function $3x + 5y + z$, for example, is linear" (p. 15). In linear equations, the solution of one equation can be generalized and applied to other solutions of other equations. In a linear world, a small cause results in a small effect, and a large effect is obtained by adding up small effects.

In contrast, nonlinearity entails the product of two or more distinct variables instead of their sum, and there is no coefficient for all of the variables. Thus, in nonlinear equations, a small change in one variable can cause a disproportionate, sometimes even catastrophic, influence on other variables (Briggs and Peat, 1989; Larsen-Freeman, 1997). Nonlinear interactions almost always make the behavior of the system more complicated than would be predicted by summing or averaging (Holland, 1995). For example, in a nonlinear system, correlations among the participating elements remain relatively stable and constant for a large range of values of the variables, but when a certain critical point is reached, the correlations split up, and the equation describing the system plunges into a new behavior, so that prediction of the end point is not possible (Briggs and Peat, 1989). Moreover, because nonlinear equations are individual and peculiar, the solution of one equation cannot automatically be generalized and applied to the solutions of others. The nonlinear and open systems that Poincaré, Heisenberg, Planck, and Prigogine described render determinism, reductionism, and predictions futile. Nonlinearity exerts its unpredictability in the complex phenomena we find all around us—the behavior of forest slime molds, the formation and behavior of ant colonies, a sudden hurricane or an earthquake, the immune system, the rise and fall of cities, economies, and civilizations and so on.

Summary of Classical Dynamics and New Science

In summary, classical dynamics perceived the universe as determined by and reducible to linear mathematical formulas. Although it recognized that there are random influences on the system from outside, such influences were conceived as inconsequential and were disregarded. In classical dynamics, the sum of the parts was considered to be the same as the whole, and thus, defining mathematical formulas of parts and summing them was conceived to be the way to understand and predict the whole. Also, since the universe of classical dynamics was a closed system, it was basically static and maintained equilibrium, where time was reversible and no spontaneous patterns emerged.

Table 1.1. Classical Dynamics and New Science

Classical dynamics	New science
Deterministic	Stochastic
Systems are reducible to formulas	Systems are not reducible to formulas
Closed systems are investigated	Open systems are investigated
Equilibrium states are investigated	Far-from-equilibrium states are investigated
See the universe analytically	See the universe holistically
The whole is the sum of the parts	The whole is more than the sum of the parts
Linear equations are used	Nonlinear equations are used
Time is reversible (ahistorical): accumulation of experience is not counted	Time is irreversible (historical): accumulation of experience is counted
No spontaneous self-organization is noticed	Spontaneous self-organization is noticed and investigated
Static aspects of systems are investigated	Dynamic aspects of systems are investigated

In contrast, the new science finds the universe to be a whole that is not determined by or reducible to linear formulas for parts that constitute the whole. Stochasticity, rather than determinacy, rules the universe, and thus, prediction is not possible. The systems of the universe are open, so that they are dynamic and under the inexorable influence of external inputs. The influences include random ones, which can make a disproportionate difference and cannot be disregarded through approximation. These influences create systems that are far-from-equilibrium states in which spontaneous self-organization emerges through irreversible time. Table 1.1 summarizes the differences.

Complex Adaptive Systems and Emergentism

Complex adaptive system (CAS) was a term coined by scientists who gathered at Santa Fe Institute to construct a common theoretical framework for complex systems. Since its founding in the mid-1980s by George Cowan, the institute has been the hub of research activity on complexity and currently boasts the participation of such renowned scholars as Nobel laureates Murray Gell-Mann, Philip Anderson, and Kenneth Arrow (Waldrop, 1992).

Such diverse phenomena as cities, the immune system, the central nervous system, the ecosystem, and stock markets can be called CASs. Defining the characteristics of a CAS will need decades of further research,[1] but for now, CASs are generally described in terms of three salient attributes: CASs are systems of

---

1. For a more detailed discussion of the characteristics of CAS, refer to Lee (2003).

complex structures in which patterns emerge dynamically through local interactions among many agents in spite of the absence of preordained design; small inputs into a CAS can cause major changes (the whole is more than the sum of its parts); and these phenomena also show a general tendency of "coherence under change" (Holland, 1995, p. 4).

Briggs and Peat (1989) agree that one defining characteristic of complex systems is nonlinearity. As discussed above, a small change in one level can result in an unpredictable, disproportionate, and even catastrophic change at another level through feedback. Waldrop (1992) also explains that emergence is an omnipresent phenomenon, which can be observed in both nature and culture. For Waldrop, emergence means that under the right set of circumstances, local interactions among individual elements can result in a system of higher complexity that transcends the characteristics of individual elements, even when there is no top-down master plan. Waldrop uses the example of water to illustrate the emergence phenomenon:

> Take water, for example. There is nothing very complicated about a water molecule: it's just one big oxygen atom with two little hydrogen atoms stuck to it like Mickey Mouse ears. Its behavior is governed by well-understood equations of atomic physics. But now put a few zillion of those molecules together in the same pot. Suddenly you have got a substance that shimmers, gurgles and sloshes. Those zillions of molecules have collectively acquired a property, liquidity, that none of them possesses alone. In fact, unless you know precisely where and how to look for it, there is nothing in those well-understood equations of atomic physics that even hints at such a property. The liquidity is "emergent." (p. 82)

Examples that show this property of emergence abound in nature. A water molecule is created from one oxygen atom and two hydrogen atoms, but water has characteristics that do not exist either in oxygen or in hydrogen. We cannot derive the properties of a protein from the genes that control its formation. Nor can we derive the properties of an organism from the proteins that compose it.

However, neither the scientists at Santa Fe Institute nor scholars elsewhere have yet discussed the possibility that language may be an example of a CAS and emergence. This is not surprising given the fact that the institute includes mostly "hard scientists" and some economists. Their focus naturally falls on the tangible physical world, and the world of symbolic semiosphere, which contains language systems, does not often draw their interest.

Realizing that linguistics can benefit from the findings of complexity theory, we argue here that language is a CAS that emerged through local interactions among participating agents, since it conforms to all of the characteristics of a CAS that have been identified so far. However, we will need a bit of imagination and willingness to apply the principles of CASs in order to understand language as a

CAS, because it will be the first time for language and its evolution to be investigated as a CAS.[2] We examine below whether principles of CASs are compatible with language.

We now turn to the principles of CASs that scientists have identified so far. These principles hold true for all CASs, whether the particular system in question concerns the earth's climate or an ant colony. We argue that the phenomenon of language emergence conforms to these principles as well and that the observed compatibility between CAS principles and language emergence strengthens the possibility that languages are CASs and that such patterns as syntax, phonology, and pragmatics emerged through interactions.

Aggregation

The first principle of CAS is aggregation (Holland, 1995). Aggregation requires two conditions: a mass of agents and aggregate interaction among the agents. Holland notes that large numbers of active agents, diverse in both form and capability, make up CASs. Johnson (2001) supports this view and argues that a mass of agents is necessary for a collective behavior or a pattern to emerge. For example, a river is composed of a mass of water molecules. Only when a large enough number of water molecules aggregate and interact with one another can a pattern of river flow emerge. A city also emerges only when a large number of agents, including people, commercial enterprises, and administrative organs, aggregate and interact.

A question to ask here is whether or not a large enough number of agents existed some time in hominid history for language to emerge. We will discuss two kinds of agents: the number of hominids and items of a representation or communication system.[3] We argue that with the formation of hominid social groups, more words emerged and that eventually, when a large enough pool of words came into being, linguistic patterns such as syntactic, phonological, and pragmatic rules also emerged.

---

2. In order to understand language as a CAS, we need to clarify two concepts. First, we need to carefully investigate what would constitute "agents" in the process of emergence of language as a CAS. Second, we also need to illustrate what we mean by "interaction" among agents and items. If we are discussing a relatively simple CAS, such as an ant colony or a body of water, the problem of terminology may not be too serious. Individual ants are agents of the colony, and their chemical and tactile communication represents their interaction. In a body of water, water molecules will be the agents, and their interaction will be chemical and physical. When we try to understand more complex structures, such as human society, economy, or language, finer definitions are necessary. Unfortunately, such a discussion is beyond the scope of this chapter. Interested readers are encouraged to refer to Lee (2003).

3. It is not clear what would constitute the items of a representation system. However, we arbitrarily use "word" to mean a meaning-bearing communicative item.

Dunbar (1998) argues that language evolved as a grooming method when the number of individuals in hominid communities surpassed the point at which physical-contact grooming would be possible. He shows that the ratio of the size of the neocortex to the rest of the brain correlates with primate group size. If the ratio is high, the group size tends to be large, and vice versa. Dunbar calculated that the group size of hominid societies in the middle Pleistocene was about 130, which made it impossible for all members physically to groom one another. To maintain group cohesion, therefore, hominids had to devise a new way of grooming, which resulted in the birth of language. What we learn from Dunbar's argument is that a large enough aggregation of agents may have occurred in the phylogeny of hominids about 1 million years ago and that this may have satisfied the first condition of CASs and emergence.

We also can question whether there were enough words in some hominid communities to make the emergence of linguistic structures, such as grammar and phonology, possible. Evidence on this matter will never be conclusive, but strong speculations can be made from animal-communication research, primatology, and child language-acquisition studies. It is a well-known fact that most mammals, birds, and fish have a restricted number of displays, generally between 15 and 35 (Moynihan, 1970). Miller points out that the average primate knows about 5 to 20 distinct calls, and the unusually intelligent bonobos, such as Kanzi, have about 250 words in their command (Miller, 2000). Lieberman reports that Washoe, a common chimp, had about 150 words (Lieberman, 2000). The average human adult English speaker knows about 60,000 words (Miller, 2000).

Considering the fact that the chimpanzee brain hasn't evolved much since the divergence of the hominid and chimp lines about 7 million years ago (Allman, 1999), it is logical to assume that the first hominid group had at least 5 to 20 meaning-bearing vocalizations and that the vocabulary size has grown to 60,000 in the process of human evolution since then. There may be a relationship between the size of vocabulary and the emergence of syntax. Lieberman (2000) reports that chimps, with about 150 words in their lexicon, already had simple aspects of syntax. Greenfield and Savage-Rumbaugh (1990) report that their subject (Kanzi, a *Pan paniscus*), which had about 250 words, used productively and without redundancy "protogrammatical rules" such as "action or actions precede agent," "action precedes object," "actions of chase and tickle precede actions of hide, slap, and bite." From these findings, they conclude that Kanzi had a primitive version of an ergative grammar system. Bates and colleagues demonstrate that human children begin to apply grammatical rules when the vocabulary in their expressive lexicon exceeds about 600 words (Bates, Dale, and Thal, 1995; Bates and Goodman, 1997).

Synthesizing the above data, we can speculate that at some point in the history of human evolution, some hominid group(s) grew in population to about 130 members. They also developed about 150 words and had simple aspects of language organization, as Lieberman's chimps did. When the size of their lexicon increased to about 250, they probably developed a slightly more complex organization, as Savage-Rumbaugh's Kanzi did, and a more complex structure like that of Bates's children formed when the number of vocabulary words increased to about 600. This vocabulary size could have created the right environment for individual words to interact locally with other words and result in advanced levels of complex grammar. Locke (1998) echoes a similar idea. He believes that hominids expanded their capacity for reference, which proliferated words and which, in turn, made utterances increasingly variable and unpredictable. At this point, a means of organizing utterances for purposes of better communication came into being.

Multistrata of Building Blocks

The second principle of CASs and emergence is related to the first principle of multiple agents. Holland (1975, 1995) notes that an agent at one level serves as the building block for agents at a higher level, which, in turn, serve as the building blocks for agents at the next level. Agents of a higher level are more complex than those of a lower level, and an aggregate of agents of one level makes up a meta-agent of a higher level, an aggregate of which, in turn, makes up a meta-meta-agent of the next level. In this way, a CAS is composed of a hierarchical structure of agents. According to Holland, the biosphere is such a system: a group of proteins forms a cell, a group of cells a tissue, tissues an organ, organs an organism, and organisms the entire ecosystem.

Holland's concept of multistrata in a CAS is also evidenced in human society and in language. Breaking down the entire human race into ever finer constitutive groups, one passes through ethnic communities, kin or clan groups, and families, until one reaches the level of individuals. In terms of interactional groups, we can imagine a typical conference or a party. A small number of people temporarily form a group and talk among themselves, neighboring groups form a loosely connected metagroup, the cohesion of which may depend on eavesdropping or overhearing, and these metagroups form the entire party. In terms of language, phonemes form syllables, which then form morphemes; morphemes form words, words form phrases, and the process continues, until we end up with speech acts, stories, and so on.

Local and Random Interactions

The third principle of CASs is that agents of CASs interact locally and randomly. Johnson (2001) states that the whole process of emergence can occur only through local and random interactions between agents, without any predetermined goal, design, or top-down command. "Local" in this context means two things. First, each individual meets only neighboring agents and does not necessarily interact with other agents. Second, each agent is unaware of the whole picture, that is, the state of aggregate interactions involving all agents. "Random" in this context means that meetings between agents occur, to great extent, by chance. According to Holland (1975), a CAS is composed of a network of many agents acting in parallel; agents in this system constantly react to actions of neighboring agents.

Johnson (2001) illustrates this point by using an ant colony as an example. In a colony, each individual ant only communicates *locally* with its immediate neighbors, encountered *randomly* during its daily activities. The communication, which occurs via semiochemicals (pheromones) and tactile sensors, encodes task recognition, trail attraction, warning, and necrophobic behavior. Based on the frequency with which an ant meets certain pheromones, tactile contacts, and gradients of the chemicals, the ant switches its job from nest building to foraging or to raising pupae. No individual ant knows the state of the entire colony or assumes the responsibility for directing the overall operation. "Queen ant" is a misnomer for what is merely another individual agent performing its duty of laying eggs according to its interaction with other ants that attend it. The queen ant is neither aware of nor responsible for the state of the entire colony. Only through these unplanned local and random interactions among individual ants does global behavior of the whole colony emerge, which is called collective intelligence (Johnson, 2001) or swarm intelligence (Hoffmeyer, 1996).

The interaction among agents in the process of language emergence conforms to this principle. First of all, the predominant mode of interaction for hominids in a group must have been local, except on ritual occasions or in group hunting activities. Individual agents probably remained ignorant of the big picture regarding the community at large. The situation is the same today. No individual in any human society knows the whole state of interactions among its members. Parents don't know what their children are talking about to their peers. Neighbors don't know about what their neighbors are talking about or to whom. This situation may have been mitigated somewhat after the invention of mass media, but we still are ignorant of most things that are happening in the world. The same is true for words. Words are produced and perceived only in the immediate cognitive and social situation of their human users. When linguists use words, words from the domain of, say, molecular biology are not likely to be involved. Since human users remain ignorant of the state of the whole society, words that depend on these users must be ignorant of it as well. There is no reason to believe that the situation was different in hominid societies.

The second condition—randomness of interactions between individual agents—is another that we can take for granted. Some meetings may be planned, but most are random within broad constraints of societal organization. A person who goes to school on a given day might run into friends, colleagues, school personnel, or even tourists. On the way to school, he or she might see other motorists, police, pedestrians, or panhandlers and interact with some of them. These meetings occur randomly. In the same way, interactions between words are random and realized only through encounters of their hosts. The meetings of hosts are random, so the meetings among words cannot help being random. Once again, there is no reason to believe that the situation was different in hominid societies. The recognition of randomness as an important part of every interaction is one of the great achievements of new science. Traditionally, science has disregarded randomness as inconsequential, but chaos and complexity theories recognize its vital role in the process of pattern emergence. Indeed, randomness lies at the heart of the emergence of diverse and unpredictable patterns in CASs.

Tagging

According to Holland (1995), tagging is a CAS mechanism that enables or facilitates otherwise simple agents to form highly adaptive aggregates. These aggregates make selections among agents or objects that would otherwise be indistinguishable. In other words, tagging is the mechanism by which interactions among agents become directed, or biased toward particular direction, and facilitated when the local and random interaction takes place. Examples of tags abound in nature. A banner in a rally directs, biases, or facilitates interactions among rally participants, and visual patterns and pheromones perform similar functions in selective mating among animals. Trademarks, logos, and icons direct, bias, or facilitate commercial interactions in an economy.

At present, it is not clear what the tags would be in interactions among the agents in language emergence. For now, we present some speculation and leave the matter for further investigation. Rigorous research on the structure of interaction among people, such as discourse analysis and conversation analysis, will help advance our understanding of the matter. One possible tag in linguistic interactions may be announcements that configure the interpretive context for utterances to come. If someone announces, for example, that he or she is going to tell a story, other people in the group will tend to listen rather than initiate different conversation topics of their own or look away. Words such as *what, when,* and *where* may serve as tags as well, in that they frequently lead questions rather than statements. Conjunctions such as *because, since, if,* and *that* are followed by clauses rather than by prepositional or noun phrases. Certain intonations can induce a particular structure of utterances over others. Similarly, certain gestures, facial expressions, or postures invite particular responses. It is quite likely that there are elements in language that perform taglike functions by directing, biasing, and facilitating linguistic interactions.

Internal Model and Pattern Match

Holland (1995) argues that CASs dynamically formulate internal models that perceive and select patterns in the torrent of inputs to which CASs are exposed. When these patterns in the environment are perceived, the internal models go through changes, and the changes affect the CAS's future ability to capture the patterns when it encounters them again. The models thus enable CASs to anticipate. Through this interaction between internal models and patterns of input from the environment, selection and adaptation of the models take place. Some models will survive and persist if their predictions enhance the survival of the CAS, just as others will perish if they don't facilitate it.

Johnson (2001) describes this characteristic as "pattern match." According to Johnson, CAS agents are marked by the ability to learn. Learning, in his sense, is an ability of a system to alter behavior in response to patterns found in the immediate environment. For example, the immune system learns because it alters its behavior in response to antigens found in the environment. Cities learn because they alter themselves in response to their changing environments, such as changes in traffic systems, population size, industries, and so on. For an ant colony, learning would be defined as the change of tasks based on accumulated chemical and tactile information.

Humans match patterns instinctively. If a child is moved to a community where a different dialect is spoken, the child will speak the dialect in no time. Pattern matching by newborns to caretakers' behavior has been well documented (Elman et al., 1996). Schumann (1997) also notes that the human organism has an innate tendency initially to "seek out interaction with conspecifics" who are their caregivers and then gradually interact with "others in the individual's network of social relations" (p. 1). Through these instinctive interactions, humans match patterns of their neighbors. Donald (1998) argues that mimetic capacity had long been in place before the emergence of language. Tomasello (1999) also argues that imitative learning is a human-distinct capacity, and imitation is a primordial pattern-matching process.

It is not clear how words match patterns with neighboring words and learn from the interactions among themselves. Although we lack a conclusive explanatory model for this, we are not without some tantalizing clues. For example, some English verbs followed by the particle *to* of the infinitive tend to be phonologically reduced. *Have to* is reduced to [hæftə], *got to* to [gɑɾə], *ought to* to [ɑɾə], *want to* to [wʌnə], and so on. What we observe here is that strings of phonemes in similar environments tend to change in a similar way. In other words, words match patterns and change; that is, words learn. Grammaticalization and lexicalization scholars have already investigated this type of change, and more research on the subject may shed light on the pattern-matching behavior of words.

Flow

Holland (1995) states that input of resources to a CAS flows through a network of nodes and connectors in the CAS. Nodes are CAS agents, connectors designate possible interactions among the nodes, and a resource is what flows through the network. For example, in the CAS of the central nervous system, nerve cells are the nodes, and interconnections among the nodes via synapses are connectors. Electrical pulses and chemical information are resources that flow over the network. In the ecosystem, species are the nodes, food-web interactions are the connectors, and biochemicals are the resource. In the Internet, personal computers are the nodes, cables that connect the personal computers are the connectors, and messages are the resource.

Networks of flows have two properties: a multiplier effect and a recycling effect (Holland, 1995). Because of these two properties, nonlinear changes can occur on the network, or on the resource, itself. The multiplier effect takes place when an input to a node passes through connectors to other nodes, inducing a chain of changes. This phenomenon is called a multiplier effect because an input can cause multiple changes while it travels over the whole network. The recycling effect also occurs in the flow of resources over the CAS network. An input of energy is recycled again and again when it travels from one node to another. Take, for example, a tropical rain forest, where nutrients travel from plants to herbivores to predators and to plants again. While the resource travels through the network, it is recycled again and again and causes multiple changes to the nodes via a chain of reactions. While an input causes a cascade of reactions throughout the network, the initial input transforms both itself and the network with nonlinear effects. Both the flow of the input and the network, far from remaining fixed, represent patterns that reflect changing adaptations as experience accumulates over time.

In the system of language, the nodes are probably human individuals, the connectors are the social web of human relations, and the resources are the linguistic information that flows over the network of individuals and their social web. When a piece of linguistic information (for instance, a newly coined word) travels over the nodes of individuals through the connectors of the social web, the information causes a cascade of changes to the individuals' linguistic knowledge by the multiplier effect and is recycled whenever an individual passes it to another individual. In addition, this linguistic information transforms itself and the social web in a nonlinear manner while it passes through the network.

Bottom-Up and Indirect Control

According to Johnson (2001), "indirect control" is one of the principles of emergence. What he means by this is that the aggregate behavior of the whole system is indirectly controlled by the local rules its individual agents follow but not directly by top-down master rules. For example, one of the rules for ants in a colony may be summed up as follows: "If I meet the semiochemical A with X gradient Y times, I will switch my work to foraging." These low-level rules ultimately control the macro behavior of the whole colony and contribute to unexpected behavior by the whole group. Holland (1975) makes a similar argument when he claims that control in a CAS is achieved only through highly dispersed influence. He uses the example of the brain. Each neuron in the brain affects only those neurons to which it projects. There is no master neuron in the brain that dictates the behavior of each individual neuron. Through this locally dispersed control among neurons, however, coherent behavior of the whole brain emerges.

Indirect control of linguistic behavior may have been operative for hominids as well. Hominids' responses to others in their community occurred at local levels, without the presence of a mastermind to dictate all of the details of interaction among individuals. There could not have been top-down design of linguistic structures in hominid societies, either. It is conceivable that words about things induced the rise of words about attributes; words about moving objects, such as animals, may have led to words expressing motion, which then evolved into verbs. These controls all remained indirect and did not dictate the overall structure of utterances.

In modern times, however, tremendous efforts are made to directly control how people use language. The effort is usually realized through education, publication manuals, and mass media. Behind this trend of direct control of linguistic behavior lies the ideology of prescriptive grammar on the matter of what constitutes "proper language." Based on this phenomenon, some might argue that language control can be direct. Nevertheless, we should keep in mind that this trend is a fairly recent one in the course of human history and that this influence has been limited to only those who can afford the education, which is still out of reach of most of the population of the world. In addition, even those who receive formal education don't always follow the prescriptions made by grammarians. Such situations alert us to the fact that indirect control of linguistic forms is never absent.

Feedback and Circular Causality

Although bottom-up control is found at the very heart of CAS dynamics, it also induces a kind of top-down influence. This bidirectional influence can be described as "circular causality" (Kelso, 1995). Local interaction among agents leads to bottom-up control, but the resulting structure exerts a top-down influence on these local interactions through circular causality. Johnson (2001) agrees that feedback is another principle of CASs and emergence: "all decentralized systems rely extensively on feedback for both growth and self-regulation" (p. 133). Waldrop (1992) also illustrates this principle of emergence clearly by describing the same thing in three different ways: positive feedback, increasing returns, and self-enforcement. He states that positive feedback may magnify small accidents of history or nature into major differences in the outcome under a favorable set of conditions.

To illustrate this tendency, Waldrop tells the story of how the VHS video format came to dominate the market even though it was technologically inferior to Beta. This dominance started with only a slightly larger market share that VHS vendors were lucky enough to gain in the beginning. Video stores hated the idea of having to have two different types of tapes for every movie and went with the market leader. This boosted VHS's market share even more, which in turn gave the video stores a greater incentive to choose VHS. A small initial difference grew rapidly through positive feedback until VHS became the only product in the market.

Positive feedback in language behavior may be seen in the adoption of new words and forms. The more people use an item, the more it will be accepted and used by others. Such increasing returns may be illustrated by the use of the word *cool*. This word, the canonical meaning of which is to describe a temperature condition, started to be used "in order to emphasize how good or marvelous you think something is" (*Collins Cobuild English Language Dictionary*, 1988, p. 313) in informal English among young people. Nobody knows the exact origins of such usage, though a rough timeline might be obtained (English dictionaries published in the 1960s, for example, do not carry this definition). We can imagine how this usage may have emerged through positive feedback. One person or a group of people may have used the word to refer to something valued (e.g., a style of music), which gradually spread until it became prevalent among the population.

Feedback is the pivot of our conversational life as well. Conversation analysts have shown how speakers and listeners actively coparticipate in discourse. Far from being passive recipients of information, listeners actively co-construct the conversation through their continuous feedback to the speakers.

Lock-In

The last principle to be presented here is that of "lock-in" (Waldrop, 1992). A CAS allows patterns to emerge dynamically and to undergo changes, but once macro group characteristics appear, the CAS becomes resistant to further change, in a process known as lock-in. The case of VHS video tapes discussed above is an example of this phenomenon. Waldrop (1992) also illustrates this point with the example of the standard keyboard layout—QWERTY—used today.

According to Waldrop, the QWERTY keyboard layout was designed in 1873 by an engineer named Christopher Scholes, not to help typists type with greater ease or speed but to slow them down, because typewriting machines of his day tended to jam if the typist went too fast. Scholes's design was a small and insignificant accident in history. However, because of the layout's superiority in terms of preventing jams, the Remington sewing machine company chose it and mass-produced typewriters using it. This drove more typists to learn the QWERTY layout, leading other typing machine companies to choose it as well, which, in turn, forced more typists to learn the system. Finally, QWERTY became the standard layout used by millions of people, and the layout was essentially "locked in" forever. It is interesting to note that this layout is still used in computer keyboards even though computers are inherently jam-free.

The innatist idea of UG may be another example of lock-in. When Chomsky's book *Syntactic Structures* was first published in 1957, it had a slight advantage over Skinnerian behaviorism in terms of its explanatory power on the matter of child language acquisition. This initial advantage may have attracted some researchers who were frustrated with behaviorism, but once these researchers started to produce articles and books, they attracted more and more researchers and students in an ever spiraling process. This positive feedback has continued to enforce the UG idea for the last half-century, and the theory seems to have obtained the status of a lock-in now. This does not mean that it is necessarily correct but only that the theory itself came under the relentless momentum of CASs. In this light, UG theory is not unlike VHS videos or QWERTY keyboards. It dominates not because of its superiority but because of the self-reinforcing mechanism of positive feedback and lock-in.

Waldrop's lock-in also applies nicely to language. The human language system may have been only one of many possible communication modes. Languages also could have taken radically different patterns (Carstairs-McCarthy, 1998). For example, there is no biological or economic necessity for a language to have case or gender inflections, as German does, or two aspectual forms, as Russian does. English speakers have no problem communicating without either of these features. Although native speakers of Latin doubtless felt that several different noun paradigms of Latin were natural or even indispensable aspects of the language, this opinion is hardly likely to be shared by speakers of other languages. These systems are not necessarily efficient in terms of communication, nor do they enhance the biological fitness of the users of the language. Like VHS, QWERTY keyboards, and UG theory, these linguistic systems may be seen as examples of the lock-in principle.

Conclusions

This chapter has investigated whether complexity theory can provide a theoretical foundation for language evolution. Examining the principles of the theory and compatibility between the theory and language leads us to conclude that the theory indeed may shed light on the question of language evolution. In *The Language Instinct*, Pinker (1994) wrote, "Language is not a cultural artifact. . . . Instead, it is a distinct piece of the biological makeup of our brains" (p. 18). The position we are taking here is squarely opposite to Pinker's. We argue that language is not a part of biology but a cultural artifact that emerged out of interaction among hominids. We also argue that languages are not genetically but rather culturally transmitted to us.

TWO

Evidence for Language Emergence

In chapter 1, we argued that languages are complex adaptive systems (CASs) and that they emerged out of interactions among hominids and are culturally transmitted. We also described the principles of CASs and emergence theory, argued that the general characteristics of CASs are compatible with those of language evolution, and briefly discussed the ways in which early hominid societies might have been conducive to the emergence of languages. One important task remaining is to investigate the properties of languages and linguistic interactions among agents in order to develop more stringent arguments that would show that the principles of CASs and emergence are really characteristic of languages. Advances in computer technology have given us a powerful tool with which to further investigate this compatibility. By designing local interactions among agents that take place without preconfigured grammatical structure and showing that grammarlike patterns can emerge purely out of these local interactions, computer simulations can strengthen the position of emergentists. Emergentists can also try to investigate historical examples of language change in order to show that languages and grammars do emerge. Even though there is no way to prove that languages emerged as other systems described above, since there is no fossil evidence of the languages used by Pleistocene hominids, these studies can help us formulate stronger theories.

This chapter explores what evidence exists to support the thesis of this book: that languages are interactional artifacts and belong to the category of CASs. The first section of the chapter presents three simulation studies, which show that simple interactions among agents can produce unexpected and unpreordained grammarlike structures shared among the populations. In the next sections, we discuss linguistic pattern emergence that has been occurring throughout history, specifically pidgin and creole languages, Nicaraguan Sign Language, and historical linguistics. We then present traditional interpretations of these phenomena and new interpretations from the perspective of languages as CASs. We conclude that languages are open systems in which incessant energy input (interactions) results in spontaneous pattern emergence as in any other system in a far-from-equilibrium state. The patterns are grammar, phonology, semantics, pragmatics, and so on.

Experiments Supporting Language Emergence

With recent advances in mathematical theories, computer technology, and robotics, simulation experiments can now test hypotheses about language emergence. These experiments are not without their limitations. The most critical is a simulation's inability to capture the complexity and intricacy of human interactions. Moreover, simulations cannot conclusively prove emergence rather than genetic evolution of language. These experiments can, however, show the possibility of language emergence. The area is still young but promising. As technology advances and results of simulation experiments accumulate, more sophisticated and closer-to-reality experiments will help us better understand the process of language emergence.

Kirby's Simulation

Kirby's simulations (1998) involve three central components, each of which has four neighbors: above, below, to the right, and to the left. The first component represents speakers, the second utterances, and the third acquirers. In the first phase, all speakers randomly produce utterances according to their particular grammars. After the first phase, all acquirers take samples of the utterances produced by the speakers closest to their position in the array (the four neighbors). The utterances are used to set the acquirer's grammar, after which the acquirers take turns becoming the speakers, and the previous speakers become acquirers sampling utterances of their neighbors.

  Through this simulation, Kirby showed that syntaxlike structure can emerge through repeated production and parsing without predetermined, complex sentence structure. Kirby argues that languages evolved historically to be optimal communicative systems and have adapted themselves for their own survival and propagation in transmission from generation to generation. Human language-learning mechanisms also evolved in order to learn the languages more efficiently.

Batali's Simulation

Batali (1998) performed a mathematical and computational simulation experiment to see whether structured meaning can emerge through local interactions among individual agents without any external guidance over how the system ought to develop. According to Batali, "some of the grammatical regularities manifest in human language could emerge as a result of non-genetic cultural processes among a population of animals with the cognitive capacities required for communication, but who do not initially share a co-ordinate communication system" (p. 406).

Batali's experiment involved a number of agents designed to do two things: produce tokens that bear structured meanings, and assign interpretations to tokens produced by other agents. The agents had no tokens in common. Initially, the agents' communication system was indeed chaotic. Few agents produced the same tokens for the same meaning, and none of the agents was able to understand tokens sent by others. However, as the simulation proceeded, each agent started to learn to interpret tokens sent by the other agents and succeeded in sending tokens that other agents learned to interpret. This group of agents eventually developed a highly accurate communication system, and they even created novel combinations of meanings.

This experiment showed that simulated agents can learn meaning-bearing tokens by only observing the behavior of others. Batali concluded that early hominids had a theory of mind and would have exhibited systematic regularities, through which they expressed structured meanings without any innate language-specific traits. Some of the grammatical regularity of modern human languages might also have emerged from these systems.

Steels's Robotics

Steels (1998) echoes this view. According to Steels, cultural evolution, such as evolution of language, follows Darwinian selection, and in order for anything to evolve in a Darwinian way, three requirements must be met: a mechanism of information preservation, a source of variation, and a feedback loop between the occurrence of a specific variation and selective success. Steels argues that an individual's language memory is the mechanism of information preservation, like genes in biological evolution. Speech errors are sources of variation, like mutations and crossovers. Finally, minimizing cognitive effort and maximizing communicative success constitute a feedback loop, analogous to reproductive success.

Steels's experiment involved robots equipped with language-game programs. The robots had onboard computational resources, a battery, left and right motors, and approximately 30 sensors, including those for vision. Interacting with other robots in the robotic ecosystem, which included a charging station to which access was gained through competition, these robots came to command form-meaning correlations, lexicon, and phonology. Steels concluded that "language is an emergent phenomenon. Language is a mass phenomenon actualized by the different agents interacting with each other. No single individual has a complete view of the language nor does anyone control the language....Language spontaneously forms itself once the appropriate physiological, psychological and social conditions are satisfied, and it becomes more complex due to its own dynamics and pressure to express an ever-expanding set of conceptualizations and speech acts" (p. 384).

Pidgins and Creoles

Unlike the case of computer simulations, it is not possible to use real human beings in experiments to see whether linguistic structures can emerge through simple interactions. Probably the closest situations to the experiment in history are the emergence of pidgins and creoles, the invention of Nicaraguan Sign Language, and language change investigated by historical linguists.

Traditionally, pidgins are understood as communication with words and holistic phrases without grammar, that is, without developed patterns, and creoles are understood as fully developed languages that have complex grammar and occur only when children are exposed to the pidgin while they are acquiring their first language (Bickerton, 1990). The argument behind these definitions has been that a pidgin does not have structures and patterns because it is learned and spoken by adults who have already passed a critical period for language acquisition. On the other hand, creoles have grammar because they are learned by children who are in a critical period and thus, based on their innate grammar, use a pidgin as raw material to create a creole.

However, we argue that pidgins are not without structure, although the patterns are not as complex and sophisticated as those of fully developed languages; that the classification as pidgin and creole is not categorical, but these languages occupy not-clearly-defined areas in a spectrum of systems, which are infinitely diverse; and that creoles with very complex structures do arise in populations made up of adults. This point is especially important. If complex linguistic structures, or full languages, emerge among adults, they must arise out of interactions, because adults either don't have innate grammar at all (Schachter, 1988) or have only limited access to it (White, 1987). If they are right, adults are not supposed to develop a full language. Apparently, this is not the case. Creoles have arisen through interaction among adults and probably will continue to do so.

Structure of Pidgins

A pidgin arises when speakers of two or more different languages are brought into contact for the purpose of work or trade without having opportunity or need to learn the other's language properly. For example, in the 1800s, Russians and Norwegians would trade every summer, and they developed a pidgin called Russenorsk[1] (McWhorter, 2001). Both groups needed to communicate to trade, but they didn't have to learn the other party's language thoroughly. What they did instead was to learn pieces of each other's language and mix them into a makeshift communicative system that would serve only for trade and some social

---

1. Russenorsk is considered to be either a jargon (Sebba, 1997) or a stable pidgin (Romain, 1988), but the definition doesn't affect the validity of our argument here, and it will be treated as a pidgin.

interaction. They developed a few hundred common words without much of what would be called grammar by the standard of modern syntax. Bickerton (1990, p. 121) presents an example of Russenorsk used by a Russian sea captain and a Norwegian one who are trying to barter flour for fish:

(2.1) Word-for-word translation to English

1. R [Russian seller]:   What say? Me no understand.
2. N [Norwegian buyer]:   Expensive, Russian-goodbye.
3. R: Nothing. Four half.
4. N: Give four, nothing good.
5. R: No brother. How me sell cheap? Big expensive flour on Russia this year.
6. N: You no true say.
7. R: Yes. Big true. Me no lie, expensive flour.
8. N: If you buy—please four pud (measure of 36 lbs).
9. [N:]   If you no buy—then goodbye.
10. R: No, brother, please throw on deck.

According to Bickerton, the above language has virtually no grammatical items. Verbs are often missing, and when they appear, they don't have subcategorized arguments. When several clauses appear together, they are structurally unconnected. In other words, "both words and utterances are simply strung together like beads, rather than assembled according to syntactic principles" (Bickerton, 1990, p. 122). However, Bickerton's conclusion is completely modern-syntax-written-style-centric. Although the above segment of interaction looks devoid of complex grammatical apparatus from the point of syntax of written styles of modern languages, it already shows systematic combinations of words. First, the negative marker "no" is systematically placed in front of the verbs it negates in lines 1, 6, 7, and 9. Second, modifiers are consistently placed before the modified items in lines 5 ("big expensive flour," "this year") and 7 ("big true," "expensive flour"). Third, an intensifier, "big," is used systematically in lines 5 and 7. Fourth, the longest utterance in the extract (line 5) has no copula and thus is seemingly ungrammatical. However, Russian has no copula in present tense, and, therefore, with respect to the copula, this utterance is no less grammatical than the same utterance would be in Russian. This utterance also has an intricate constituent structure, which does not match Bickerton's idea that words in pidgins are "simply strung together like beads." The constituent structure is perhaps:

[[[big [expensive]] flour] [on [Russia]] [this [year]]]

In addition to the patterns mentioned above, Russenorsk even developed an all-purpose preposition, *pa* (McWhorter, 2001).

Other examples of pidgins show patterns, too. Sometimes the contact between two linguistic groups is constant, as on Hawaiian plantations. Diverse pidgins arose during the period from the 16th to the 19th centuries, when European colonialism brought speakers of different languages as workers and slaves into tropical coasts and islands such as Hawaii, where the workers and slaves were forced to work together and to communicate with one another. In a normal immigrant situation, the immigrants would learn the language of the native speakers of that region, but these workers and slaves didn't have sufficient access to the target language, because they were living in strictly stratified societies where contact between the European owners or managers and the workers and slaves was minimal. Furthermore, the Europeans were drastically outnumbered by the slaves (Bickerton, 1990). The following extracts are examples of Hawaiian pidgins investigated by Bickerton (1990, p. 120):

(2.2) Utterance of a Korean native speaker
Aena tu macha churen, samawl churen, haus mani pei.
And too much children, small children, house money pay.
"And I had many children, small children, and I had to pay the rent."

(2.3) Utterance of a Japanese native speaker [italicized words are Hawaiian]
Ifu laik meiki, mo beta *make* time, mani no kaen *hapai*.
If like make, more better die time, money no can carry.
"If you want to build [a temple], you should do it just before you die. You can't take it with you!"

In analyzing the extracts, Bickerton argued that the pidgin consisted of short strings of no more than four words whose order was quite variable and devoid of grammatical items except those that were relatively rich in meaning. The verbs didn't have necessary argument structure. Once again, Bickerton's interpretation of the utterances is completely modern-syntax-written-style-centric. What he misses is that even these few examples show systematic order of verb and object.[2] In example 2.2, the object ("house money") precedes the verb ("pay"), and in example 2.3, the object ("mani: money") precedes the verb ("hapai: carry"). Both of the examples show OV word order.

In other examples of pidgins, more sophisticated grammar patterns or structures are observed. When Europeans invaded North America, Native Americans learned English for the purpose of basic communication for trade and brief interactions during which they spoke a pidgin English. McWhorter (2001) shows an interesting example that was uttered when an Indian woman rejected a white suitor (p. 136, citing Leechman and Hall, 1980):

2. Bickerton (1990) included one more example, uttered by a Filipino. The utterance doesn't include an object to verify whether it has VO order or OV order.

(2.4)

You silly. You weak. You baby-hands. No catch horse. No kill buffalo. No good but for sit still-read book.

This utterance may seem to lack structure from the perspective of English syntax, because it does not contain subjects, copula, number marker, correct negative marker, and so on. However, we can see that the speaker positioned words in a very systematic way. First, the theme ("you") comes first, and attributes of the theme ("silly"/"weak"/"baby-hands") follow. Second, a negative marker ("no") precedes predicates ("catch"/"kill"/"good"). Third, transitive verbs ("catch"/ "kill"/"read") precede their objects ("horse"/"buffalo"/"book"); therefore, the example shows systematic VO word order. The bottom line is that pidgins do have systematic patterns.

As mentioned earlier, the distinction between a pidgin and a creole is not categorical. Romaine (1988) says that pidgins have independent structures of their own that are not from the substratum and superstratum languages. She also argues that a pidgin can expand without its being acquired as a first language by children and that there are few structural differences between an expanded pidgin and a creole that may develop from it. Bickerton's notion that a pidgin is without structure or pattern doesn't seem to hold.

Dynamic Changes of Pidgins

The term *pidgin* covers a range of communication systems that have different levels of structural complexity and functional capability. Furthermore, pidgins are not static but dynamically change in terms of their linguistic characteristics depending on their social conditions. In other words, pidgins develop into linguistic systems of greater complexity as the complexity of social interaction increases (as in the case of Tok Pisin, discussed below), or they die out when there is no further need for them (as in the case of Russenorsk). Depending on circumstances, a pidgin may die out at any time or evolve into a complete language slowly or quickly. For this reason, classification of pidgins into categories in absolute terms is not possible. When researchers use different category names for diverse pidgins, the names should be understood as intending to capture the idealistic characteristics of some cases of pidgins. However, the classification of pidgins provides us with a convenient way to understand their developmental process. Sebba (1997) schematically describes the stages of pidgin development according to their linguistic characteristics and social conditions. He argues that a pidgin may evolve from a jargon into a stable pidgin, usually via a process of tertiary hybridization (see below), when appropriate circumstances are met. A stable pidgin, in turn, may become an extended pidgin over time, again when appropriate circumstances are met. At any of these stages, creolization of the pidgin may occur. The rest of this section is Sebba's description of these stages.

A jargon is formed when just two linguistic groups are in contact in a limited social context only periodically; therefore, it has only limited range of social functions, such as seasonal commerce. Since the contact is not continuous, it is not transmitted from generation to generation but is reinvented in an ad hoc fashion. Linguistically speaking, it is minimally structured. Its vocabulary is unstable, and its grammar is inconsistent. A jargon may evolve into a stable pidgin via tertiary hybridization. Tertiary hybridization occurs when a pidgin comes to be used between speakers of different language speakers, none of whom is a native speaker of the superstrate language that provides the basic lexical items. In this situation, the pidgin comes to be used as a lingua franca by speakers of diverse mutually unintelligible languages.

The transition from a jargon to a stable pidgin depends on the social functions of the language. If some circumstances arise in which the jargon speakers are in greater contact in diverse social situations, the jargon will develop into a stable pidgin, and otherwise, it will not. The critical momentum of this development is the scope, continuity, and frequency of interaction among the speakers. The linguistic characteristics of a stable pidgin are that the semantic, structural, and phonological variability of the preceding jargon stage is reduced; relatively firm lexical, phonological, and grammatical conventions are established, although they are still narrow and limited; the grammatical structures may be independent from those of the source languages; and the speakers' target language is now the pidgin, not the lexifier language (Muhlhausler, 1986, cited in Sebba, 1997).

If a stable pidgin comes to be used for a more diverse range of functions or domains, it moves forward and develops into an extended pidgin. The most important characteristics of an extended pidgin are that it may function very much like a first language for many of its speakers, "with the full referential range and expressive capabilities of any other language" (Sebba, 1997, p. 106), and that expansion of its functions may result in the creation of new genres of communication with stylistic variations. For example, a stable pidgin may be used only for spoken communication between traders, but an extended pidgin may be used in religious activities, as well as in trade. This would result in the pidgin being used in such diverse genres as church newsletters, hymns, sermons, scriptural translations, and so on. A pidgin in this stage has a good chance to become a creole, a full-fledged language.

Before we discuss creolization, it should be noted that scholars do not necessarily agree on what a creole is. If it is defined as what arises from a pidgin only when children acquire it as a first language, this definition is based on a social-generational issue. If it is defined as a language with fully developed grammatical structures, not necessarily with native speakers, it is based on linguistic characteristics of the language. However, both of the definitions cause problems. First, as a pidgin evolves, it may become the main language used by speakers in a stable community, as when migration of rural people into an urban area brings together people from diverse language backgrounds. In this situation, the pidgin is used in various domains in everyday interaction, even within the family if the family members have different first languages. When children are born in this family and the community, they may acquire the pidgin as their first and native language. According to the first definition of creole, this language is a pidgin to adult speakers and a creole to the children. Then the classification of it either as a creole or as a pidgin doesn't capture the whole identity of that language.

The second definition is problematic, too. The terms *pidgin* and *creole* were only arbitrarily coined by researchers, and there cannot be a clear-cut line between a pidgin and a creole in terms of structural complexity in the real world. Even the concept of complex structure is also arbitrary, not necessarily reflecting reality. It is not really possible to say that one pidgin is more complex than another except in such cases as when one is a simple jargon and the other is an extended pidgin. Because of this difficulty, when structural complexity and the grammatical apparatus of a language are used to classify it as a pidgin or a creole, the classification will always be controversial.

The process of creolization is not uniform. Sometimes extended pidgins evolve into creoles gradually through nativization when the right social circumstances are met. However, creolization can occur at any stage of a pidgin. Even a jargon can creolize without going through stages of stable pidgin and extended pidgin, as when children are born where the only lingua franca used by adults is a jargon. The process is called "abrupt creolization" by Thomason and Kaufman (1988, cited in Sebba, 1997), and it occurs within a short period of time, such as just one generation.

Rise of Creoles among Adults

Historically, unusual situations sometimes arise in which people are forced to use a pidgin as their primary language. Hundreds of people come to use the pidgin all day for decades, and this situation tends to transform a pidgin into a creole, that is, a full language with ways to express precise concepts with a systematic grammar, complete with tense, number, gender, and so on.

McWhorter (2001) argues that contrary to the traditional claim that a pidgin becomes a creole only when children are exposed to the pidgin, adults do transform pidgins into creoles: "The adult: pidgin/children: creole formula is in fact an oversimplification.... In most recorded cases, adults accomplished the transition from pidgin into creole long before significant numbers of children even acquire it" (p. 145).

McWhorter introduces the history of a creole called Tok Pisin, which developed in Australia and the various South Sea islands in the late 1700s and is used as a native language in Papua New Guinea today.[3] McWhorter argues that Tok

---

3. Wurm (1977) estimates the number of Tok Pisin native speakers to be 1 million (cited in Sebba, 1997).

Pisin started as a pidgin and developed into a creole by adults; Sebba (1997) also agrees that it became a creole through nativization of a pidgin after decades of use without native speakers of its own. The adult speakers worked in plantations in Australia, Fiji, and Samoa. The language was brought home to diverse islands by those who worked on the plantations. The pidgin speakers continued to use the language in communication among people speaking different native languages. Tok Pisin today shows fully developed grammatical structure and is considered a true language. McWhorter explains how some structural patterns of the language have developed through history.

Early examples of the language[4] show that some grammatical items had already emerged. For example, "stop" from the English word "stop," was used to mean "to be," and "by and by," also from English, was used as a future marker. The early form "stop" was later changed in its function to a progressive marker, and "by and by" was phonetically simplified to "bye" and became an auxiliary with its function corresponding to the English "will." "Save," which was from Portuguese, was used to mean "to know" and later went through a functional change and came to be used as a habitual event marker. In addition, tense and aspect markers, such as "pinis," from "finish," became a perfective marker, and "bin," from "been," became a past-tense marker. Also, the English word "along" was changed to "long" and used as an all-purpose preposition. A determiner, "wanpela," developed to mean "a" from the English "one fellow," and "dispela" came to mean "this" from the English "this fellow." Tok Pisin also developed the causative marker "im" from the English "him." The following example shows these grammatical morphemes of Tok Pisin (Muhlhausler, 1997, cited in McWhorter, 2001, pp. 143, 144):

(2.5)

Em I go long market.	She goes to market.
Em I **save** go long market.	She goes to market (regularly).
Em I go long market I **stop**.	She is going to market.
Em I go long market **pinis**.	She has gone to market.
Em I **bin** go long market.	She went to market.
Em **bai** go long market.	She will go to market.
boil/boil**im**	water boils/make water boil
hariap/hariap**im**	to be in a hurry/to make someone hurry
lait/lait**im**	a light shines/to make something shine

Nicaraguan Sign Language (NSL)

Pidgins and creoles show how a new language can emerge when two or more groups with limited common linguistic resources are put in contact. Grammaticalization

---

4. McWhorter (2001) included as early examples of Tok Pisin material recorded in the 1850s.

(discussed below) shows how new patterns arise diachronically in one language through interaction among the language speakers. But the remarkable case of Nicaraguan Sign Language shows how language emerges out of no language.

History of Nicaraguan Sign Language (NSL)

In most countries, deaf people spontaneously form their own communities. However, deaf people in Nicaragua had little contact with one another because of various sociocultural factors. There was no unifying national education system for deaf people, societal attitudes isolated deaf individuals, and marital patterns generally precluded marriage between deaf people, which prevented hereditary deafness. Thus, there was no chance for them to form a community in which they could communicate and associate (Senghas, 1995a; Senghas and Coppola, 2001). As a result of this isolation, the only language they used consisted of home signs that helped them and their family members make do in daily life. In 1977, the first school for deaf children was opened with 25 students in the capital city of Managua, and the number of students increased to 100 in 1979. In 1983, a vocational school for deaf teens was opened, and the children from the Managua school could continue to associate with their peers through the secondary school. The enrollment of the two schools surpassed 400 that year. Finally, for the first time in the history of Nicaragua, deaf people had a community in which a common communication system could emerge.

All of the students in the schools had hearing parents. Furthermore, the teachers were all hearing people, and they didn't know anything about sign languages (Senghas, 1995a). The teachers initially tried to teach the children to lip-read and to speak Spanish, and the students were not allowed to sign in class. The teachers' efforts had little success. Later, they tried to teach finger-spelling, but that strategy failed, too. The children started to sign spontaneously among themselves on buses and on the school grounds, and a basic signing communication system emerged. When new students entered the school, senior students naturally passed down the sign system to them, and more complex structures emerged in time.

When the deaf children first came to the school, they had only idiosyncratic home signs, crude gestures developed within the children's families. They served basic communicative needs in the family and mostly had the form of pantomime with iconic similarity to the referent. For example, "to drink" was expressed by a thumb gesturing toward the mouth, "to eat" by a flat hand with the fingers bending back and forth in front of the mouth. This sign system is called Mimicas.

The first generation of students soon spontaneously developed a sign system called Lenguaje de Signos Nicaraguense (LSN), a pidginlike sign language, which is still used. When later generations of students entered the school, they were exposed to LSN by senior students. Later generations developed a more complex sign system called Idioma de Signos Nicaraguense (ISN), or Nicaraguan Sign Language, which is like a creole (Senghas, 1995a).

Studies and Findings

Realizing that lip-reading and speaking or finger-spelling were ineffective, the Nicaragua Ministry of Education invited an American sign-language specialist, Judy Kegl, to visit the schools in 1986, hoping that she might shed light on the problem. Then a task force, called the Nicaraguan Sign Language Project, was formed to conduct research on the community and the sign language. Since then, many studies have been conducted. We give here a synopsis of the results of the studies, arranged according to the chronological development of the sign language.

Number of Arguments per Verb

Senghas (1995a, 1995b, 1995c) divided her subjects into two categories. In the first group were 13 people who entered the school before 1983, and in the other group were 12 people who entered in 1983 or later. Her subjects had to tell a story about a two-minute animation they had just watched. The results showed that those in the second group used verbs with two or more arguments more than twice as often as the subjects in the first group.

Another study (Kegl, Senghas, and Coppola, 1999) corroborated this result. LSN signers tended to allow only one argument per verb. Therefore, they signed for "the woman pushes the man" in the following ways:

1. Woman push man get-pushed.
2. Woman push man react.
3. Woman push man fall.
4. Woman push man cry.

On the other hand, the ISN signers produced more than one argument per verb, such that they signed for "the woman pushes the man" as follows:

5. Man, woman push.
6. Woman push man.

Inflections and Agreement per Verb

In sign languages, use of space is central to the grammar. Alterations in the movement or direction of body and hands from or to the neutral location constitute morphological devices that mark person, number, thematic roles, temporal information, deictics, agreement, and so on (Kegl, Senghas, and Coppola, 1999; Senghas and Coppola, 2001). Senghas (1995a, 1995b, 1995c) compared the number of inflections per verb used in the storytelling by the two groups (the one that entered the community before 1983 and the other that came in 1983 or later). The inflections included markers of number, person, position or orientation, and aspect. The result was significant and showed that members of the group that entered the school before 1983 used fewer inflections (X=1.71) than members of the later group (X=1.93).

Senghas also compared the two groups in terms of the number of agreement markers used for each verb. Agreement was observed when two constituents (e.g., the verb and its argument) were marked by the same functional inflections in order to co-index them. If both a verb and its argument were marked for plural, they were considered to exhibit agreement. The result was that the earlier-entering group used fewer agreement inflections (X=0.66) than the other group (X=0.94).

Word Order

Another study (Senghas, Coppola, Newport, and Supalla, 1997) examined how word orders evolved as time passed. The subjects were divided into two generations: those who entered the community in 1980 or earlier and those who entered in 1985 or later. Members of both groups entered the community before the age of six. In this study, subjects watched videotaped events that were designed to elicit a single sentence each. The stimuli were designed to elicit verbs of one animate argument (class 1: e.g., "cry"), verbs of one animate argument and one inanimate argument (class 2: e.g., "tap"), verbs of two animate arguments (class 3: e.g., "push"), and verbs with two animate arguments and one inanimate argument (class 4: e.g., "give").

The results showed that the first generation produced predominantly NV sentences for class 1 verbs ("man cry") and NV or NNV for class 2 verbs without a consistent order between the two nouns ("cup man tap"). When there were two animate arguments, the first group consistently used two verbs, one of which was for the agent and the other for the experiencer. The word order was NVNV, in which the first noun was always the agent ("man push woman fall"). When there were one inanimate and two animate arguments, two verbs were produced, in which one was for the animate agent and the inanimate theme and the other was for the recipient, such as NNVNV ("man cup give woman receive").

The most distinct contrast between the first generation and the second generation was found in class 3 and class 4 verbs. The second generation didn't actively use word orders of the first generation, such as NVNV. Instead, the second generation produced two adjacent verbs without intervening nouns ("man woman push fall" and "man push fall woman"). Another characteristic word order of the second generation was to drop noun arguments frequently. In a later study that reanalyzed the same data used for the 1997 study, Senghas (2000) found that the second generation consistently used directional movements of body and hands within a sentence and across sentences. The second generation was also found to interpret the directional movement to be coding thematic roles of arguments. Senghas argued that this development was the emergence of a morphological device to mark arguments. The frequent omission of nouns by the second generation was probably the result of the developing morphological system.

The Age Factor

Senghas (1995a, 1995b, 1995c) investigated how age factors influenced individuals' language learning. She divided the subjects of each group into three subcategories: those who were younger than 6.6 years old when they entered the school, those who were between 6.7 and 10.0 years old, and those who were between 10.1 and 27.5 years old. The subjects in the first two groups used verbs with two or more arguments more than twice as often as those in the third group. The same tendency was also observed in the number of inflections per verb and agreement markers per verb. The subjects who entered the community when they were young used more than twice as many inflections and agreement markers per verb as those who began signing at an older age.

The development of Nicaraguan Sign Language started from idiosyncratic home signs and gestures that the first generation of students brought with them to the school. As time passed, the early generation of deaf children developed a pidginlike sign system that had the following characteristics: it depended on the consistent use of word order to express basic grammatical relations when there were two animate nouns; when the signers employed word order, they consistently placed agent nouns before patient or theme nouns; it had only minimal morphological structure; the argument structures were simple; and sentences had many redundant segments, and signing was slow. As more time passed, the later generations of children developed a more sophisticated language system, and it is now a fully developed language. Its characteristics are that word order changed to permit two consecutive verbs, which was interpreted as incipient stage of serial verb emergence; it developed more complex morphological structures, which allowed the signers to omit noun arguments frequently; the argument structures became more complex, and, therefore, there were more arguments for verbs; and redundancy decreased, increasing signing speed.

Historical Linguistics and Grammaticalization

Historical linguistics provides insights about what changes occur diachronically in one language and how they occur. It also shows how one language diversifies into mutually unintelligible multiple languages. We describe here findings from historical linguistics regarding how languages change. All human languages are continually transforming into what eventually will be so different that they will be classified as new languages. French, Spanish, Italian, Portuguese, Romanian, and Catalan are all different languages today, but they all came from Latin, which is also only a variant of Proto-Indo-European, which was spoken 4,500 to 6,500 years ago and was the ancestor of most languages spoken in Europe and the northern part of South Asia today (Comrie, 1992).

Even when a language maintains its name, its grammar may go through radical changes. A language spoken only a few hundred years ago may not be recognizable to speakers of the same language at a later time. English spoken in the 10th century could not have been understood by English speakers of the 15th century (McWhorter, 2001). English speakers today, who have no difficulty reading articles or novels written a century ago, may be reluctant to accept this idea. However, modern English is an exception rather than a norm in this regard. According to McWhorter (2001), the speed of linguistic change decreases when literacy of a population increases. As more members of a language community learn how to read and write, the shared writing system of the language exerts an inhibitive influence on language change as printed forms become available as standards. The reason English hasn't changed much over the last century may be that the general population obtained literacy.

General Trends of Language Change

Comrie (1992) argues that linguistic complexity increases diachronically and that there are four general trends in language change. First, morphophonemic alterations are caused by the absence of the alterations. Proto-Germanic language did not have morphophonemic alterations, but its descendants, such as English and German, have them. In Proto-Germanic, the singular form of mouse was /mu:s/, and its plural form was /mu:si/. In modern English, they are /maus/ and /mais/, and in modern German, they are /maus/ and /mo?ze/. This example shows that a morphophonemic alteration indicating the number of the noun took place in the process of development of English and German, but their ancestor did not have it.

Second, phonemic tones, such as in Chinese, arise from a nontonal origin. Comrie says that the first languages must have lacked tonal oppositions and must have arisen only later in the history of language evolution.

Third, the distinction between nasalized and nonnasalized vowels develops in languages that initially do not have that distinction.

Fourth, morphology develops from an isolating structure, in which each word has invariable structure and morphology is absent, to an agglutinating system, in which affixes are readily segmentable and are formally and semantically regular and productive, such as regular plural or past-tense markers of English. An agglutinating system develops into a fusional structure, which does not involve readily segmentable units, such as internal vowel change for plurals or tense in English (*mouse-mice, sing-sang-sung*). In other words, all affixes are derived from independent lexical items, and fusional morphology can be traced back to affixes whose segmental nature has been eroded.

Comrie argues that more complex structures arise from less complex structures. McWhorter (2001), on the other hand, discusses five general trends of language change without necessarily presuming an increase in complexity in the change process. First, sounds tend to erode and eventually disappear over time, especially when they are unaccented and also especially when they are affixes. In addition, sounds, especially vowels, mutate and transform into new ones. Changes of sounds can result in changes of grammar. Latin had six forms for number and person affixes. The affixes eroded, and in French, only three forms were left in spoken form (five in written form). The erosion of sounds resulted in obligatory pronouns in French, which were barely needed in Latin. Latin had case endings on nouns, but they disappeared in French. The repercussion of the missing case endings incurred by sound erosion is that French came to have a relatively rigid word order, which had been much freer in Latin. Another characteristic regarding sound change is that it tends to spread to most instances of a sound in similar environments in the whole language. McWhorter's example of this tendency is that the sound *uh* is changing into the sound a in English, as in the first vowel in *shut up*. This tendency spreads into other instances, such as *but* and *what*.

A second general tendency in language change is that a grammar pattern tends to generalize into an across-the-board rule. For example, in Old English, there were diverse forms of plural endings, but only one form, −*s*, is left today with only a few remnants of the past, such as *mouse/mice*. The −*s* ending rule generalized to almost all plural markings of nouns.

Third, all languages continually create new usages of words and phrases that have expressive power, but the expressive force gradually diminishes through time. The English word *terrible* was first used to refer to truly horrifying things, but it is now used for less and less grisly phenomena.

The fourth general tendency is that rebracketing naturally happens as a result of reinterpretation of the boundaries of words. In English, *orange* and *apron* were originally *narangi* and *napron*, but [a [narangi]] and [a [napron]] were somehow reinterpreted as [an [orange]] and [an [apron]] via rebracketing. This kind of reinterpretation of word boundaries sometimes becomes common enough to be generally accepted among the population, and new words are created. Rebracketing also happens on a larger scale to create new sentence structures, such as [be going [to V]] is reinterpreted as [be gonna [V]].

The last tendency McWhorter notes is related to the semantic scope of lexical words. Through time, the meaning of a word or an expression can undergo processes of narrowing, broadening, or drifting. The English word *hund*, which meant any dog, narrowed down to mean only a hunting dog today. On the other hand, the word *dog*, which was used to refer to a particular breed, underwent a meaning-broadening process and came to mean any dog today. Sometimes a word's meaning just drifts. There may be a close enough relationship between one meaning and another after one step, but after several steps, the original meaning of the word is not easily reconstructable from the most recent one. Consider the English word *silly*. The word meant blessed in Old English, innocent around A.D. 1400, weak in 1633, simple or ignorant later in Middle English, and finally, foolish today.

Another general tendency of language change, most frequently discussed and probably most prominent, is referred to as grammaticalization. It is related to the third and fourth tendencies of McWhorter and the fourth tendency of Comrie but needs to be discussed separately, because the topic occupies a central position in historical linguistics today. Generally speaking, grammaticalization means that a lexical word or phrase with a concrete semantic content comes to lose the semantic content and serves as a segment that only expresses an aspect of grammar in a certain context. Once grammaticalized, the form continues to develop more grammatical functions (Hopper and Traugott, 1993). In this process of grammaticalization, a gradual transformation takes place from lexical word to grammatical word, to clitic, and even to inflectional affix. The direction of change is from lexical to syntactic to morphological. This progression tends to take a strong unidirectionality in the history of individual words of languages of the world (Hopper and Traugott, 1993).

Motivation for Language Change

Why do languages change at all, and why do they do so in those ways? Sociolinguistics focuses on the role of sociocultural influences. Language change must be influenced by social, cultural, political, and technological changes, to name a few. However, it is fair to say that change in language occurs even without those external factors, considering that languages also rapidly change even in isolated hunter-gatherer societies in which societal changes are minimal for thousands of years (McWhorter, 2001).

A group of researchers, mostly from the pragmatics camp, focuses on the role of speakers and hearers. They argue that the motivations for language change are "maximization of efficiency via minimal differentiation on the one hand, and maximization of informativeness on the other" (Langacker, 1977, cited in Hopper and Traugott, 1993). The economy-of-speech argument is probably valid, but it still cannot explain why such diverse patterns of language occur in the world when people have the same biology and operate under the same economic principles.

Both of the above arguments may have some validity. However, what they are missing is that languages are likely to be open dynamic systems in which patterns spontaneously emerge only via local interactions without top-down teleological design. The reason that there are such diverse structures in languages of the world is probably that languages, as CASs, don't work in a deterministic way; they are unpredictable. Hopper and Traugott (1993) cautiously mention the difficulty of prediction regarding language change:

> Although it is possible to describe change in terms of the operation of successive strategies of reanalysis (rule change) and analogy (rule generalization), the important question remains why these strategies come about—in other words, what enables the mechanisms we have outlined, most especially those involved in grammaticalization. It is tempting to think in terms of "causes" and even of "explanations" in the sense of "predictions." However, the phenomena that give rise to language change

are so complex that they will perhaps never be understood in enough detail for us to state precisely why a specific change occurred in the past or to predict when one will occur and if it does what it will be." (p. 63)

Traditional and New Interpretations

We have so far raised the question of why the phenomena occur as they do. Although there are diverse explanations, the generative linguistics position is most frequently preferred. Generally speaking, generative linguists think that the existence of innate grammar in the brains of children who have not passed the critical period takes central position in the explanations of those phenomena. According to Bickerton (1984), pidgins grammaticalize under the influence of the UG in the generations of children who acquire the pidgin as a native language. In other words, a pidgin becomes a language with grammar only when it is aided by innate grammar, or "bioprogram." The primary investigator of Nicaraguan Sign Language, Senghas, echoes Bickerton's idea. She thinks that Nicaraguan Sign Language developed from simpler, pidginlike language to more complex and creolelike language as a result of the innate ability that only children have: "All children have a special inborn ability not only to learn language, but to surpass the language of the environment when it is weak, and to create a language where none existed" (Senghas, 1995a, p. 551). Generative linguistics focuses on the role of child language acquisition to explain grammaticalization as well. For example, Lightfoot (1989, cited in Hopper and Traugott, 1993) argues that linguistic changes from one generation to another are caused by the fact that different children select different parameters from among different possibilities, which are a genetically coded restricted set of structures.

The generative linguists' assumption that grammar is a genetically defined entity is problematic and is questioned in many areas, such as genetics (Deacon, 1997) and neuroscience (Elman, 1993; Bates, Thal, and Janowsky, 1992). Furthermore, it is unclear how generative linguistics can explain how fixed genetic codes of humans can subserve 7,000 different languages.[5] However, generative linguists seem to be correct when they say that children have a different ability to acquire a language. Children's ability to acquire their community languages with great ease and regularity, even in stimuli-poor environments,[6] is truly remarkable. This point has been used by generative linguists to argue for the existence of

---

5. Pagel (2000) says that there are 7,000 languages in the world today. Considering that numerous languages have died throughout human history, we cannot even speculate about how many languages have existed.

6. Many scholars (e.g., Sampson, 1997) do not agree with the poverty-of-stimulus argument of generative linguists and says that there is sufficient and adequate linguistic input to children.

a grammar organ in the brain, and it was this ability that originally drove Chomskians to believe that there must be a genetically transmitted grammar module in the brain. In order for the languages-as-CASs theory to be valid, we should be able to explain this age factor without positing the existence of innate grammar.

Connectionists are among the groups that speak to this issue. They design computers to learn in ways thought to be similar to the activity and structure of human brains. Their computer networks are composed of three layers, or nodes: input, output, and hidden units. Learning in these networks takes place as the network receives input sequences, processes them through the hidden units, and produce sequences through the output nodes. The net has no innate preprogrammed structures except that it has a bias to give more attention to some aspects of the input than others. One of the researchers in this camp, Elman (1993), found in an artificial-neural-network simulation experiment that the very limitations in resources available to a child's brain still in the process of maturation may, in fact, be a necessary prerequisite for learning complex systems such as language and grammar. In his experiment, fully mature neural networks could not learn complex systems such as relative clauses and number agreement. In his framework, children can learn grammar with ease and regularity precisely because their neural network is immature and going through maturation.

Kuhl (2000) also provides a neurobiological explanation for why infants, rather than adults, acquire a community language with greater facility and regularity. The domain-general learning strategies of infants are different from those of adults, and this very difference accounts for infants' ability to acquire the ambient language with ease. Children characteristically employ learning strategies of pattern perception and statistical (probabilistic and distributional) computational skills. Using these strategies, they detect and exploit statistical properties of their ambient language and form a strong bias toward these properties so that they can perceive them more easily later. For instance, once a child detects a phoneme in his or her ambient language, a bias toward that particular phoneme is established such that it, and not other phonemes, will be more easily recognized in the future.

Kuhl (2000) even suggests that this learning strategy of infants may have influenced the nature of language as well. This point has profound implications for understanding language emergence, since it suggests that languages may have evolved in the process of human adaptation, psychological and physiological. The research conducted by both Elman and Kuhl indicates that the superior ability of children to acquire languages exists in the relative immaturity of neural structure and in the different physiology and psychology of children. This is especially interesting because human beings are very distinct from other primates (and from almost all other animals) in that they are born with much less mature brains.

The human bipedal gait, which is believed to have started with *Australopithecus* and to have been completed in *Homo erectus* (Jurmain, Nelson, Kilgore, and Trevathan, 2000), made it necessary for the human female to have a narrow pelvis to support locomotion. This anatomical change made it hard for a neonate with a big brain to pass through the birth canal of its mother. Thus, human babies are born with very immature brains. They have to undergo a long period of neural maturation after birth, and it is precisely during this period that socialization and acquisition of community language take place. If the maturation process is the secret of acquiring language, as Elman and Kuhl suggest, then the long period of maturation can explain why human children can learn such a complex system as language with remarkable regularity and facility. With the advancement of knowledge about how the human (infant and adult) brain works, there is no doubt that we will get a better explanation. We need not be frustrated by the current dearth of scientific explanation, nor need we jump to the conclusion that there must be a magical grammar box in the brain.

We now try to construct an argument that the phenomena investigated in pidgins and creoles, Nicaraguan Sign Language, and historical linguistics render support to the idea that languages are CASs and that patterns such as grammar and phonology spontaneously emerge via interactions among agents that participate in the interactions.

Languages, Open Systems, and Far-from-Equilibrium State

In an open system, there is continuous energy input from the outside, and this energy flow results in spontaneous pattern emergence. As Prigogine (1988) said, an open system evolves from an equilibrium state to a near-equilibrium state to a far-from-equilibrium state when there is an accumulated influx of energy. In the last stage, the system responds to the outside influences nonlinearly, patterns and order emerge out of chaos through self-organization, and the system continuously renews itself. CASs being studied at Santa Fe Institute are open systems that are mostly in a far-from-equilibrium state.

In order to argue that language is a CAS, we need to discuss two issues: whether languages are open systems and, if they are, what constitutes energy inputs; and whether they are in a far-from-equilibrium state when patterns such as grammar and phonology appear. First, it would appear that all languages (except dead languages such as Latin and Sanskrit or artificial languages such as Esperanto or computer languages) correspond perfectly to the definition of open systems. An organism, which is an open system, takes continual energy inputs from intakes such as nutrients, water, and air. Likewise, if we perceive linguistic interactions among people to be energy inputs to the system of a language, we can say that languages take energy inputs. Whenever a linguistic interaction occurs between two people, this interaction is feeding into the amorphous and nonphysical system of language, or linguosphere. In other words, all living languages are subject to constant inflow of energy; therefore, they are open systems.

Second, all living languages in the world seem to be in the far-from-equilibrium state of Prigogine's trichotomy. As in any other system in this state, in languages, the accumulated influx of energy of interactions is so great that patterns and order such as grammar and phonology emerge nonlinearly through self-organization, and languages continuously renew themselves. This point is evidenced by research in historical linguistics (see above). As Comrie (1992) argued, patterns such as morphophonemic alteration, phonemic tones, and the distinction between nasalized and nonnasalized vowels occur in languages. All living languages are always changing. In this process, patterns emerge and disappear nonlinearly, new languages evolve, and some languages totally change into different languages. In other words, languages continuously renew themselves through accumulated influx of energy. Some languages in danger of extinction today because of the decreasing population of their native speakers are probably in a different state. They are not likely to be in a far-from-equilibrium state, because not a large enough number of interactions are occurring in that language; therefore, they are lacking in energy input. Thus, the systems are withering and dying out.

Prigogine's trichotomy also explains the evolution of pidgins and creoles and Nicaraguan Sign Language with regard to the difference in complexity of patterns between the early stages and the late stages of those linguistic systems. An early stage of a pidgin, such as a jargon stage, or the early period of Nicaraguan Sign Language, or the Mimicas stage, probably did not reach a far-from-equilibrium state because of a lack of enough energy input with a limited number of interactions. This is probably why early pidgins and early Nicaraguan sign languages have only limited patterns and simple structures, as discussed above. On the other hand, in the later stages of those linguistic systems, more interactions took place, and as energy input increased, the systems approached far-from-equilibrium states, and when a threshold was crossed, complex patterns of grammar and other rules emerged spontaneously in the linguospheres. The process of development from a jargon to a stable pidgin to an extended pidgin and finally to a creole and the process of development of Nicaraguan Sign Language from Mimicas to LSN to ISN may occur as these linguospheres move toward, reach, and cross the threshold to a far-from-equilibrium state.

The Predictability Issue: Deterministic versus Stochastic

Studies of pidgins and creoles and historical linguistics support the idea that languages are CASs. In a CAS, it is intrinsically impossible to predict what patterns will emerge at what time. The same is true of languages. First, it is not possible to predict what types of patterns will emerge in a pidgin or a creole. Although some would say that there is a typical creole syntax (Carden and Stewart,1988; Bickerton, 1984), Romaine (1992) argues that creoles are quite diverse. She also argues that the grammatical structures of pidgins and creoles are independent from those of the substrate and superstrate languages. Furthermore, one cannot predict when creolization will occur. As discussed above, creolization occurs either abruptly from a jargon or a stable pidgin without going through extended pidgin stage or gradually via the last stage of pidgin. Also, some pidgins evolve into creoles, others stay as stable pidgins for a long time, and still others die out. Some creoles have no antecedent pidgin (Mufwene, 2001). Creoles evolve either when there are children acquiring a pidgin, as Bickerton (1990) argue, or only among adults, as McWhorter (2001) and Mufwene (2001) argue. Therefore, we cannot predict what structures a creole or a pidgin will develop in the end, when a creole will develop from a pidgin, or even whether a pidgin will ever evolve into a creole (Sebba, 1997). These factors can be influenced by any variable in a catastrophic way. This unpredictability is a hallmark of CASs.

The same situation is observed in historical linguistics. We discussed above how semantic scopes of lexical words unpredictably narrow, broaden, or simply drift. This is only an example. McWhorter (2001) says, "Language changes stem from the inherent randomness of general language change" (p. 49). He also says, "Language evolution . . . is largely a matter of chance, like the eternal transformations of that clump of lava in a lava lamp" (p. 44). Languages can change in myriad directions, and their destinations are simply unpredictable. The unidirectionality hypothesis of grammaticalization appears to be contradicted by the unpredictability principle of CAS, but it is not. What the unidirectionality hypothesis captures is a general direction of change of lexical items to grammatical items. This general direction is similar to water boiling when heat is applied. What is unpredictable is what kind of patterns will appear in the body of water when it boils (see chapter 1). Likewise, in the process of grammaticalization, it is not possible to predict when and in what form grammatical items will appear or whether they will ever appear. Hopper and Traugott (1993) warn: "There is nothing deterministic about grammaticalization and unidirectionality. Changes do not have to occur. They do not have to go to completion, in other words, they do not have to move all the way along a cline. A particular grammaticalization process may be, and often is, arrested before it is fully 'implemented,' and the 'outcome' of grammaticalization is quite often a ragged and incomplete subsystem that is not evidently moving in some identifiable direction" (p. 95).

Local Interactions, Pattern Match, and Bottom-Up Control

As discussed above, in a CAS, patterns emerge only through local and random interactions but not by top-down control or preordained design (Holland, 1995; Johnson, 2001). Individual ants interact with other ants in the colony only locally and randomly, but a collective behavioral pattern of the whole colony appears. Without this principle, diverse and unpredictable patterns could not emerge. Otherwise, all patterns would be determined by design through top-down control, and, therefore, only those patterns of the design would emerge and all patterns would be predictable. In addition, in a CAS, pattern emergence is possible because of the pattern-matching ability and adaptive internal models of agents (see chapter 1). The processes of emergence in pidgins, creoles, Nicaraguan Sign Language, and historical language changes all conform to these principles.

A scenario presented by McWhorter (2001) captures these principles of CAS well. As discussed above, McWhorter says that in all languages, there is a tendency for sounds to erode and finally disappear over time. The process of the erosion and disappearance occurs through local and random interactions and the pattern-matching abilities of people. When the process of erosion of a particular sound in a particular position begins, a few people may tend to pronounce the sound less distinctly in casual speech. This tendency is detected, used, and spread by some others who are engaged in interaction locally and randomly with them. When a new generation comes along and grows up hearing the reduced version of the sound, they come to regard the reduced version as the default pronunciation. A few people among the new generation may carry the erosion process further and pronounce the particular sound even less distinctly. This less distinct rendition of the sound will be detected, used, and spread among people again. Through reiteration of this process, a generation may come along that will perceive no sound at all at the position.

In this scenario, the interaction occurs among individuals, that is, locally. There can be more global interactions, such as at gatherings or religious services, taking place from time to time, but most interactions are likely to occur between individuals. The interaction is also random to a great extent, because meetings among individuals cannot be totally planned. Some social institutions, such as family, school, workplace, church, and so on, may define and bias the opportunity for and frequency of meetings among individuals. However, the institutions don't prevent random meetings across these institutional boundaries. In sum, the interactions among individuals that foster the disappearance of the particular sound at the particular position in McWhorter's scenario are local and random.

In addition, the disappearance of the sound is possible because of people's pattern-matching ability and adaptive internal models. When people hear a reduced version of a sound, they may accept the new pattern and even try it. When the new pattern is used by and spread among people, through a positive feedback process, individuals will hear the new rendition of the sound more frequently and will increasingly come to perceive it to be normal. The pattern-matching tendency is also observed in the area of grammar. As McWhorter noted, when a pattern of grammar appears, it tends to generalize into an across-the-board rule, as evidenced in the English plural marker. One pattern is matched by other instances in similar contexts and spreads throughout the language. During this process of pattern matching, the internal model in an individual's mind with regard to the sound or the grammatical pattern will go through adaptive change so that the individual can perceive and use the new rendition of the sound or grammar pattern more easily in the future.

The human ability to detect a pattern and imitate it is of utmost importance in the history of human evolution (Tomasello, 1999). When Tomasello refers to the distinct human ability to imitate, he means that we can not only duplicate behavior of others but also discern the intention of others when they are engaged in the behavior. Applying this ability to the reduced-sound scenario above, we may not only copy the reduced sound of a speaker, but we may also infer, consciously or unconsciously, that the reduced sound may constitute an internal model in the speaker's mind. When this inference occurs, we may actively match the speaker's sound pattern, because the speaker, having the reduced sound as the internal model, will also understand our reduced sound better. When the speaker understands us better, we can convey what we want to convey, and our speech act can be successful. New patterns of language may appear via this fine attunement between conversing individuals. Finally, when a new generation comes along and accepts the reduced version as default, the collective internal model of the people of that generation becomes completely different from that of previous generations.

Aggregation

As discussed in chapter 1, aggregation is necessary for CASs (Holland, 1995). Aggregation means two things: there should be many agents, and there should be aggregate interaction among the agents. The cases of pidgins, creoles, and Nicaraguan Sign Language testify that aggregation is also necessary for linguistic patterns to emerge. Generally speaking, only simple linguistic patterns appear when there are a limited number of agents and a limited number of interactions, but more complex linguistic patterns emerge when there are a large number of agents generating a large aggregate interaction.

In early pidgin situations, such as the jargon stage and the stable pidgin stage, the number of interacting pidgin speakers is limited because the social domains of the pidgin are confined. The lexicon is probably also small. In other words, the number of agents (people and lexicon) is small. In this situation, the pure number of interactions occurring in the pidgin will also be limited. As Holland (1995) and Johnson (2001) demonstrate, diverse and complex patterns won't emerge in this situation, and truly early pidgins won't have complex linguistic structures. On the other hand, when a pidgin creolizes either gradually or abruptly, interaction in the pidgin occurs by more members of the community (sometimes most members of the community) in diverse social domains. The lexicon is probably large as well. This condition satisfies the aggregation principle of CASs, and more complex and diverse linguistic patterns will emerge. In sum, pidgins have simple structures as a result of the limited number of participating agents and interactions, but creoles have more complex and diverse patterns because they have a larger number of agents and interactions. This point can also explain why there is no clear-cut line between pidgins and creoles. Pidgins and creoles are to be understood as two extreme points in a continuum of complexity. At one extreme on the continuum are early pidgins such as jargons, and on the other are creoles. There are all levels of complexity between the two extremes, and any line drawn between stages will be controversial. And, of course, creoles can develop without an antecedent pidgin.

The process of the development of Nicaraguan Sign Language can be explained from this perspective as well. NSL developed from home sign to Mimicas to LSN and finally to ISN. Two kinds of changes accompanied these transitions. The first was that the population of signers was cumulatively increasing as new students entered the school every year. When the school opened in 1977, 25 students were enrolled, but the number increased to 400 by 1983. If we take the students who graduated from the school into count, the number of people in the signing community of the country probably now exceeds several thousand. In addition, considering the cumulative number of interactions that must have taken place in the population since 1977, the increase in the number of interactions during the period must have been exponential.

The second change was emergence of more complex linguistic structures. Nicaraguan Sign Language started from the idiosyncratic home signs and gestures of the first generation. It developed into a system of simple argument structure and minimal morphology, which finally evolved into a more complex and sophisticated language system, complete with serial verbs, anaphors, complex morphology such as verb inflections, and complex but nonredundant argument structure. And now NSL is a full-blown language. Complex linguistic patterns emerged only when there was a sufficient aggregation of agents and interactions.

Multistrata

As discussed in chapter 1, Holland (1975, 1995) notes that CASs are composed of multistrata of agents. An agent at one level serves as the building block for meta-agents at a higher level, which, in turn, serve as the building blocks for meta-meta-agents at a next higher level. Agents of a higher level are more complex than those of a lower level. Human linguistic communities are structured in this way. A language itself is structured in this way. A change at one level can result in a change in the next level, which, in turn, brings about another change in the next level after that, and so on. When a chain of change occurs, the scope of change is nonlinear; therefore, a small perturbation at one level can cause a catastrophic restructuring at a higher level.

Research in historical linguistics testifies that this principle of CASs is operating in language change. McWhorter (2001) demonstrated this point using the development of French from Latin. The sound erosion of six number and person affixes and case endings in Latin resulted in only three forms of the first and none of the second in French. The change that started in Latin as erosion of sounds brought about the changes from a no-pronoun system to an obligatory-pronoun system and from a free-word-order system to a relatively rigid word order. The change at the phonetic level resulted in changes in morphological systems, which, in turn, resulted in changes in syntactic systems, which resulted in a different language.

Conclusions

The topic of language evolution is one of the most important issues facing linguistics. It not only addresses the phylogeny of language, but it also speaks to the question of what language is. If languages evolved through human biological evolution, innatists such as generative linguists would have support for their position that there is a UG in our brains, and we, who study the neurobiology of language, would have to try harder to find the neural basis of UG. However, chapters 1 and 2 of this book take a different approach to the source of language structure. From the perspective we provide, humans did not need to evolve either language genes or grammar modules in the brain. Like any other complex system in nature, languages follow the principles of CASs, and linguistic patterns have emerged dynamically through self-organization.

To reach this conclusion, we investigated how modern science overcame the problems of classical dynamics. The nature of classical dynamics was deterministic and reductionistic. It did not explain the intrinsic unpredictability and indeterminacy of the universe, nor did it address spontaneous pattern emergence. The theory of CASs was born in this realization. It tries to capture how complexity appears and works unpredictably, indeterminately, and nonlinearly. It tries to explain how patterns emerge spontaneously and dynamically through self-organization. The theory of CASs is still young, but it has been successful in explaining the dynamics of many phenomena in nature and in society, such as weather and climate, the immune system, the stock market, the development of cities, and so on. We believe that language evolution can be understood from the perspective of this theory.

We have also investigated the principles of CASs, how CASs work, and whether languages follow the same principles. We found that languages are compatible with the principles of CASs, and this compatibility argues that languages are genuine CASs. Finally, we have provided evidence of the emergence of patterns in languages. The evidence was drawn from connectionists' simulation experiments, pidgin and creole languages, Nicaraguan Sign Language, and historical linguistics. The investigation of this evidence supports our thesis that language is a CAS, born of massive interaction among language users.

THREE

The Implications of Interaction
for the Nature of Language

In many ways, Chomsky's early claims about the nature of language are extremely attractive. In an attempt to understand the human mind, it seems natural to begin with language, the most obvious attribute unique to the species. Smith (1999) argues, in agreement with many linguists, philosophers, anthropologists, and sociologists, that "despite the complexity and variety of animal communication systems, no other creature has language like ours" (p. 7). To look at language in order to uncover the nature of the human mind may therefore appear quite logical. However, we would like to suggest that it is interactional tendencies—an "interactional instinct" (see Lee and Schumann, 2005), if you will—that are intricately involved in shaping the characteristics of human language. Moreover, it is only by examining language in its close relationship with such interactional tendencies that we may truly understand how language works or, more specifically, how language that requires an evolutionary and neurobiological explanation works.

The notion of a universal grammar (UG), a set of innate grammatical principles shared by all human languages, is a common theme among modern linguistic paradigms. Such paradigms see language as "a sort of biologically inherited coding system for our biologically inherited knowledge base" (Sampson, 1997, p. 3) and view grammar as the key to its uncoding.[1] O'Grady (2005) remarks that one of the principal points of consensus to have arisen among linguists regarding the inner workings of language is "the idea that the core properties of language can be explained by reference to principles of *grammar*" (p. 1, emphasis added). When contemplating what aspects of language to examine and explain, it again may

---

1. This belief has led to the practice of using *language* and *grammar* interchangeably in linguistics.

appear quite logical to begin with grammar as a formal property, since it is this aspect of language that is most obviously distinct from other forms of (animal) communication. Other reasons grammar has taken center stage may be more practical in nature; grammar is the most concrete and easily accessible feature of language, and it can be examined without much technological aid beyond per-haps printed materials. However, relying predominantly on printed materials (or sentences fabricated by academics) has led researchers to make claims based on the complexities of grammar endemic to writing. The priority given to grammati-cal structure in linguistics is not merely based on the practicality of examining something so immediately observable and available for analysis. Rather, the focus on discovering autonomous and genetically based grammatical principles has generated claims that are both neurobiological and evolutionary (e.g., Bickerton, 1981, 1984; see also Chomsky, 1975, 1991).

This chapter is a prolegomenon to a biological investigation of language. Before we begin extensive studies of the evolution and neurobiology of language, we must decide what our database will be. We have to decide to what characteri-zation of language biological accounts must be responsible. We must ask our-selves where we should look for language that will allow us to better understand the grammar and language with which the brain evolved to cope. The brain faces language with all of its imperfections—pauses, repeats, restarts, repairs, and so on. We cannot reject these discourse elements a priori as noise, which is often what is done in linguistics. These elements may turn out to be crucial to produc-ing language, comprehending it, and learning it. In addition, by turning to language that is familiar to those who are highly literate and by examining written language and isolating sentences, we, as analysts, have been creating a problem that the brain was not required to solve. It is not that sentences are uninteresting; they may show functions of words or constructions in writing or reveal connections between such functions in speech and writing; they may also reveal what the brain is capable of learning after schooling and with the luxury of time and reflection. Indeed, "not everyone is equally capable of combining clauses into a well-integrated sentence with subordinate adverbial clauses, participial phrases and relative clauses introduced by a preposition plus a WH word" (Miller and Weinert, 1998, p. 20). Isolated sentences or complicated syntax endemic to academic prose are simply inappropriate data for the theory that linguists have set out to prove. This chapter, therefore, considers conversation as the primordial form of language and as a form of language that first evolved in the environment of evolutionary adaptation. One aim here is to expose the kinds of information that more naturalistic approaches (such as conversation analysis and discourse analy-sis) can provide as a rationale for using these data in the initial explorations of the biological foundations of language.[2] By "naturalistic," we mean to indicate

2. This is not to say that other schools of linguistics, such as the Columbia school (CS) and cognitive grammar (CG), have nothing to add here. Both of these schools have

that these approaches look at linguistic forms and elements in naturally occurring spoken language.

Given the scope of this chapter, we will not elaborate in much detail on the insights that neurobiological and evolutionary studies may bring to this discussion, except to iterate a lesson expounded by primatologists and animal biologists studying evolution and animal behavior, a lesson from which linguists would benefit: "[One's] interest in the evolutionary origins of behavior highlights the need for making observations in settings like those in which the behaviors evolved" (De Waal and Tyack, 2003, p. xii).

Along these lines, several language and discourse researchers have begun to take seriously the fact that speech and/or conversation are the most natural habitats for language.

- "[O]rdinary conversation is the prototypical form of language, the baseline against which all other genres, spoken or written, should be compared" (Chafe and Tannen, 1987, p. 390).
- "[C]onversation is the most common and, it would appear, the most fundamental condition of 'language use' or 'discourse'" (Schegloff, 1979, p. 283).
- Spoken language is the "primary genre from which all other genres were derived" (Bakhtin, 1986).
- "[I]nteractive language use is the core phenomenon to be explained—all other forms of discourse are, however, interesting, derivative in every sense, ontogenetic and phylogenetic included" (Levinson, 2006, p. 85).

Specifically with respect to grammar, Hayashi (1999) notes that many researchers now recognize "that the grammatical organization of language is intimately

approached language in innovative and useful ways with respect to language use, in particular by stressing the importance of the sign and contextualized meaning in linguistic research. CS takes as a premise an interactive writer/speaker and reader/hearer. Additionally, CS purports that only in the communicative force is the linguistic signal made sense of by inference-making individuals. This is evident in Contini-Morava's (1995) review of the principles of CS, one of which states that "the theoretical units that are postulated must be consistent with the communicative goals that language is used to accomplish" (p. 2). Likewise, CS, realizing that language is a system managed by human users, asserts that linguistic forms will be influenced by human biases and abilities. In both CS and CG, the units of language cannot be separated from their users and their communicative functions. (For insightful CS analyses, see Contini-Morava and Goldberg, 1995; Contini-Morava and Tobin, 2000; Reid, Otheguy, and Stern, 2002; and Contini-Morava, Kirsner, and Rodriguez-Bachiller, 2004. For relevant studies in CG, see Langacker, 1987, 1991, 2002; Fox, Jurafsky, and Michaelis, 1999; and Talmy, 2000.) Yet many functional schools of linguistics, including CS and CG, are still, for historical reasons, wedded largely to written language, which is a very rarefied, secondary type of language. For these reasons, we do not draw significantly from either of these two schools.

intertwined with various organizations of human conduct in social interaction, and therefore that a proper understanding of what we call 'grammar' cannot be obtained without regard to interactional matrices in which it figures" (p. 476). Schegloff (1996c) similarly remarks that "it should hardly surprise us if some of the most fundamental features of natural language are shaped in accordance with this home environment in copresent interaction—as adaptations to it, or as part of its very warp and weft. For example, if the basic natural environment for sentences is in turns-at-talk in conversation, we should take seriously the possibility that aspects of their structure—for example, their grammatical structure— are to be understood as adaptations to that environment" (pp. 54–55).

When language is recognized to consist of primary forms (e.g., conversation) and secondary forms (e.g., writing), it becomes clear that what needs to be explained are not complex syntax and ambiguities but how language is used socially to accomplish actions with coparticipants. This is true whether one's interests in language center on grammar or elsewhere. Believing that language has some sort of biological roots may be warranted; claiming that these roots are not of a social nature is, at the very least, unusual when studying language in its most natural setting, that of casual conversation.[3]

What Is the Problem, Really? Isn't All Language the Same?

The fundamental problem until now has been that linguists have been struggling to provide a neurobiological account of language based on inappropriate data. This is exacerbated by the fact that students in linguistics are being trained to view human language as a uniform category and to believe that what we *can* do with language (even if unnatural) best represents language for which we need to provide an account. In an introductory graduate syntax seminar, for example, the following sentence was given to demonstrate certain structural properties of underlying structure:

(3.1)
John likes his neighbors and Bill does too.

At first glance, there does not seem to be anything unusually difficult about understanding this sentence. Linguists may note that it is ambiguous. It is unclear whether Bill likes his own neighbors[4] or John's neighbors.[5] Sentences such as this

---

3. Or, perhaps more appropriately, talk-in-interaction, as it is called by conversation analysts.
4. This is sometimes referred to as sloppy identity.
5. This is sometimes referred to as strict identity.

have informed the field of linguistics; they tell us that one sentence may have more than one meaning, which generally implies more than one possible hierarchical structure (or syntactic tree). In order to come to terms with such sentences, formal properties of syntax must be wrestled with—notions such as pronominal binding and c-command.[6] The following is another example from the same seminar:

(3.2)

John's mother had tried to persuade Bill to visit her when he was asked to.

This sentence appears to be somewhat more complicated; one may notice that it is unclear who is doing the asking and to whom *her* refers, whether it is *John's mother* or someone else. This complexity may simply be a result of the sentence's length and the number of referents that need to be indexicalized (see Deacon, 1997, 2003, for more on indexicalization in language). However, linguists have "solved" these language difficulties by examining and comparing the structures of such sentences and sentences similar to them. The ambiguity in sentence 3.1 could merely be a problem of coreference (what can corefer to *his*) and not an issue involving internal structure at all (in this case, c-command, the structural principle being demonstrated with such a comparison of sentences). However, when example 3.1 is compared with example 3.3 below, in which *Bill* does not bind *his* (and so *his* cannot refer to *Bill*), c-command (and not simply coreference) makes the correct prediction for 3.3.[7]

(3.3)

The girl that John knows likes his neighbors and Bill does too.

When we examine casual conversation or talk-in-interaction, we find very few sentences like this. In fact, we often do not find sentences (as traditionally

---

6. "The hierarchical structure of sentences has long been diagrammed such that branches of the phrase structure tree correspond to clauses. In such diagrams, pronouns generally can only refer to referents that are higher than they are in the phrase structure diagram. The most widely accepted generalization is that a pronoun cannot be coreferent with a noun phrase that c-commands it" (Harris and Bates, 2002, p. 4). C-command is a structural relation between two entities: "If A c-commands B, A is higher in the structural hierarchy than B. More formally, A c-commands B iff A does not include/dominate B and the first node that dominates A also dominates B" (Guasti, 2002, p. 424). To take simple examples, in the sentence *Mary believes herself to be a kind person, Mary* c-commands *herself*, and so coreference is possible; however, in **Herself believes Mary to be a kind person, Mary* does not c-command *herself*, and so they cannot corefer. These structural constraints on coreferencing are defined by three binding principles (principles A, B, and C), where "binding" refers to the relation between the pronoun and its antecedent. See Napoli, 1996, pp. 384–387, for a more detailed introduction to c-command.

7. For a functionalist account of c-command, see Harris and Bates (2002).

defined) at all. Example 3.1 would most likely not be ambiguous to those for whom the utterance was intended (such interactional considerations are how the brain comes to understand language), and examples 3.2 and 3.3 would very likely never be uttered at all, for reasons that we hope to illuminate throughout this chapter.

Understanding language in the circumstances in which it most likely evolved (interactional circumstances) is imperative given the neurobiological and evolutionary basis of linguists' research, particularly syntactic inquiries. However, the study of syntax often attempts to discover principles underlying quite complicated constructions and their ambiguities divorced from the real world, as illustrated above. Traditionally, decontextualized sentences are fabricated to demonstrate a particular construction or contrast, and in the cases in which sentences by real language users are explained, they are typically from written and formal genres and often demonstrate structures that do not occur in conversation and sometimes even very rarely in written genres. Gapping constructions (*I prefer musicals and my sister plays*), as examined by Tao and Meyer (Tao and Meyer, 2006; see also Schumann et al., 2006), were found to be extremely rare in speech as well as in writing. When gapping constructions were used in writing, they were common to one particular genre: journalistic writing. Yet Tao and Meyer note that gapping has been a construction to which linguists have dedicated much time. In fact, they estimate that 160 articles have been published attempting to explain gapping, while only 120 instances of gapping actually occurred in the 1-million-word corpus they examined. If our goal is to provide an accurate evolutionary and neurobiological account of language, then it is unclear why we have spent so much time trying to explain the writing of journalists.

To take another instance, tough movement was one of several types of constructions examined by Chipere (1998). He found that uneducated native speakers of English could not appropriately understand such sentences by syntax alone but had to rely on the semantic plausibility of the sentences to understand them correctly. When uneducated speakers were presented with semantically implausible sentences, such as *The bank manager will be hard to give a loan to*, they could not correctly determine who was doing the asking and who was doing the giving. However, sentences such as *The criminal will be hard to give a loan* to presented little difficulty. Contrastively, both educated native speakers of English and educated nonnative speakers of English could appropriately understand these constructions even when communicating semantically implausible situations. This again reminds us that not all language requires a neurobiological explanation. Clearly, constructions such as gapping and tough movement are not part of our most natural linguistic abilities and thus not deserving of an evolutionary and neurobiological account; rather, this kind of language is a specialized skill that requires training and literacy.

Different Kinds of Language: How Different Is
"Different," and Why Do Differences Matter?

Miller and Weinert (1998) report that there are aspects of spoken grammar that can be viewed as "not just less complex but different" from grammar in written genres (p. 21). This should come as little surprise given the primacy of speech. Ong (2002), for example, describes characteristics common to oral cultures that likely influence the grammatical differences that Miller and Weinert illustrate. Ong notes that the language of primary oral cultures (cultures with no or very little contact with literacy) is additive (rather than subordinative), aggregative (rather than analytic), redundant, conservative, close to the human life world, agonistically toned, empathetic and participatory (rather than objectively distanced), homeostatic, and situational (rather than abstract) (pp. 37–57). While the conversational extracts discussed below are taken, as far as we know, from fully literate participants, many of these characteristics that Ong ascribes to oral peoples also apply to these real-world, interactive situations among literate coparticipants (although perhaps to varying degrees).

Ong remarks about oral cultures that "when all verbal communication must be by direct word of mouth, involved in the give and take dynamics of sound, interpersonal relations are kept high" (p. 45). Ong also writes, following Malinowski (1923, pp. 451, 470–481), that "among 'primitive' (oral) peoples, generally language is a mode of action and not simply a countersign of thought" (p. 32). While certain aspects of conversation among fully literate individuals may differ from those of primary oral cultures (perhaps with respect to discourse organization), these two aspects (the importance of interpersonal relations and language as a mode of action) are characteristic of ordinary talk even among educated native speakers who have, it may be assumed, powerful connections to the literate world.[8] These characteristics thus are not unique to oral cultures but are common to much ordinary oral communication, and such aspects of orality should be kept in mind when examining the data extracts presented below.

Writing, in contrast to oral language, is a very recent technology (roughly 5,000 years old). Ong refers to writing as a technology, by which he means that it requires "the use of tools and other equipment." In this way, he claims that "writing is completely artificial" and that "there is no way to write 'naturally'" (pp. 80–81). No one would argue that writing needs an evolutionary or neurobiological explanation, because no one would argue that writing is biologically inherited. And yet our assumptions and knowledge about grammar and language are often based on the kind of language that is unique to writing (or to those who write frequently). Ong, in discussing the inappropriateness of the term *oral literature*, remarks on a progression in understanding orality that parallels the

8. If one were to examine less ordinary situations, such as classroom interaction, business meetings, or presentations, it is likely that these characteristics of oral cultures that Ong describes would diminish.

development in linguistics. This progression, like the progression of linguistics, can roughly be described as backward. His words, although maintaining a different focus from ours, eloquently describe the consequences of such a backward approach to studying language varieties:

> With their attention directed to texts, scholars often went on to assume, often without reflection, that oral verbalization was essentially the same as the written verbalization they normally dealt with, and that oral art forms were to all intents and purposes simply texts, except for the fact that they were not written down.... [T]he relentless dominance of textuality in the scholarly mind is shown by the fact that to this day no concepts have yet been formed for effectively, let alone gracefully, conceiving of oral art as such without reference, conscious or unconscious, to writing. This is so even though the oral art forms which developed during the tens of thousands of years before writing obviously had no connection with writing at all. (p. 10)[9]

Of course, studying the language use of literate individuals and individuals with close ties to the literate world complicates matters;[10] however, what is

9. In a similar vein, Miller and Weinert (1998) also acknowledge the consequences of applying written-language norms to spoken-language data: "when the formal theory gives rise to a theory of first language acquisition the problems become even worse, because the essential principles and parameters of the theory, developed on the basis of written language, are applied to the acquisition of spontaneous spoken language" (p. 5).

10. While this is certainly true, there are many parallels between Ong's descriptions of the language of oral cultures and the oral language of literate individuals. For example, Ong describes the language of oral cultures as aggregative rather than analytic and discusses how oral cultures often use "clusters of integers, such as parallel terms or phrases or clauses" (p. 38); this also seems to be a characteristic of casual conversation among literates, as is shown in the following, from Langellier and Peterson's (2004) book *Storytelling in Daily Life:* "my brother got a licking for smoking / my sister got a licking for smoking / I got a licking I still don't know to this day why" (p. 52). To take just one more example, Ong depicts the language of oral cultures as redundant, which is also illustrated in another example from the same source (the subscript numbers note the clauses that are redundant):

> And she sat I thought on the seat
> I went around to the driver's seat and I looked across and my god she's not there[1]
> [Laughs to self] my god where is she?[1]
> And I run around the car and she had slipped[2]
> She was laying underneath the car[2]
> [everyone laughing]
> and when I get nervous I giggle
> and she says "leave me alone.[3] I'll get up.[4]"
> "just leave me alone.[3] I'll get mad enough in a minute and I'll get up."[4]
> Well sure enough she did.[4] She got up.[4] (Langellier and Peterson, 2004, p. 54)

important to remember is that not all language is equal in terms of its naturalness, and linguists, by first examining the written variety, have created categories and have been led to assumptions that simply do not apply to oral language, which is clearly primary as far as the brain is concerned. Similarly, linguists frequently create sentences to analyze. As such, they have no way of knowing if or how such sentences/utterances would be used in naturalistic interaction. Additionally, they have no way of knowing to what extent their literacy skills influence these created sentences.

With the proper technology (paper, pencil, and sometimes a trained syntactician), we can understand *The cat the rat the dog chased bit ran.* We can understand this sentence because we have the tools to construct a visual diagram and ample time to reflect on what this sentence could mean. Linguists have argued that this sentence is well formed and is part of native English speakers' *competence* (part of the language faculty that is our biological inheritance). They have claimed that we do not actually use such sentences because of our *performance* limitations—limited processing capacity, constraints on memory, and so on (see below for more on competence and performance distinctions). Just as we have learned to manipulate this sentence with the help of other resources, we have also learned to use and understand the grammatical constructions in writing. More important, however, is understanding how sentences such as *The cat the rat the dog chased bit ran* would have become part of our biology when they are not instances of language that the brain actually encountered or experienced. This question remains unanswered.

Pinker (1999), while he believes that language is not inherently interactional but a biological inheritance, also warns against believing that all language deserves a neurobiological explanation. Pinker reflects on a question he is frequently asked concerning his notion of a language instinct: How can language be a biological endowment, a human instinct, when there are so many improper usages of language? To address this contradiction, Pinker argues that while laypeople view grammar as prescriptive rules (e.g., avoid dangling participles), linguists view grammar descriptively. Pinker reminds us that "prescriptive and descriptive grammar are simply different things" (pp. 3–4). He describes prescriptive rules as "inconsequential decorations" (p. 4) and as "so psychologically unnatural that only those with access to the right schooling can abide by them . . . they serve as shibboleths, differentiating the elite from the rabble" (pp. 5–6). Pinker, although he supports a biological or genetic basis for language, correctly argues that "there is no need to use terms like 'bad grammar,' 'fractured syntax' and 'incorrect usage' when referring to rural, black and other nonstandard dialects" (p. 14). Clearly, the issue of incorrect usage is not just relevant to nonstandard dialects. Incorrect usage is not (or should not be) an issue for any dialect. If it is used and understood by a native speaker, how can it be wrong? To be sure, usages can be wrong in writing, the gatekeepers having enforced rules of clear and logical prose, but by what criteria can an utterance be considered wrong in speech? Although Pinker does not directly address the differences between writing and speech, he does claim in support of our view that "the aspect of language use that is most worth changing is the clarity and style of written prose. The human language faculty was not designed for putting esoteric thoughts on paper for the benefit of strangers, and this makes writing a difficult craft that must be mastered through practice, feedback and intensive exposure to good examples" (p. 14).

Pinker even notes that writing is for strangers and therefore lacks the interactional basis of using language for interpersonal communication and social action. So, why, to support a biologically inherited language faculty, do linguists spend so much time explaining structures that are not natural but are artifacts of the norms of written prose? To be fair, linguists do not only examine complex sentences specific to writing; they also consider seemingly simple sentences such as *John likes himself*. However, it is often the case that such simple sentences are understood and explained only in comparison to more complex sentences, because it is only in more complicated sentences that hierarchical (or underlying) structure can be revealed (for example, c-commanding with respect to *John likes himself*). When considering what needs to be accounted for in terms of evolution and neurobiology, we should not need to account for aspects of language that do not happen at all (such as *The cat the rat the dog chased bit ran*) and do not happen naturally without years of training and technological aid (such as gapping constructions). Miller (2002) also makes a plea for researchers to make the appropriate distinction between oral and written language. Miller remarks that nativists "assume a large endowment of innate linguistic knowledge, without which it would (allegedly) be impossible for children to acquire the complex structures of any language. Once the complexities of written language are seen as learned over a longish period of schooling, once spontaneous spoken language is recognized as being relatively simple and once it is recognized that children do receive negative evidence (Sokolov and Snow, 1994), nativist theories lose their *raison d'etre*. This is the most important consequence of paying attention to literacy and the distinction between spoken and written language" (p. 473, cited in Tarone and Bigelow, 2005, p. 86).

For these reasons, it is to interactional settings containing natural and spontaneous spoken language[11] (casual, ordinary conversation) that we must turn to find the grammar and language that are actually suitable for the goal of linguistics. When we examine this sort of grammar and language, not only do we see a wholly different variety of language, but we also cannot help but see its interactional motivations.

---

11. Ong (2002) points out that there are very few societies today that are untouched by the influence of writing and print, which he calls primary orality. This is compared with secondary orality characteristic of cultures that rely on advanced technology. These differences may also need to be more carefully considered when contemplating the sort of language the brain naturally encountered.

There is clearly something unique about interaction, especially face-to-face discourse, among humans that is necessary for our understanding of how language works (see Joaquin, 2005, for how interaction is a precursor for the ontogeny of symbolic formation and referencing). Children cannot acquire language without interaction, and the use and manipulation of language reveals its dynamic and flexible nature,[12] which interacting participants can exploit in order to accomplish social goals. The essence of interaction has been demonstrated empirically in experiments such as those conducted by Clark and Wilkes-Gibbs (1986) and Schober and Clark (1989). In these experiments, one subject explains to a second subject in a face-to-face setting how to perform a certain task. A third participant listens to the entire interaction but is not allowed to participate. The two subjects who receive the instructions—the interactant who receives them directly/interactively (in face-to-face conversation) and the over-hearer—are then told to complete the task. Although the participants who merely overhear the instructions have the same content and information as the interacting participants, they are not able to complete the task as successfully as the interacting participants do. Bavelas (1999) argues that "this measurable difference in performance demonstrates that a dialogue is more than the utterances of individuals; it is a unique event created by those individuals, moment by moment" (p. 6) for the given situation at hand. These experiments are also telling in that they demonstrate the fundamental character of natural conversation and the sort of language that is its foundation; it is inherently interactional (which is precisely why *talk-in-interaction* seems the more appropriate term when compared with *language* or *grammar*). The linguistic units being deployed (the grammar) are not the only available resource by which interactants glean meaning or accomplish tasks (as these experiments demonstrate).

The Role of Context

The brief illustration above of how language is typically considered has raised perhaps one of the most important issues in language studies: what to do with context. Goodwin (2000a) contends that such a separation of the elements of natural spoken discourse is inadequate: "When action is investigated in terms of contextual configurations, domains of phenomena that are usually treated as so distinct that they are the subject matter of entirely separate academic disciplines, e.g., language and material structure in the environment, can be analyzed as integrated components of a common process or the social production of meaning and action" (p. 1490).

---

12. "Indeed, a language which afforded only discrete units, whose boundaries were rigid and fixed, would constitute a problem rather than a solution to the recurrent of real-time interaction" (Ford, 2004, p. 31).

Of course, in linguistics, language is by and large examined outside the context in which it exists. Sentences (or, less frequently, utterances) have either been extracted from their contexts and examined as individual, isolated, and independent units (as is sometimes the case in corpora studies) or have been fabricated and thus never existed in a natural context at all (as is usually the case in formal linguistic research).

While using extracts from natural discourse entails real language by real users, much of what gives grammar its shape is the context in which it occurs, both linguistic and situational (see Mikesell, 2004a, 2004b). It is therefore difficult to understand a particular focal construction that was uttered or used without examining it embedded in its natural surrounding.[13] The problem with fabricating sentences is even greater given that even if one believes in the existence of some innate grammar module, it would most likely not have evolved to understand or produce sentences such as examples 3.1 to 3.3 above.[14] The sorts of problems that are examined in such sentences are problems for analysts and not problems that the brain naturally faced when acquiring language. The point is that such sentences were constructed not by real language users but by skilled academics well trained in manipulating syntax; they were not designed to be understood by one's recipients; they were not embedded in a specific context or environment for which linguistic decisions by both the speaker(s) and the hearer(s) were based. Language in conversation has been shown to be "locally managed, party-administered, interactionally controlled, and sensitive to recipient design" (Sacks, Schegloff, and Jefferson, 1974, p. 696), important features to consider when attempting to understand natural language use by social language users. Within the same research paradigm, Lerner (1996) argues, "the action accomplished by the interposed talk hinges on the context of its occurrence" (p. 267). This is also true of the grammar that assists in accomplishing such action.

13. This is because a fundamental semiotic constraint of language is its property of indexicalization (see Deacon, 1997, 2003, for a general discussion and Mikesell, 2004a, for an application).

14. In fact, even after having to consider example 3.3 for its ambiguity and possible syntactic analyses, we still have difficulty understanding all of the logical readings supposedly available for this sentence, perhaps precisely because of the lack of context. Those who study syntax are often told to imagine contexts so that the various readings of different attachments of adjuncts and complements would be made available. Yet what is provided by context is precisely what cannot be intuited through such mental exercises. In fact, as the studies by Clark and colleagues show, what context affords cannot even be observed. Of course, schooling and practice with prose have given many of us ample opportunity to learn how to understand and produce such sentences, sometimes even effortlessly (see Ong, 2002, and Tannen, 1982, for a discussion of the relationship between spoken language/orality and literacy).

When language is treated as autonomous (i.e., when grammar is viewed as an independent system), everything else that plays a part in language use gets treated as either irrelevant context or noise; however, everything else matters to how language is produced and understood (especially when it is examined with respect to "the production and interpretation of human action"; see Goodwin, 2000a). In light of this, it is understood that a particular grammatical structure does not invariably serve one single function. This is precisely because contextual considerations are important for language (grammar) use. For instance, Schegloff (1997), in examining other-initiated repairs, observes that a particular linguistic form typically used to initiate repair may be employed for a different function in a particular context. He notes that "an utterance's function or action is not inherent in the form of the utterance alone, but is shaped by its sequential context as well" (p. 538).

Context is crucial; the brain evolved and language emerged through reliance on context in order to make meaning of the linguistic signal.[15] We know that language learning depends to a certain extent on the context in which it is learned, beyond merely the need for language input (see Tomasello and Kruger, 1992; Tomasello, 2002). Grammar does not function alone, and speakers and hearers work together collaboratively to coconstruct meaning from grammar as well as from the circumstances in which it is embedded. In 1966, Berger and Luckmann asserted that "most conversation does not in so many words define the nature of the world. Rather, it takes place against the background of a world that is silently taken for granted" (pp. 172–173). Decades later, many language researchers are still neglecting the context by examining only the words, only the grammar, or only the talk. Context, whether linguistic or situational, should not be ignored in the study of language or in the study of grammar.[16] This theme will be reiterated below. Sanitized syntax is not something the brain naturally encounters; therefore, context-free grammar is an antineurological and antievolutionary concept. It must be remembered that asking why the brain *can* understand sanitized syntax is an entirely different question from the one linguists have set out to answer.

15. Although the role of context involved in written texts has been debated, the richness of the context is clearly different from that of talk-in-interaction (even by highly literate individuals). This difference between spoken and written language is probably reflected in structural characteristics of both forms.

16. Similarly, Everett (2005), based on his findings of Piraha grammar and the cultural beliefs that constrain it, has argued that "linguistic fieldwork should be carried out in a cultural community of speakers because only by studying the culture and the grammar together can the linguist (or ethnologist) understand either." He also notes that studies of grammar that extract isolated patterns "are fundamentally untrustworthy because they are too far removed from the original situation" (p. 633).

Grammar in the Wild

> When one considers the grammatical structure of language as a set of social resources that is in the first instance situated in the hands of participants who can deploy and exploit (and play with) these used-in-common features of sociality, then the ground for grammatical description shifts from the structures of language to the structures of practice. (Lerner, 1996, pp. 238–239)

Many linguists and syntacticians believe that language (grammar) did not evolve for communication. The reasoning is essentially that if grammar were to have evolved for communicative reasons, it would not be as complicated as linguists believe it to be.[17] For instance, Chomsky (1991) writes that language "can be used . . . in specific language functions such as communication; [but] language is not intrinsically a system of communication" (pp. 50–51). He later argues (Chomsky and Lasnik, 1993) that "in general, it is not the case that language is readily usable or 'designed for use' (p. 18). Similarly, Newmeyer (2003) claims that "grammars are not actually well designed to meet language users' 'needs' (p. 682). While there is general consensus among linguists with regard to why language did not evolve, there is less agreement about why language did evolve, a question also worth exploring. From an evolutionary perspective, nonfunctional elements are less likely to evolve, and even characteristics that seem superfluous (e.g., the male peacock's tail) may have an important function to play, even if that function is not immediately obvious. It is therefore unclear why grammatical features would have become genetically hardwired if they served no useful purpose. In the view argued for here, language is social; it is a cultural artifact. With this in mind, Chomsky, Lasnik, and Newmeyer make a valid observation. Nonfunctional elements are seen in cultural artifacts, and, indeed, some aspects of language may not be well designed to meet communicative needs. The emergence of nonfunctional aspects of grammar is particularly evident when examining the cultural artifact of writing. Normative rules such as "Do not end sentences with prepositions" have no apparent functional motivation. But nonfunctional features appear to be less common in the grammar of conversation, given that these patterns emerge out of the interactions among participating agents (see chapter 1 herein) accomplishing real-world tasks and solving real-world problems.

This section attempts to dispel some common assumptions of linguists by synthesizing findings from two important areas of research: conversation (and to some extent discourse) analysis and usage-based linguistic approaches.[18] These

17. All data discussed in this section will be from spoken English discourse; however, similar findings are continually being observed for various other languages, including, but not limited to, Swedish, Dutch, Chinese, Russian, Estonian, and Japanese. Also please note that all names in this chapter's transcripts are pseudonyms.

18. This includes, for example, functional linguistic research and corpus-based research, both of which examine real language use.

areas share tenets that make their work particularly relevant to our understanding of grammar in spontaneous and natural conversation. Both research areas claim that real language use is what needs to be examined and/or explained, they both appreciate the importance of context in structuring the grammatical output although to differing degrees, and they show how spoken language is intricately adapted to our communicative needs. In essence, both approaches understand episodes of language to be "produced and understood not as self-contained events, but strictly within a shared context of situation" (Robins, 1971, p. 35). This fundamental commonality, however, is also the source of their difference. Where usage-based linguists (e.g., many functional linguists) often remove an isolated instance of grammar from its natural context in order to examine it, whether it be a sentence, a clause, or verbal argument, conversation analysts examine some focal item embedded in its context so as to understand the function that the focal element serves with respect to the larger interactional sequence. Examining contextualized language is a lesson that functional linguists are beginning to learn but one that is, unfortunately, still not the norm in language research.[19]

Only when we view fabricated strings of words isolated from any normal context and without the support of ecology may we be tempted to make the claims that language structure is not "well designed" for the needs of language users. Ellis (2002) underlines that language is a communicative resource and as such most likely arises and develops out of interaction; similarly, McCarthy (1998) contends that "discourse drives grammar" (p. 78). Halliday (1973) argues that "language is as it is because of what it has to *do*" (p. 34, emphasis added).

The Contribution of Conversation Analysis to Understanding Grammar in the Wild

Conversation analysis (CA) has given linguists invaluable insights in understanding the interactional basis for language. Grammar and language are often not the focus of CA research, given that it is "an approach that looks for social categories as they are oriented to by participants in social activities" (Ford, Fox, and Thompson, 2002b, p. 5). Nevertheless, conversation analysts, to discover such social categories, must understand how grammar and language are used and function in ordinary conversation.[20] Furthermore, conversation analysts whose

19. We do not intend to argue that examining decontextualized constructions is never useful; it can be, depending on one's aims. We do, however, intend to argue that when examining language in support of an evolutionary or neurobiological account, an examination of contextualized language use, especially in spoken spontaneous speech and conversation, is necessary.

20. See Ford, Fox, and Thompson (2002b) for what conversation analysis can offer to discourse-functional linguistic approaches in examining language use.

research does focus on grammar often attempt to examine linguistic forms "that enable us to do conversation, and recognize that conversation tells us something about the nature of language as a resource for doing social life" (Eggins and Slade, 1997, p. 7). Here we will review several important contributions of CA to the study of the grammar of interaction and conversation.[21] These contributions include the basic unit of conversation (the turn-constructional unit), its forms, and its interactional relevance to participants with respect to turn-taking; the use of multiple resources, for instance, in the anticipatory completion of two-part grammatical constructions; an interactive understanding of a formal linguistic notion (constituency); and the social nature of grammar, illustrated below by pseudo-cleft constructions and verb selection/argument structure. There are, of course, many other findings of CA that are consequential to an understanding of grammar; the following discussion, however, will be limited to these four domains.

The Turn-Constructional Unit, Its Forms, and Its Relevance to Participants for Turn-Taking

Schegloff (1996a) argues that "units such as the clause, sentence, turn, utterance, discourse—are all in principle *interactional units*" (p. 10). While all of these units in conversation are interactional, there is one basic interactional unit of conversation: the turn-constructional unit (TCU), whose defining feature is that it can be spoken and heard as possibly complete in talk-in-interaction. TCUs come in four grammatical forms: sentential, clausal, phrasal, and lexical (Schegloff, 2000b, p. 42). While it has been argued that sentences in spoken discourse are perhaps not a valid unit and are ill defined, most conversation analysts accept that sentences, as most generally defined (subject plus predicate), do occur in ordinary conversation.[22] Such sentences, however, have no special status in CA research. Rather, a sentence can constitute a single, complete turn, just as a clause, a phrase, or a word can. Additionally, a single turn can be made up of several TCUs or one TCU. Because a single TCU can be heard and uttered as possibly complete, it is important interactionally. A TCU is essential for speaker transition, a project to which participants are oriented in conversation, as noted

---

21. When regarding language as being intricately connected to interactional tendencies, the most natural environment in which to examine language would be not merely conversation but casual, ordinary conversation seemingly without a specific task or activity to which the participants are attending (Drew and Heritage, 1992). However, it is just this sort of conversation that has received the least amount of attention (Eggins and Slade, 1997, p. 23).

22. See Ford (2004) for a discussion of the dangers of conversation analysts turning to linguistic structures for accounts of turn-taking: "when conversation analysts gesture toward linguistic structures usable for interaction, they gesture toward research yet to be done, research that must be based on CA methods rather than apart from them" (p. 31).

by Ford (2004), among others: "the timing of turn initiation is an essential semiotic resource for human interaction" (pp. 27–28). Coparticipants (whether selected as next speaker by the current speaker or whether self-selected as next speaker) will often begin their turn at or just prior to (in terminal overlap with) the current speaker's turn (see Schegloff, 1996c, for more discussion of TCU endings; see lines 12 and 17 of ex. 3.4 and line 16 of ex. 3.5 for examples of terminal overlap). This illustrates just how attuned participants are in interaction to taking their turns with little silence intervening between the end of the current speaker's turn and the start of a new turn.

While speakers and hearers attend to the grammatical form of a TCU to project possible completion, it is not the only resource used to determine possible completion of the current speaker's turn. Fox (1999) states that "it has long been clear that recipients attend to prosodic and gestural features of the talk, as well as to grammar, in determining when a speaker might be done with his or her turn" (p. 52). Similarly, Schegloff (as well as others) has shown that not only grammar but also prosody and action are oriented to by participants.[23] These three resources—grammar, prosody, and action—together indicate the possible completion of the current speaker's turn (see Sacks, Schegloff, and Jefferson, 1974, for more on turn-taking in conversation). Ford and Thompson (1996) examined the interaction of these three resources in conversation to determine speaker transition. They wanted to determine if grammatical form was a more powerful determinant of speaker transition, that is, if speaker transition was most frequently associated with grammatical completion of a TCU. Ford (2004), in her summary of the 1996 study, reports that change of speaker more frequently occurs at places where all three of these interactional resources—grammar, prosody, and action—come together to signal possible completion. She argues that this finding "calls into question the centrality of grammatical projection to turn taking" (p. 37).[24] In short, grammar does not work alone in providing this interactional resource.

23. However, both prosody and action may require less attention than the grammatical shape of a TCU where possible completion is concerned. Schegloff notes that while he has come across instances in which parties will begin their turns when a speaker's TCU is grammatically possibly complete but not prosodically possibly complete (there is no final intonation), the reverse does not seem to happen (personal communication). Similarly, recent psycholinguistic research conducted at the Max Planck Institute of Psycholinguistics has shown that Dutch speakers rely on lexicosyntactic shape, not intentional contours, to predict turn endings in speech. From this experimental finding, the researchers conclude that "grammar is not just a means for semantic representation of predicate-argument relations (of different construals thereof). Syntactic structure is also an inherently temporal resource for listeners to chart out the course of a speaker's expression, and to plan their own speech accordingly" (De Ruiter, Mitterer, and Enfield, 2006, p. 532).

24. Ford reminds readers that this finding by no means eradicates the need to look at the particulars of each individual interactional episode.

Examples 3.4 and 3.5 demonstrate how all three of these resources are important in projecting possible turn completion and when speaker transition can appropriately occur. Example 3.4 illustrates how the use of prosody—in this case, how pitch peaks (a syllable with more stress)—can signal an upcoming possible completion.

(3.4) TG, 2:09–17 (Schegloff, 2007, p. 271); arrows mark lines with pronounced pitch peaks)

```
09   Bee:        Wha:t?
10   Ava:        I'm so:: ti:yid. I j's played ba:ske'ball t'day since
11        →      the firs' time since I wz a freshm'n in hi:ghscho[ool]
12   Bee:                                                     [Ba::]sk(h)et =
13               b(h)a(h)ll? (h)[(°Whe(h)re.)
14   Ava:                      [Yeah fuh like an hour enna ha: [If.]
15   Bee:                                                     [hh] Where
16        →      didju play ba:sk[ etbaw. ]
17   Ava:                        [(The) gy:]:m.
18   Bee:        In the gy:m?
```

Many years ago, Pike (1945) defined pitch level as a relative voicing frequency. While there has been debate in the literature about the accuracy of measuring frequency and pitch levels, it has been observed that there are generally four pitch levels in American English: extra-high (1), high (2), mid (3), and low (4). The exact frequency of each pitch level will depend on the individual speaker; while a 4 for one speaker may be different from that of another speaker, their respective 4s will be relatively the same rise in frequency to their respective 3 pitch levels. Declarative utterances and WH questions in English often (although not always) are produced in a 3-2-4 pattern (similar to the rising-falling tone of Halliday, 1967), where the numbers correspond to a pitch level. The 2 corresponds to the primary stress of a declarative statement. Once the primary stress is heard, it is likely that the declarative utterance will come to an end with the following falling syllable or word.

In line 11 above, a pitch peak (relatively more stress) occurs on *high* of *high school*. This extra stress makes it evident to Bee that the intonation of Ava's utterance following this pitch peak will decline and shortly following this decline will come to possible completion (following the normal intonation contour of declarative utterances). Line 16 offers another example of prosody projecting possible completion: the first syllable of *basketball* also receives a pitch peak, indicating that the completion of Bee's utterance is approaching. In both instances, the recipients (Bee in line 12 and Ava in line 17) are able to use the pitch peak to project that the current speaker's turn is coming to possible completion. In fact, they are able to project possible completion so well that in both cases, the recipient takes her turn in slight overlap (terminal overlap) with the current speaker's turn. Terminal overlap is not interruption; neither speakers nor hearers orient to terminal overlap as interruption, and it is a common practice in conversation that eliminates any intervening silence between turns by different speakers. This common practice again demonstrates how participants are oriented to fluent speaker transition. Of course, prosody is not the only resource in these examples that enables the projection of completion; in both lines 11 and 16, the turns are also possibly complete with respect to grammar and action.

If we turn our attention to the beginning of this example, we see how a single lexical TCU (a single word) can be possibly complete in line 9. Ava hears Bee's lexical TCU as possibly complete and immediately comes in to take her turn in line 10. She does so without any silence intervening, as is shown in the transcript by no marking of a pause or gap.[25] Ava in line 10 follows with a sentential TCU that is both grammatically and prosodically complete. However, upon completion of this TCU, Bee does not come in to take a turn; she does not hear this TCU as making up Ava's full turn. It is a general practice that when someone states his or her physical or emotional state, he or she will follow with an account of that state. If someone announces that he or she is "so tired" and does not provide an account, the first thing one is likely to do is ask why that person is "so tired." Bee expects to hear more; she expects Ava to take additional TCUs within this turn to provide the account for her declared physical state, and this is exactly what Ava does. In this way, *I'm so tired* does not make up a complete turn (only a complete TCU), and both participants are oriented to this fact, which is demonstrated by Bee not coming in to try to take a turn and by Ava not manipulating the talk to guarantee her additional TCUs.[26] What this shows is that a sentence, although traditionally considered to be a complete unit of analysis in linguistics, may not be considered as such by individuals in a certain sequential context, whereas a word may be.

Example 3.5 also shows how a TCU can be grammatically and prosodically complete and nevertheless the action that is carried out via the TCU projects more to come.

(3.5) Debbie and Shelley, 2:13–24 (Schegloff, raw data)
```
13  Debbie:   well Shelley: that's how it sou::nds.=
14  Shelley:  =w'll a-=
15  Debbie:   =I mean I'm jus telling you how it sou:[nds.
16  Shelley:                                         [I understand that
```

25. Silences in CA are indicated in the transcript by parentheses, so a half-second silence would be transcribed as (0.5); a silence so brief that it is essentially unable to be timed is called a micro-pause and would be transcribed as (.). See the appendix to this chapter for additional transcription symbols. Additionally, pauses and gaps are different objects; while pauses are within turns, gaps are between turns.

26. Speakers can, for instance, speed up or cut off their talk to try to maintain the floor when their current TCU is coming to possible completion and is thus in danger of being heard as making up a complete turn. Ava does not employ any such tactics here, showing that she is aware that this single TCU is not in danger of being heard as a complete turn.

```
17                    bu- ya I- I mean its not- its not just that:t I mean Iwalw
18                    I was excited to go befor:e and I still wanna go its jus I
19                    mean I don't wanna spend the money: and I know I have other
20                    responsibiliti:es: an,=
21  Debbie:    →      =butif- but th- see this is what I'm see:in. I'm
22                    seeing well that's okay but if Mark went you would
23                    spend the mo::ney.
24  Shelley:          we:ll that's not true either=
```

Before line 13 of this example, Debbie has accused Shelley of backing out of a trip because her boyfriend is no longer able to go. Shelley in lines 16 to 20 continues to deny that this is the reason for her deciding not to go. In line 21, Debbie again presents the situation from her perspective: *see this is what I'm see: in..* Although this TCU is both grammatically complete (as a sentential TCU) and prosodically complete (as indicated by the period at the end of this TCU marking falling intonation), the action is incomplete. The addressee therefore understands that transition is not relevant at this point, and she does not come in to take a turn. Fox argues that "it is not just that a particular language is deployed to fulfill the needs of turn-taking; rather, that language is almost certainly shaped by turn-taking needs" (p. 53; see also Schegloff, 1996c).

Anticipatory Completion: Two-Part Constructions

Hearers and speakers seem to attend to grammar inasmuch as it serves their needs to anticipate when a turn will come to possible completion and thus when they may be able to take a turn. Several lines of evidence demonstrate that this is so. Nonspeaking participants will often gear up (with an in-breath or perhaps a response cry, as defined by Goffman, 1978) just before possible completion of a current speaker's turn in order to begin their own turn at or just before the moment of turn completion or, as in example 3.6, in order to complete the current speaker's turn simultaneously for or with the current speaker:

(3.6) (Lerner, 1996, p. 249)
```
1  Fran:      BUT WHUT UH YUH GONNA DO, YUH JUST GONNA SPREAD
2             THAT STUFF ON THE DRI:VEWAY?=
3  Mike:      = >'s gonna load [up with it<
4  Steve:                     [I'm not gonna spread it
5             on the dri:[veway, I'm gonna dump't
6  Fran:  →              [Aih! You gonna dump it
7             (0.4)
```

The response cry *Aih!* in line 6 is uttered just before the second clause of Steve's utterance, *I'm gonna dump't.* Fran shows that she is able to project exactly when the second clause of Steve's turn is going to come. She gears up with a response cry just before the start of the second clause and, in doing so, is able to coconstruct the end of Steve's turn simultaneously with him. As was demonstrated in examples 3.4 and 3.5 above, speakers also frequently begin their own turn just prior to possible completion of the current speaker's turn—in terminal overlap.

Perhaps even more convincing evidence of the interactional importance of grammar to conversational participants involves anticipatory completion of a two-part grammatical construction. Common examples in English include *if-then* or *when x, y* constructions. In example 3.7a, the first part of this grammatical construction, *when I called* him, is likely to be followed by a second clause, in this case *I told him that I didn't have the money.*

(3.7a) Debbie and Shelley, 3:21–22 (Schegloff, raw data)
Shelley: when I called him I told him that I didn't have the money . . .

Participants in conversation not only seem to be oriented to possible completion of a TCU in order to take a turn, but they are also oriented to the completion of the first part of a two-part construction. Lerner (1996) notes that "practice ordinarily associated with the boundaries of a TCU, is also available for use at internal boundary points" (p. 251). For instance, participants can often use the grammatical tendencies in two-part constructions as a powerful interactional resource, as in example 3.7b.

(3.7b) TG, 7:17–20 (Schegloff, 2007, p. 275)
```
17   Bee:   hh Yihknow buh when we walk outta the
18          cla:ss.=
19   Ava:   =nobuddy knows wh't [wen' on,]
20   Bee:                       [Wid- hh]h=
```

Ava, using Bee's two-part (*when x, y*) grammatical construction, is not only able to project when Bee's turn will come to possible completion but is also able to project the content of Bee's turn. She is thus able to complete Bee's turn for her. Ava utters the second part of this two-part construction seamlessly, without hesitation and with no silence following the first part uttered by Bee (this is indicated in the transcript by the equal signs adjoining the two turns). This projectability afforded by such two-part grammatical constructions is quite powerful, in that a recipient can use them to demonstrate to the current speaker that he or she is not only listening but is also understanding the speaker so well that he or she can actually complete the turn just as the speaker intended.

Once again, grammar is not the only resource that allows this projectability; actions that commonly occur in pairs in conversation also provide a similar resource, because they have sequential ordering similar to that provided by two-part grammatical constructions. Lerner describes one of these two-part actions as "disparaging reference + complainable," as illustrated in example 3.8a.

Vic's disparaging reference *He's a bitch* is immediately followed by a complaint, *he didn't put in the light on the second floor.* Lerner comments that this "two-part format provides an additional resource for projecting the form of TCU completion," and this projectability can be used by addressees to cocomplete the TCU that is under way (p. 255). This is especially true at the end of a TCU, as seen in example 3.8b.

(3.8a) (Lerner, 1996, p. 255)
Vic: He's a bitch he didn' pud in duh light own dih sekkin flaw,

(3.8b) JS (Lerner, 1996, p. 255)
1 Joe: oh hundreds of automobiles parked around there en people walkin
2   across the bridge you know? en all a' these go:dam people onna
3   freeway [were stoppin-
4 Edith: [were rubbernecking

In example 3.8b, this two-part format allows Edith to project the completion of the complaint that Joe has begun after his disparaging remark and complete it along with Joe. We see that projectability is an attribute not only of grammar but also of other resources of conversation. The role of grammar is essentially a progressive unfolding of linguistic units in a linear and temporal fashion. These aspects of grammar are related to Lerner's (1996) notion of "sequential adjacency": the "words that are produced reveal reflexively that they represent progress for the turn-so-far toward a (next) possible completion" (p. 258; see Lerner, 1996, p. 257, on serial and sequential adjacency).

CA's Contribution to Understanding Formal
Linguistic Notions: Constituency

Work in CA has also contributed to the understanding of constituency, a structural notion that has proven useful for both generative and functional-based approaches to grammar. CA has "provided evidence for how such 'classic constituents' might actually be oriented to by participants as resources for social action in a conversation" and can thus be regarded as "formats for strategic interactional functions" (Ford, Fox, and Thompson, 2002a, p. 15). Ford, Fox, and Thompson (2002a) note that the study of turn-taking shows how participants attend to grammatical constituency in interaction (although conversational analysts usually do not describe it in these terms). Essentially, they argue that it is constituency that allows for smooth turn transitions at the possible completion of a TCU, and it is therefore constituency that underlies the overwhelming occurrence of transitions with no overlap or silence, two alternatives that have interactional import and are imbued with social meaning. They examine constituency as relevant to the interactional use of increments, defined as "any nonmain-clause continuation of a speaker's turn after that speaker has come to what could have been a possible completion point, or a 'transition-relevance place,' based on prosody, syntax, and sequential action" (p. 16), the three resources for projecting possible turn completion described earlier (see Schegloff, 1996c, 2000a, for more on increments).

(3.9) (Ford, Fox, and Thompson, 2002a, p. 20)

```
01   John:   An' how are you feeling?
02           (0.4)
03   →       these days,
04   Ann:    Fa:t. I can't- I don't have a waist anymore,27
```

Example 3.9 illustrates in line 3 a type of increment that Schegloff (1996c) has called an "extension"; it is syntactically and semantically parasitic on the utterance, which has, prior to it, come to possible completion. Ford, Fox, and Thompson call these types of increments *"constituents of* prior turn units" (p. 17). They also discuss a second type of increment, one that is not parasitic on the prior utterance but is independent or a "free constituent" and most frequently (15 of the 19 instances occurring in their data) an "unattached NP" (see line 7 in ex. 3.10).

(3.10) (Ford, Fox, and Thompson, 2002a, p. 26)

```
01   Mike:   The guy ended up turnin' around'n goin back 'cause
02           [he wasn't about to sell it
03   Curt:   [°(Oh Christ).
04           fifteen thousand dollars wouldn't touch a Co:rd,28
05           (0.7)
06   Curt:   That guy was (dreaming).
07   →       Fifteen thousand dollars [ for an original Co:rd,
08   Gary:                            [ Figured he'd impress him,
```

Ford, Fox, and Thompson found that these two types of increments are similar, in that they emerge "where there are identifiable problems faced by the speaker in pursuing uptake from a recipient" (p. 18). For example, in 3.9, they note that John's intended recipient, Ann, who is noticeably pregnant, is looking at her dinner plate and not gazing in his direction when he comes to possible

---

27. The transcription methods differ depending on the disciplinary background of the particular researcher from whom the conversational extract is being reproduced. Unless otherwise noted, transcription notations are from Jefferson (1985), which can be found in the appendix to this chapter. All extracts reproduced of an isolated utterance do not follow any particular transcription method, given that their original use was to demonstrate a grammatical aspect of spoken discourse rather than an interactional tendency of conversation/talk-in-interaction.

28. A Cord is an antique car once popular in the 1930s.

completion (see Goodwin, 1979, for a detailed account of the problematic nature of an unattending recipient in interaction). In fact, there is no uptake by Ann but rather a 0.4-second silence. They note that it is so important for John to secure an attending recipient that he removes a bite of food from his mouth to add the extension, which more clearly specifies his intended recipient and attracts her gaze and a response. Ann clearly hears this increment as directed to her and a question about her pregnant state. The increment thus has created a new point of possible completion to which a recipient can attend and in which speaker transition can successfully and smoothly take place, which the authors describe as a "reinterpret[ation] [of the prior unit] as still in progress" (p. 26).

Contrastively, example 3.10 includes an unattached-NP increment (line 7). The authors point out that in overlap with Mike's turn, Curt provides a turn showing his appreciation for and his stance toward the story Mike is finishing. Not receiving any response from Mike, Curt provides a second attempt to demonstrate his understanding of Mike's story (*That guy was dreaming*). After Mike again does not provide any acknowledgment of Curt's demonstration of understanding, Curt adds an increment, an unattached NP (*Fifteen thousand dollars for an original Cor:d*). The authors note that this increment is produced "in a scornful tone" and thus "provides yet another display of Curt's assessment of and stance toward the 'antagonist' of the story' (p. 27). They suggest that this unattached-NP increment "can be seen as a display of specific appreciation for the outlandishness of the antagonist's actions" and is thus "serving to summarize, evaluate, and assess the absurdity of anyone thinking they could get a Cord for fifteen thousand dollars" (p. 27). In addition, given Mike's lack of responsivity to Curt's assessments, it can also be seen as an attempt to secure a recipient response from Mike.

These two types of increments are different, in that "extension increments, as *constituents of* the preceding clause, continue the action of that turn, while unattached NP increments, though not new turns, do the functionally separate action of assessing or commenting on the prior turn material" (p. 18). That is, the former do not work to produce a separate action, while the latter do work at producing a new action. The authors argue that this serves as an indicator for the sort of response or alignment that the speaker is expecting from his or her recipient (p. 26).

Constituency is important theoretically because constituents are the building blocks of the hierarchical, internal structure of grammar. Constituency has therefore been believed to be part of our mental representation. Indeed, in the 1960s and 1970s, experimenters tried to demonstrate that constituency was "psychologically real," using what was then the new experimental design of click monitoring during sentence parsing (Fodor and Bever, 1965; Fodor, Bever, and Garrett, 1976; Ladefoged and Broadbent, 1960). It turns out that examining the use of grammar in conversation suggests that constituency matters for participants in real time. Not only are the placements of increments and turn-taking accomplished with respect to constituency boundaries, but the placement of continuers[29] seems to occur here as well (although this has not been examined systematically or with constituency in mind). Lerner (1996), for example, shows that continuers are often placed after the first component of a two-part construction, leading one to believe that this may be a reasonable hypothesis. Constituency may merely be common collocations of phonological strings that can be exploited in both predictable and flexible ways and that frequently occur in doing discourse (see Hoey, 2004, for further discussion of grammar as collocations). Common collocations may be mentally represented inasmuch as that means that the brain does the work in understanding them. But why would this imply that constituents are any more special than colors or lexical items, which presumably also have mental representations? While such linguistic studies may show that constituency is a relevant phenomenon for people in using language/grammar, these studies do not clearly show that constituents evolved as part of a genetically inherited language faculty.

The common belief that grammar is fixed or functionless does not hold up in conversation. Participants use grammar flexibly (see Ford, 2004); however, grammar undoubtedly is sequentially predictable in many ways, and it is in some sense this predictability that allows participants to manipulate it, use it as a marking place to be able to project possible completion of a TCU, and accomplish coconstructed actions with coparticipants. Interlocutors are oriented to grammatical structure, but they are so oriented usually to carry out actions.[30] Moreover, grammatical patterns can change in language use depending on their discourse functions (see Tao, 2007, in which he shows how the independent use of *absolutely* emerged from its dependent use, in part because speakers tend to use it with positive collocates in discourse and thus as a turn-initial discourse marker similar to the change-of-state token *oh* discussed by Heritage, 1984). Such emergence of new grammatical patterns is perhaps why Lerner (1996) argues that instead of grammatical structure, "a more felicitous term might be 'grammatical practice'" (p. 268).

The Social Nature of Grammar: Two Cases

Pseudo-Cleft Constructions   Lerner discusses several devices that allow hearers to intervene before the current speaker's turn comes to possible completion.

---

29. Continuers have been described by Schegloff (1982) and are frequently used by the hearer in conversation during extended bouts of talk to demonstrate to the current speaker that although the turn is coming to or has come to possible completion, it is understood that this is not a place where the hearer intends to come in to take a turn. In other words, continuers are used to show that one understands that the current turn is expected to continue. Typical continuers are *uh-huh* and *mm-hm*.

30. Schegloff (personal communication) has noted that participants in talk-in-interaction are sometimes attuned to form for form's sake, as is evidenced in some cases of repair.

Some have already been mentioned, but there is one additional instance that is particularly interesting in terms of the way grammar is used to accomplish this task. Lerner notes that word searches are designed for coparticipation; they invite the hearer to aid in finding the desired word, as in example 3.11.

(3.11) GL:DS (Lerner, 1996, p. 261)

```
1   L:   he said, the thing thet- thet- sad about the uhm black uhm
2        (0.3)
3   P:   muslims,
4   L:   muslims, he said is thet they don't realize ...
```

Lerner notes that L's first utterance is a so-called pseudo-cleft construction,[31] and so it is designed for P to do the completion of the preliminary component of this particular structure. In theoretical syntax, pseudo-cleft constructions are one type of test for determining constituency that allows analysts to decide whether or not a string of words is a constituent precisely because the string can be manipulated as an individual unit. Additionally, pseudo-clefts are often believed to stand in relationship to their syntactically unmarked (declarative) counterparts. For example, from the declarative sentence *I'd like you to clean the kitchen*, the WH-cleft construction *What I'd like you to do is clean the kitchen* is compared.

WH-clefts are also pseudo-cleft constructions, and in linguistics, they have taken the canonical form demonstrated in the sentence *What I'd like you to do is clean the kitchen*. In speech, however, WH-cleft constructions do not come in only this syntactic variety. Ross-Hagebaum and Koops (2006) searched the Santa Barbara Corpus of spoken English and found that WH-clefts often repeat the WH-clause subject in the focus phrase, *What it'd done is it caused him to be introverted*, or omit the copula (among other syntactic variances), *What they did ( ) they took the stubs and they cleaned em up*. They conclude that the "varying degrees of syntactic integration found in WH-clefts (measured in terms of factors such as subject repetition, copula omission, size of focus, placement of prosodic boundaries) are correlated with differences in discourse function." The syntactic varieties of WH-clefts in conversation clearly resemble the canonical cleft construction that linguists examine; however, the fixed version that linguists focus on is apparently only fixed in and because of writing. The varieties of cleft constructions in spoken discourse, as shown by Ross-Hagebaum and Koops, are not merely exceptional cases in which speakers were not able to produce the "correct" construction when under heavy processing constraints but are also functionally relevant.

One interactional function of pseudo-cleft constructions has been noted by Lerner in examining word searches in conversation. Word searches are typically

---

31. *It was the trash that John threw into the bag* and *It was in the bag that John threw the trash* are both cleft constructions of the sentence *John threw the trash into the bag.* Pseudo-cleft constructions are most commonly considered WH clefts such as *What John did was throw the trash into the bag* or *What John threw into the bag was the trash.*

placed in constructions that force the unknown element at the end of the unit so that they may be produced by one's interlocutors. While Lerner remarks that word searches act as a device to allow completion by another participant, the grammar also provides a resource with which this can be ensured. In syntactic theory, grammar is given no purpose (except as it defines language); it is functionless, but here we see that grammar can direct interaction and be used to create a sense of collaboration among coparticipants. Lerner (2002) has noted that there are instances that require parties to speak at the same time, which he calls choral coproduction. It also happens in conversation that an addressee will say the end of the TCU along with the speaker (as was shown in ex. 3.8b). Participants, even if they are able to predict the end of a speaker's TCU, are not required to produce it in concert. Such collaboration certainly has an interactional consequence and an effect on the interpersonal relationships of participants, all of which is made allowable in part by the nature of grammar.[32]

One Motivation of Word Selection: The Grammar of Verbs   How participants in conversation select words has been discussed in CA in varying respects. Much of the research on word selection deals with person reference (see Sacks, 1972; Sacks and Schegloff, 1979; Fox and Thompson, 1990; Ford and Fox, 1996; Schegloff, 1996b), although there has also been some attention to how sound and other poetic devices influence word "selection" in conversation and other forms of talk-in-interaction (see Jefferson, 1996). This section investigates a possible motivation for verb selection. This is not to say that there is only one motivation for how participants select verbs; there are probably many, depending on the context and action/project being pursued in the talk.

Mikesell (2005) shows how verb selection and the grammar of verbs (even though explicit arguments are sometimes "optional"; see the section on argument structure) can be employed strategically by speakers to accomplish interactive goals. She shows how specific verbs are used precisely because their grammatical deployment can highlight participation frameworks[33] and can be constructed by the speaker to direct the hearer to a particular understanding of a narrative climax as shown in example 3.12. In this specific case, the storyteller selects verbs that

32. Carter and McCarthy (2004) note that various uses of what they call language creativity are employed to create a sense of connection and closeness with their interlocutors. While the employment of pseudo-cleft and other such constructions by speakers to carry out an utterance that contains a word search may merely seem to be a practical use, there is likely an interpersonal aspect of employing the construction in such circumstances as well. That is, it is used by coparticipants to coconstruct or collaboratively construct utterances rather than construct them individually. Eggins and Slade (1997) also found that actions such as arguing, gossiping, and storytelling function primarily to construct social identities and interpersonal relationships.

33. Participation frameworks have been discussed by several discourse analysts. Goodwin (1996) notes that "the production of talk and other forms of action is situated

emphasize a one-participant or two-participant framework. In this example, such a selection allows the speaker to provide instructions to the addressee about how to understand the ongoing talk. These instructions, accomplished by highlighting the participation framework, also provide cues to addressee(s) about the expected reaction to display once the climax of the narrative has been reached.

The following interaction takes place between two sisters, one of whom, Darleen, works in a public-school system with young children. She begins telling a story to her sister, Laura, about a recent conflict she had with the woman who is her senior, Linda Burgess. Their mother, Pat, is also present but is not the main addressee, having already heard the story (this is also evidenced by the fact that Darleen's eye gaze is consistently directed to her sister). Darleen's and Laura's five-year-old cousin is also present but is not an active participant in the interaction.

(3.12) Asperger's, 1:14–31 (Mikesell, 2005)

1		D:	((eye roll, headroll followed by another eye roll and headshake
2			as in frustration or irritation)) Linda Burgess. Mm.
3			(1.8)
4		L:	Who's she. hh.
5		D:	(hh)**To my face.** °To my face. I wouldn't normally tell you
6			this but since we're doin' this ((reference to videotaping)).
7			To my face. Tell me. I realize I'm young, (0.9) I jus' don't
8			(.) know if she doesn't (0.5) uh realize that I'm not stupid.
			((laughter))

[5 lines omitted]

14		D:	No [wait wait
15		L:	[((laughter)) I was li:ke hh
16		D:	**Oh** it's almost- It's almost that good. Um we had a kid that
17	→		she came to me about and I: was **dead** on with this kid, °I wz
18	→		dead on. An' it turns out after the fact I'm dead on. And she
19	→		kept tellin' me she dudn' agree with me. Which is fine. She
20	→		doesn't have to agree with me you know. But I: have the
21			degree:(hh) f(h)uck(h)e:r you gon- ((raises hand to mouth))
22		L:	hh hh hnh huh ((looks to 5 year old playing at table))
23			(5.6)
24		L:	not hea::rd. ((singsong voice))
25	→	D:	whhhew Um s- she says to me um we're talkin' about this kid and
26	→		she says I don't agree with you I don't agree with you. She
27	→		says I have more experience than you do with this kind of
28			disorder.

within *participation frameworks* of various types. Like sentential grammar and grammar for interaction these frameworks provide for the appropriate ordering of relevant elements, for example participant categories such as speaker and hearer" (p. 374).

```
29        L:   What kind of disorder was it?
30    →   D:   Asperger's. And I wanted to say to her but I'm (.) too
31             professional for this. How (.) do you: kno::w what experience
32             I ha:ve and what I don't.
33        L:   I would've said that [(        )
34        D:                         [If you: have so much experience with
35             it why are you asking my: opinion.
36        L:   Oh I don't think that's unprofessional. Just don't
37             [say it that way. But say-
38        D:   [wait oh no wait. It gets better.
39             She says then to me well you do realize there's a
40             learning curve to your job.
41             (0.9)
42        P:   ooh that's what really (did it). That's what did it.
43        L:   ((laughter))
```

Darleen begins this narrative with *To my face. To my face*, which is again uttered in line 7. The repetition and stress placed on these utterances situate them as particularly salient. They invoke for the recipient a particular type of reading, one that not only views Darleen and Linda Burgess as the two key players in the narrative that is about to ensue but also emphasizes these two roles in a very powerful way. This sets the stage for the narrative, and various linguistic features are later employed to continue to emphasize the participation framework, one of which is verb selection. This participation framework is highlighted again in lines 16 to 17, when Darleen provides the background to her narrative: *she came to me about*. The selection of the verb allows Darleen again to highlight important features of the narrative, specifically the participants involved (Linda and herself), because the verb allows both an explicit agent/ subject and an experiencer, and the dynamic between these two participants positioned in this framework, because the verb situates Linda as the more agentive character, the one who made the decision to seek assistance from Darleen. Darleen does not say that they "discussed" or "talked about" this particular child in providing the background, which would highlight neither of these aspects but would instead place the two parties on more equal or neutral terms. This choice of verb is consistent with the effect of the repetition of *To my face* in highlighting the two participants, Darleen and Linda.

The grammar of a verb is traditionally examined for its structural characteristics, what slots they fill in syntax and what arguments they require. However, these structural properties are not typically examined for their interactional import. It is not merely the meaning of the verb that is significant for conveying the propositional content that Darleen wants to express. The structural properties of a verb are also important for this narrative because they enable Darleen to continually emphasize an aspect of the narrative that is, for her, central to the telling and for providing instructions to her recipient to guarantee a certain understanding, to which we will return shortly.

Throughout the narrative, Darleen continues to select verbs that allow her to highlight a two-participant framework. Such an emphasis is consistent with other aspects of the narrative (a more detailed account is provided in Mikesell, 2005). In lines 18 to 19, with the indirect quote *And she kept tellin' me she doesn't agree with me*, the verb *tell* invokes the same participation framework important for the telling. The focus is drawn again to the participation framework in this same utterance with the negated form of *agree*, for which the prepositional phrase *with me* is optional, even by formal rules of syntax.[34] On the surface, it may seem that *with me* is not communicatively necessary (and perhaps thus violating Grician maxims) in this specific circumstance; the characters of the narrative have been explicitly referred to and are easily indexed in the earlier sequence. In addition, the utterance that occurs in line 18, in which Darleen expresses that she assessed this particular child correctly, makes it clear that it is *me* (Darleen) with which *she* (Linda) does not agree. In this way, the "optional" prepositional phrase does not reduce any potential ambiguity in the proposition about who the participants are or with whom Linda disagrees but is included to bring this specific participation framework back into the forefront. We see an emphasis on the participation framework yet again in lines 20 and 25 and twice in lines 26, 27, and 30. This is clearly an important feature of the telling.

Mikesell argues that emphasizing the participation framework in this particular episode allows the storyteller to provide instructions to the addressee to pay particular attention not only to what was said but to who was saying what to whom. Accentuating the individual characters involved, the actual actors displayed in dialogue, in turn accentuates the fact that these two individuals are not working unitarily toward a common goal, that of helping the child in question. Rather, the telling focuses not only on the talk that is exchanged or the actions that transpire in this interactional episode but also on the participants themselves (*she says to me; she doesn't agree with me*), allowing Darleen clearly to display her own stance toward this relationship. All of these subtle instructions enable the recipient to align with the teller appropriately when she comes to the story's climax in lines 39 to 40. These instructions are important because the climax[35] is delivered as an indirect quote and in a deadpan manner (with little intonational contour or embodiment of the quoted talk), thus allowing her recipient to display on her own accord and without immediate prompting by the storyteller just how Darleen was in the right.

---

34. See also Goodwin (2000a), who examines three girls playing hopscotch, one of whom uses a pronoun that is "optional" in talk. He remarks that "the fact that the pronoun is being produced when it could have been omitted suggests that it is doing some special work" (p. 1469).

35. The climax, *She says **then** to me well you do realize there's a learning curve to your job*, contains speech being reported—*well you do realize there's a learning curve to your*

We see again that the structure of a verb is important for talk-in-interaction, not for the structural integrity of the syntax but rather for interactional outcomes. The participation framework was highlighted at the outset of this narrative not by a particular syntactic construction but also by the proposition it entailed (*To my face*). However, this participation framework, clearly important to the telling, is again picked up and emphasized in the grammar. Clearly, participation frameworks can be highlighted by propositional content (as in *To my face*); however, for most of the narrative, Darleen uses verb selection and argument structure to do the job. When examining isolated sentences or made-up sentences, such robust connections between grammar and interaction would go unnoticed. Neglecting contextual and interactional considerations, in turn, neglects powerful resources that the brain relies on to make sense of language. In this one episode alone, grammar, prosody, and facial expression (in delivering the narrative climax), the prior talk and knowledge of the participants (in this case, Pat has already heard the narrative and responds first after the story climax), and so on, are all employed for both the speaker to design the narrative and for the hearers to interpret it according to the speaker's design. This process reflects the interactional contingencies of the moment (Goodwin, 1986) and allows the interlocutors a shared understanding. Janssen (2007) has similarly argued that speakers rarely explicate the reason for focusing on a particular frame of reference or situation; rather, he argues, "when trying to understand what a speaker means, we try to determine how our interpretation of the utterance involved is compatible with our interpretation of the current frame of reference" (p. 354), and "speakers offer phonetic cues which enable their addressees to determine what situation matters, and why" (p. 357). In the example discussed here, we see how grammar is used to coconstruct a particular frame of reference (or participation framework) in which the interlocutors work to share a similar understanding of the situation. Although the focus of this examination was on one particular grammatical aspect, a thorough understanding of this grammatical feature was only possible by understanding a variety of interactional features normally considered to be independent or unrelated to grammar itself.

Reflections on What CA Contributes to Understanding Grammar in the Wild

This section has presented some cases of grammatical features (constituents, pseudo-clefts, argument structure) of English that meet interactional goals. We

---

job—which receives little animation. In the original presentation of this example, Mikesell focused on the nature of reported speech being used and discussed the consequences of ensuring an appropriate stance from recipients at the narrative's climax by presenting a neutral or objective presentation of the climax rather than an animated version of it. Darleen's highlighting of the participation framework via verb (and argument) selection, in part, does the work of guaranteeing an appropriate uptake of the unrevealing climax.

do not say that these grammatical features *only* meet the interactional pursuits discussed in the particular examples shown above. CA has shown that the actions being accomplished in interaction are what speakers and hearers orient to, and the grammar is merely a tool, a resource, for accomplishing this action. As such, specific grammatical features can be used to accomplish a variety of goals, and there is often not a one-to-one correspondence between a grammatical construction and an interactional aim. Yet grammar may not merely be *a* resource available to language users; it is perhaps one of the most powerful (Schegloff, personal communication). Regardless, the study of language must also consider context, the semiotic surround, and environment; if one wanted to understand how sailing works, one could not just understand the shape of the sail without understanding how that sail is used in various wind patterns and water currents. In Janssen's (2007) proposed speaker/hearer-based grammar, he argues that the use of grammatical constructions is based on a relationship that the speaker and hearer can integrate into their conceptualization of the frame of reference in the light of their interpretation of the current situation, their knowledge of the world, and possibly the situation communicated in previous utterances and sometimes even utterances to come. To focus on the interactional import of linguistic resources, language studies must be rethought to include the milieu in which grammar is used as well as the other systematic resources that are employed in concert with grammar.

The discipline of CA has provided valuable insights to the study of natural spoken discourse. Eggins and Slade (1997), however, note three drawbacks of the discipline for the study of casual conversation, the main focus of their own work: "its lack of systematic analytical categories," "its 'fragmentary' focus, and "its mechanistic interpretation of conversation" (p. 31). They claim that appropriately addressing these drawbacks "requires a shift of orientation away from conversation as a form of social interaction that is incidentally verbal, and towards conversation as a linguistic interaction that is fundamentally social. Rather than seeing conversation merely as good data for studying social life, analysis needs to view conversation as good data for studying language as it is used to enact social life" (p. 32).

They again emphasize the interactional basis for language in concluding that casual conversation seems "to clarify and extend the interpersonal ties that have brought [participants] together" (p. 67).

The Contribution of Usage-Based Approaches to Understanding Grammar in the Wild

Object Complements in Conversation

Thompson (2002) addresses predominant assumptions held about complements, which she claims "are generally agreed to be clausal arguments of predicates" (p. 125). She provides Noonan's definition to illustrate: "by complementation we mean the syntactic situation that arises when a notional sentence or predication is an argument of a predicate (cited from Noonan, 1985, p. 42)." Common assumptions addressed by Thompson are that complements are a homogeneous (or unitary) category, that they are arguments, and that they are subordinate to their clauses, clauses that Thompson calls complement-taking predicates (CTPs).[36] Analyzing the 425 examples of finite indicative complements from her database of spoken American English, she concludes that complements should not be viewed as arguments; in fact, she argues that there is little evidence based on how participants treat complements for the category of complement at all: "the syntactic behavior of the commonly recognized complement types for English (e.g., infinitives, *that*-complements, gerunds, and question-words) is highly disparate, and, to my knowledge, there exists no evidence to support their being considered to be the same category" (p. 127). She argues that these constructions are rather better characterized as "main verbs plus several kinds of finite and non-finite clauses" (pp. 127–128).

She also finds that complements are not subordinate to their CTPs, as is typically presumed; she argues that "it's the CTP whose 'profile' is 'overridden' in complement utterances" (p. 131). To show this, however, she underlines the importance of examining how complements are organized "with reference to particular courses of action that the participants are engaged in doing" (p. 131). She shows how such courses of action involve the complements just as much as they involve the CTP. Specifically, she notes that a speaker's stance is often expressed in the CTP phrase, whereas the action—for example, an aligning agreement (as in ex. 3.13) or the main interactional aim (as in ex. 3.14)—is expressed in the complement. In other words, she describes the CTP phrases as providing a frame in which the action can be expressed. She notes that the majority of CTPs in her corpus (82 percent) provide an epistemic frame and occur in the most varied forms as compared with other functioning types of CTPs, such as evidential, which make up 13 percent, and evaluative, which make up approximately 4 percent (p. 137).

(3.13) At a birthday party, after Kevin was discovered to have lettuce on his tooth, everyone has jokingly commented on it, and Kendra has asked for a toothpick (Thompson, 2002, p. 132)

Wendy: . . . everybody's getting uh, tooth obsessed.
Ken: I guess **we a=re**.

In example (3.13), Ken's complement (in bold) is equally as important, if not more so, in terms of its interactional significance as the CTP I *guess*. It is the complement that provides the "aligning agreement" to Wendy's summary in the independent clause. The I *guess* is interactionally important because it lessens the alignment epistemically; however, the complement *we are* is equally

---

36. Thompson deals only with finite indicative clauses. She uses "complement" for the clause that is the subject or object of the predicate.

important because it expresses the actual alignment (compare the difference interactionally of Ken uttering *I guess* without the aligning complement). One action is inhabited in the CTP, and the other action is located in the complement, but both are clearly necessary for the interactional accomplishment of this single TCU.

(3.14) Frank and his young son Brett have noticed that Brett's sister Melissa appears to be about to mark on Brett's art project (Thompson, 2002, p. 132)

```
1  Melissa:  are you gonna add like the little lines that
                jut out of [these]?
2  Frank:                  [get your pen] back from that.
3  Brett:    .. yeah
4  Melissa:  it's erasable,
5            and I am not marking on it.
6  Brett:    ... I don't care if it's erasable.
7            don't touch it.
8  Melissa:  <HI I didn't HI>.
9  Brett:    ... I know.
```

In example 3.14, Melissa produces two simple main clauses in lines 4 and 5 to demonstrate her attitude toward being told, more or less, to stay away from Brett's project. In line 6, Brett responds by producing a CTP (*I don't care*), which Thompson notes expresses his "disdainful stance towards Melissa's claim" in line 4. In the complement of line 6, however, Brett reiterates Melissa's claim. This interactional episode deals with the issue of Melissa and whether or not she is going to interfere with Brett's project. The main impetus of this interaction is grammatically found in main clauses (lines 2, 4, 5, 7, 8, and 9) and the complement (the bold portion in line 6), while Brett's stance can be found in the CTP (*I don't care* of line 6). Thompson demonstrates that both the complement and the CTP are important interactionally; however, it is the complement that reflects the import of these participants.

Thompson concludes that complements occur as arrangements of CTP phrases with finite clauses rather than matrix verbs and complements. She also notes that four out of the five most-used CTP phrases can be considered fixed or formulaic as they regularly occur in simple CTP phrases, with a first-person-singular subject and without a complementizer (p. 139). *I think* and its negated and tensed variants occurred in this formulaic pattern 107 times out of the 139 times *think* occurred as a CTP (77 percent) (p. 139).

(3.15) (Thompson, 2002, p. 139)

```
K:  I think it'll be real interesting,
    ..I think it'll be a real,
      ... (H) a good slide show.
```

Thompson argues that "what we think of as grammar may be best understood as combinations of reusable fragments" (p. 141),[37] the "fragments" of complements being the CTP phrase and the complement portion, both of which can be used independently in conversation. Thompson contends that there is no evidence that CTP clauses produced independently should be regarded as "missing a clause" (p. 145). On an interactional note, she also shows the "fragments" of complements to be relevant to the production of turns and turn components.

Argument Structure and Clause Structure in Conversation

In terms of traditional linguistic foci of grammatical study, argument structure has been described as "one of the most challenging" because it "[brings] together the grammar and the lexicon, syntax and semantics" (Gropen, 2000, p. 95).[38] Simply put, argument structure refers to the number and type of arguments, or syntactic properties and their semantic roles, required by a given predicate. It has traditionally been viewed in structural terms (see Alsina, 2001; Hale and Keyser, 2002), and Tao (2001) claims that "most current approaches of argument structure can be characterized as rational and intuition-based" (p. 76). It has been noted, however, that the grammar of clauses, as well as argument structure in conversation, is much less rigid and less stable than has been proposed in formal linguistic analyses (Jackendoff, 1990; Grimshaw, 1993), very similar to the variation we saw with respect to pseudo-cleft constructions. Usage-based studies have also found that argument structure is not only less rigid than linguists have proposed but also tends to be structurally simpler.

Thompson and Hopper (2001) document several problems that arise when examining argument structure in spoken discourse. One problem involves the concept of scene, which is typically determined by imagining or intuiting the sort of semantic roles (arguments) that need to be realized or projected by a particular verb. Considering the verb *give*, it can be determined to require an agent or subject that does the giving, an object that is given, and a recipient that receives the object. This verb is thought to be stored in the lexicon as a two-place predicate structurally demanding these arguments. It has been attested that such intuitive practices are often unreliable and inaccurate for understanding how argument structure is realized in language use, especially that of conversation. Moreover, intuition often produces very neat and orderly constructions, which also seem to be uncharacteristic of conversation. Imagining what arguments a verb *should* take seems to create a division between how one conceives of a verb and how one actually uses a verb. Thompson and Hopper (2001) demonstrate various instances of unsystematic cases

---

37. Thompson notes that others have made similar claims, including Becker (1984) and Hopper (1987).

38. Arguably, this could be said of any aspect of grammar.

from natural spoken discourse, of which we will mention only a few. The verbs in examples 3.16) to 3.18 [39] have been conceptualized in terms of scenes to take concrete arguments—a doer/agent/subject, an object, and often a topic. However, these examples "do not refer to single physical events" (p. 41), making such concrete arguments difficult to conceptualize.

(3.16)
I forgot.

(3.17)
they pay in advance.

(3.18)
she brought that up.

In example 3.16, the verb *forget* (here in the past tense) is theorized to take an object (something that is forgotten), but clearly, it is often not used syntactically in this way. Similarly, examples 3.19 to 3.21 contain no lexical verb at all, making arguments particularly difficult to locate for these utterances, and again, "the notion of 'scenes' is inapplicable" (p. 41).

(3.19)
I'm **excited about it**.

(3.20)
it was **confidential**.

(3.21)
Ray's **his manager**.

Other problems Thompson and Hopper discuss involve "predicates with no argument structure," as in the following (p. 43).

(3.22)
I don't think you'**ll be getting** much **out of** that one, Wendo.

(3.23)
I think I'**m over it** faster than I would be.

(3.24)
I'**d be on** pregnancy vitamins.

---

39. These examples, being isolated and extracted to demonstrate variability in argument structure, do not follow the transcription methods of Jefferson (1985).

Thompson and Hopper note the difficulty of describing many of the utterances in their data in terms of argument structure. They claim that "this is because, among the clauses in our database with two participants, a number are 'dispersed verbal expressions'" or lexicalized expressions and have therefore been "learned as units" (p. 43). Examples 3.22 to 3.24 were three such lexicalized expressions.

Such observations of the fluidity and flexibility of argument structure require one to question the fundamental notions that are often taken for granted in the study of grammar. While Thompson and Hopper's observations of argument structure in spoken discourse are important in revealing the nature of argument structure as a real phenomenon, it is equally important to examine such structures as part of their contextualized surroundings, both linguistic and otherwise, because it is here that the interactional import of various structures is realized.

Tao (2001, 2003) has investigated the argument structure of the verbs *remember* and *forget* in context and has drawn some interesting conclusions about the usage of such verbs and the class of arguments they take. He found that *remember* is used more frequently in highly interactive types of spoken discourse and that its argument structure, as well as the argument structure of *forget*, is often simpler than has been proposed (Tao, 2003, p. 81). Evidence for this comes from the fact that both verbs are commonly (one-third of the time) used in spoken English without subjects (p. 82). He claims that, although both verbs have been argued to take complements, complement taking is not an essential feature of either verb, and in fact, it "appears to be a marginal feature of *remember* in spoken English, as over 70% of the time *remember* does not take a complement" (p. 77).

Tao presents three types of noncomplements. One is the zero-object type, as in *I remember/I forgot*. The second is shown in example 3.25, a simple NP type that includes a relative clause, and the third is shown in example 3.26, a relative-clause type. While the majority of the corpus used in this study was from interactive contexts, some of the data were drawn from university lectures, business meetings, and other professional settings. However, the fact that even in these more formal (less ordinary) settings the phenomenon appears robust suggests that these tendencies would be even stronger if their examination was limited to ordinary conversation among copresent participants.

(3.25)
I remember very carefully the statement that he made.

(3.26)
I don't remember what she has announced as her schedule.

Tao also notes that both verbs are found more often in spoken than in written discourse, which suggests that the non-complement-taking nature is a product of language use; the features of these verbs are emergent (see Hopper, 1987, 1988, 1998; Bybee and Hopper, 2001, for more on the nature of emergent grammar).

With respect to the nature of argument structure, Tao (2003) concludes that "1) inherent rationality[40] of predicates plays a limited role in grammar and thus should not be the exclusive object of research in argument structure; 2) argument structure, like other aspects of grammar, is a dynamic phenomenon, one that is to be regarded from language use" (p. 77).

Mikesell (2004a; see also Schumann et al., 2006) also examined argument structure in context. She provides several instances of "elided" arguments—subjects, objects, and topics[41]—in contextualized spoken English. These "elided" arguments are often considered obligatory in structural terms. Contrary to demonstrating that argument structure is, in fact, complicated, this study reveals that it is often quite simple structurally precisely because talk is recipient-designed, and interlocutors take account of contextual considerations. Unexpressed subjects, for instance, are easily indexicalized through other semiotic resources and contextual cues. Similarly to Thompson (2002) in her conclusions about object complements, Mikesell stresses that these arguments are not "missing" or "elided" but rather that their nonexpression is quite natural in conversation, and, if anything, they should be seen as being "explicitly added" in formal and written expression. Arguments can be "elided" with no demonstration of any problems or confusion on behalf of the coparticipants. This is true of both subjects, as in examples 3.27 and 3.28, and objects, as in 3.29 (topics are also "elided" but much less frequently; this makes logical sense when considering the interactional implications of not making topics explicit).

(3.27) JS:II61 (Pomerantz, 1984, p. 67)

```
01  E:   . . . 'n she said she- depressed her terribly
02  J:   Oh it's [terribly depressing.
03  L:          Oh it's depressing
04  E:   Ve[ry
05  L:   [But it's a fantastic [film.
06  J:                        [ It's a beautiful movie.
```

40. Tao seems to be referring to how argument structure is traditionally determined in linguistic theory—that is, by imagining logically what arguments a verb should take based on its semantics. *To kick* logically requires an argument to do the kicking and an argument that is kicked. This logical imagining or "inherent rationality" does not seem to be accurate with many verbs examined in natural conversation, as Tao demonstrates.

41. Objects and topics are sometimes considered complements (structurally, they are sisters to the head of a VP) and therefore part of argument structure. Some researchers define complements more narrowly as arguments of a verb containing a verbal component (rather than just an NP). Tao (2003) is an example of this narrow definition of complement.

(3.28) TG 10:01–07 (Schegloff, 2007, p. 278)

01
02 Bee: °(I 'unno)/ °(So anyway) ·hh Hey do <u>you</u> see v- (0.3)fat
03   ol' Vivian anymouh?
04 Ava: No, <u>hardly</u>, en if we do:, y'know, I jus' say hello quick'n,
05   ·hh y'know, jus' **pass** each othuh in th[e hall.]
06 Bee: [Is she] still
07   hangin around (wih)/(with) Bo:nny?

(3.29) DA, 2 (Schegloff, 1992, p. 1304)

01 A: Well I'd like to see you very much.
02 B: Yes [uh
03 A: [I really would. We c'd have a bite, en [(ta:lk)
04 B: [Yeh.
05 B: Weh - No! No, don't prepare any [thing
06 A: [And uh - I'm not going to
07   **prepare**, we'll juz whatever it'll [be, we'll
08 B: [No! I don't mean that. I min-
09   because uh, she en I'll prob'ly uh be spending the day togethuh.

Mikesell (2004b) argues that what matters for the interlocutors is whether the arguments are easily indexicalized by the participants in either the linguistic or situational/environmental context, which can include shared knowledge, facial expression, gesture, and eye gaze. Such examples show that semantics afforded by the interaction can motivate what gets structurally expressed, although the reverse is typically assumed. We have seen that not only are linguistic elements that are considered redundant included (as was shown in the discussion of verb selection above), but elements traditionally considered syntactically required are not mandatory.

Additionally, Halford (1990) demonstrates how spoken language is organized by discourse units, which frequently cannot be examined structurally. He discusses cases in which there is the possibility of bidirectional attachment and intonation cannot resolve the ambiguity (to which clause the string should attach). In example 3.30, it is unclear how the string *because I'm in a bad mood* is attached syntactically in this context.

(3.30)

I hate sitting around here **because I'm in a bad mood** I'll go home

Miller and Weinert (1998) provide the following example, taken from radio, of this type of construction that is particularly relevant to argument structure.

(3.31)

That's why we do **it** is because we want to make sure

In examples 3.30 and 3.31, it simply is not an issue (interactionally) where the bolded string or word is attached; in 3.31, *it* can be indexically or semiotically grounded as both the subject and the object. Interactionally these utterances are perfectly acceptable and do not require any special explanation, nor should we disregard them as merely performance errors. Tao and McCarthy (2001) support a similar position in light of the continuing debate centering on how to understand nonrestrictive *which* clauses in spoken English (see ex. 3.32 and ex. 3.33 below), a debate that has focused primarily on fabricated sentences and counterexamples.

They argue that an approach based on such fabricated sentences "could potentially conduct a debate without end, and that the only solution to such disagreements about grammaticality is to look at actual use in a corpus, and to base the notion of 'grammatical' on the repeated and patterned utterances of ordinary native speakers" (p. 655). Argument structure, although being described as quite complicated, at least from the perspective of the analysts, is, in real conversation, much simpler for the participants. Not only does the structure itself tend to be simpler in ordinary conversation, but our intuitions as analysts also are often incorrect about how argument structures of certain verbs are expressed, partly because the argument structures of verbs may change based on interactional constraints and fluctuations. This resonates in Miller and Weinert's (1998) declaration, noted earlier: "it must be emphasized that investigators of spontaneous spoken language in a number of countries have discovered that such language has syntactic structures that are not just less complex but different" (p. 21). In fact, analysts may need to consider the usefulness of the category of argument structure altogether in talk-in-interaction.

Relative Clauses in Conversation

Tao and McCarthy (2001) examined nonrestrictive relative clauses (NRRC) in spoken English using spoken corpora of both British and American English. It should now be unsurprising that they found such structures to behave much simpler and more flexibly than has traditionally been proposed. In identifying NRRCs, they state that while they "do not wish to suggest that the distinction between appositive and continuative[42] NRRC has no validity," "it is perhaps best to treat the distinction between appositive and continuative NRRC as a continuum rather than a discrete opposition," especially given the "the influence of interactional factors on the unfolding of grammatical structure" (p. 661). They also found that nonrestrictive *which* clauses frequently come packaged in one syntactic format over others, and they often serve a special communicative/interactional function over other possibilities. In other words, the authors found that these types of clauses take on both a preferred grammatical structure (71.24 percent were continuative, as

---

42. Appositive NRRCs "are embedded in the matrix clause," while continuative NRRCs "are added after the matrix clause, and act like extra sentences" (p. 654).

in ex. 3.32 below) and a "preferred communicative function" (62 percent were evaluative), "giving the speaker's attitude, opinion or stance towards the message of the immediately preceding utterance(s)"[43] (p. 662), as shown in example 3.33. These findings indicate that these types of clauses "constitute an assessment activity" (p. 655).

(3.32) Speakers are discussing problems with a furnace (Tao and McCarthy, 2001, p. 654)[44]

<speaker 1>	Otherwise you gotta come back and put the coil in **which means you gotta modify the duct work to [get that coil in there so**
<speaker 2>	[Right

(3.33) Speaker is complaining about the materialism that dominates Christmas (Tao and McCarthy, 2001, p. 663)

<speaker 1>	I know my brother goes into debt for the kids every Christmas you know like if they don't spend two hundred pound on them you know it's not enough
<speaker 2>	Mm
<speaker 1>	**which I think is silly** but that's the way of things today

The authors conclude that in order to examine the use of nonrestrictive *which* clauses, "it seems necessary, and indeed mandatory, to examine the interactional environment in which [they] occur and the interactional consequences" (p. 665). In fact, they note that the organization of turn-taking and speaker exchange (see Sacks, Schegloff, and Jefferson, 1974) is an important factor in examining and understanding the use of nonrestrictive *which* clauses in spoken discourse. They found that the overwhelming majority (96 percent) of the *which* clauses were spoken by the same speaker, a logical finding given their assessment function. However, they also found that *which* clauses are often produced in a next turn and often following some minimal uptake or "display of acknowledgment" by the listener, as in example 3.34.

43. In the discussion of the NRRCs and the CTPs (e.g., *I guess* in ex. 3.13) of object complements, both are serving the same function, that is, both grammatical forms are claimed to be used to provide one's stance. While this is true, it should also be observed that these forms are also functionally distinct, since the *which* clauses that Tao and McCarthy discuss are continuative, while the CTPs are introductive.

44. Examples 3.32 through 3.34 were taken from the Corpus of Spoken American English (CSAE) from the University of California, Santa Barbara, which consists mainly of casual conversation. The transcription methods follow the guidelines of this corpus, which is based on the concept of the intonation unit as described by Chafe (1987, 1994).

(3.34)

01   Sp 1:   Oh I - I don't remember.
02   Sp 2:   I just got liability.
03   Sp 1:   **Just liability.**
04   Sp 2:   **Which is good enough.** At least it's insured,
05   Sp 1:   Yeah

Here, the listener (speaker 1) in line 3 repeats part of speaker 2's turn, demonstrating receipt of the previous turn. Tao and McCarthy note that while the tokens that come between the first speaker's turn and their *which* clause appear neutral, they nevertheless "[seem] to function to encourage the main speaker to express his/her assessment to the recipient" (p. 667). They conclude that evaluative *which* clauses are "by no means a unilateral act on the part of the main speaker"; rather, their production is "more of a joint interactional activity" (p. 671).

Tao (2003) makes the following statement in the conclusions of his study on the argument structure of *remember* and *forget*: "it is hardly a simple matter to predicate [the verbs'] syntax by deriving it from, or, as is commonly done, decomposing, their meanings out of context, and hope to achieve a realistic explanation. Such explanations, though often precise and convenient in theory, are also often at variance with speakers' discourse practices. Only by integrating our understanding of semantic propensities of lexical entities with careful analysis of naturalistic discourse data can linguists hope to yield the best possible approximation of the nature of linguistic structures and structural evolution" (p. 92).

Reflections on What Usage-Based Approaches Contribute to Understanding Grammar in the Wild

We have thus far seen that grammar in speech usually tends to be simpler but in many respects can be seen to be more complicated for pragmatic or interactional motivations, an important relationship for understanding the kind of grammar that is a reflection of our most natural abilities. Many linguists have never really considered this kind of grammar; some have never even encountered the grammar of natural spontaneous talk. Some have never seen this kind of grammar[45] because it is less practical; it requires audio and video recordings and a careful consideration of what is often thought of as "noise" or extraneous factors and context. Yet it is this type of grammar situated in all of the "noise" that the brain

---

45. Of course, they have certainly heard this sort of grammar in the wild; however, research tends to take place with things that can be easily indexicalized or given concrete form (see Schumann et al., 2006). Thus, while linguists use the grammar of conversation, it remains unfamiliar to them for investigative purposes.

evolved to understand. It is precisely this sort of grammar that the brain is most comfortable producing and comprehending. Language most natural to our abilities does not consist of complicated sentences divorced from context. This sort of grammar is reserved for, and more or less unique to, writing or language composed offline, artificially manipulated forms of language that are a practiced skill. Problems of understanding grammar occur far more frequently in writing than in speech; this is not simply coincidence (see Schegloff, 2002, for examples of the kind of complexity that is typical of conversation). Conversation grammar is like walking; with some models (even if their gaits vary from one another) and some practice, a child succeeds to the point where the ability to walk is taken for granted. The grammar of writing and prose is like a gymnastics floor routine; perhaps most of us can manage a cartwheel, but with extensive training and the right tools (a coil-spring floor, for one), a few of us can master quite complex routines, but there is clearly more variability in our talent in gymnastics than in walking. Moreover, we would never think of examining one's ability to do gymnastics in order to understand one's ability to walk and then claim that the gymnastics floor routine is so complicated that it must be genetically hardwired.

Language in the Wild

Because conversation and discourse analysts have typically been leaders in examining language in its natural habitat and embedded in context, these two fields have perhaps made the most contribution to understanding the nature not only of grammar (see above) but also of language in interaction, that is, with all of its available resources both internal to it (the traditional distinctions including grammar and prosody) and external (the environmental and situational context and visual resources, including eye gaze, body position, gesture, and facial expression). We briefly reviewed Ong's (2002) description of oral cultures above. Discussing the homeostatic nature of oral traditions, he says that "words acquire their meanings only from their always insistent actual habitat, which is not in a dictionary, simply other words, but includes also gestures, vocal inflections, facial expression, and the entire human, existential setting in which the real, spoken word always occurs" (pp. 46–47). Again, gestures, vocal inflections, and the like are not resources known and employed strictly by oral cultures but are resources employed by even fully literate individuals in ordinary conversation and for more than merely words. Traugott (2008), a major contributor to the notion of grammaticalization, responds to Chomsky's recent suggestion in Andor (2004) by highlighting the nature of interactive language use and dispelling the misconception that communication is linguistically precise. She states: "Chomsky suggested that if language were designed for communication, then everything would be spelled out and nothing would be hinted at. This assumes that communication is transfer of information. But if we instead view communication as negotiated interaction, then hints are optimal. Each participant in the communicative event is given some leeway that allows for saving face (one's own or others'), and creative thinking beyond the immediate situation" (p. 239). Indeed, with so many other semiotic fields available for both understanding and communicating, not everything needs to be precisely encoded in the linguistic signal.

To understand better how multiple semiotic fields may be employed, we introduce a classic study in which Goodwin (1979) argues that sentences cannot be accurately examined without also examining the ecological niche in which they were originally constructed, as well as the interactive development that gives way to them. He draws this conclusion based on the close examination of a videotaped interaction in which the sentence being examined can be seen to be continually constructed based on the interactional moment-to-moment cues, essentially emerging little by little as the situational and interactional circumstances change or are realized by the speaker.

Goodwin examines the sentence *I gave, I gave up smoking cigarettes::. l-uh: one-one week ago t'da:y. aschilly*. If this sentence were examined divorced from its context, there would be perhaps little to say about it: *I gave up smoking cigarettes one week ago today actually*. However, Goodwin notes that the repetition of *I gave* can be shown to be employed by the speaker in order to secure the eye gaze of his addressee,[46] a well-documented practice in face-to-face interaction. When the speaker begins his turn, he is looking at his recipient, but the recipient is not gazing at him. The speaker restarts his turn, and the gaze of his intended recipient reaches him just as *up* is being uttered. This resource (along with others like it) has been shown to be used by speakers systematically to secure the gaze of an addressee (Goodwin, 1980).

Goodwin (1979) also notes that over the construction of this sentence, its speaker gazes at three different individuals; these three hearers are thus incorporated into the unfolding structure of this sentence. In other words, parts of the sentence are constructed for each noticeably attending addressee. When the speaker begins the sentence, he does not look toward his wife, a hearer who would already be privy to the fact that he quit smoking, but is looking at an addressee for whom this would constitute new information (in line with Grician maxims; Grice, 1975).

In contrast, in the middle of the sentence (at *one-one week ago t'day*), he is gazing at his wife. At the end of *cigarettes*, the speaker is gazing at his first addressee, for whom this information is new. He is still gazing at this first addressee when he utters /l/, which most probably is the beginning of *last week*. However, at this moment, he begins gazing at his wife, a knowing recipient, and tailors his talk precisely for this new addressee; he highlights that this is now an anniversary of his quitting smoking, something that his wife might not have

---

46. Such devices (restarts, cutoffs, sound stretches) are called phrasal breaks and are common practices employed to secure the eye gaze of a recipient (see later in the text section for further elaboration).

realized. In essence, Goodwin shows that a sentence "may not be understandable as a unit apart from the situated occasion of its production" (p. 97). Although Goodwin's own analysis of this episode is much more detailed and insightful, these brief highlights iterate the importance of analyzing even simple sentences within their contextualized settings; the participants, their relationships, and the moment-to-moment interactivity are all relevant to how the talk[47] unfolds.

It was mentioned above that eye gaze as a visual process is important for understanding how talk is constructed and designed. Goodwin (2000a, 2000b) argues for the importance of examining a variety of kinds of semiotic resources that can be shown to be relevant to the participants of any given interaction. For Goodwin, this includes visible resources such as the body (see also Schegloff, 1998; Coupland and Gwyn, 2003; Hindmarsh and Heath, 2003): "the visible bodies of participants provide systematic, changing displays about relevant action and orientation" (p. 157). He shows that the body is an equally important resource that is used to display and understand participants' orientation.

While Goodwin (2003a) points out that the bodies of interactants are an essential part of interaction, he also notes that they cannot be understood apart from the environment in which they are embedded. He provides an analysis of an archeological dig in which a student is having difficulty, and the experienced archeologist, using not only words but a pointing gesture with her hand as well as an orientation with her body, demonstrates to the student how the dig should continue (see Kita, 2003, and Haviland, 1993, for more on pointing). He notices that the hand gesture alone is not sufficient for the student to understand the teacher's instructions but that the hand gesture is only meaningful when it is seen in the contextual environment in which it was created. In other words, the gesture as a semiotic resource is no resource at all when removed from the world in which it was implemented. He likens this to watching a football player running to score a touchdown. The movement is not meaningful by itself, and an analysis of the movement of the player's body decontextualized from its environment (without the field, the lines marking the field, etc.) reveals little. In a sense, objects in the world and the world itself can become extensions of our own bodies and are integral to interaction and constructing and understanding meaning. Additionally, these resources are not static but are ever changing in response to all sort of considerations: "As interaction unfolds contextual configurations can change as new fields are added to, or dropped from, the specific mix being used to constitute the events of the moment" (Goodwin, 2000b, p. 167). While these specific examples are not of casual conversation, in that they have a specific purpose and location required for this purpose to be fulfilled, it is likely (if not

---

47. We have followed researchers of interaction and used *talk* rather than *grammar* or *language* precisely to avoid the baggage that comes with using one of these terms that are either too narrowly defined (as is the case for *grammar*) or not well defined at all (as is the case for *language*).

certain) that similar resources and constraints are necessary for an adequate analysis of talk in ordinary conversation.

What is important here is not simply that all of these elements matter for a particular action or goal to get accomplished (although this is important as well) but also that all of these resources are relied on in order to make sense of the grammar. And, of course, the grammar (the talk) is also important to understanding the orientations of bodies and gestures. When grammar as a resource fails us, prosody, eye gaze, and visual displays such as gesture, the body, and the environmental surround, as well as nonvisual cues, including shared knowledge and the prior histories of the participants, can be referred to and employed to "recover" meaning that might otherwise be lost (see Goodwin, 2003b, and Goodwin, Goodwin, and Olsher, 2002, for studies on conversation and aphasics). Similarly, when visual displays are not accessible to one's addressees, as in the case of telephone calls, grammar, prosody, and shared knowledge are the primary resources used in interaction.

One of the aims of many discourse analysts is to devise a theory of action; for our purpose, it is enough to understand that grammar (or language, depending on how one defines it) did not evolve as an autonomous system among its users but was used along with a multitude of semiotic resources, all of which were employed in concert for meaning to be made and for actions to be successfully carried out. The most natural habitat of language incorporates all of these nonlinguistic[48] resources and practices, all of which can be studied independently as autonomous systems but which were never meant to function alone, suggesting that the brain did not evolve to make use of these systems independent of the others. Rather, the brain evolved to use them in the service of interaction. In examining vision as a semiotic resource, Goodwin (2000b) states that "neither vision, nor the images or other phenomena that participants look at, are treated as coherent, self-contained domains that can be subjected to analysis in their own terms" (pp. 157–158); the same is true of grammar and other elements of language employed in interaction. To understand the grammar and language that require an evolutionary and neurobiological account, we must understand how all of these semiotic fields jointly operate. It is in this joint operation that the complexity of language becomes quite astounding; while the grammar in conversation seems to be less complex than the written or created variety that syntacticians examine, the constant monitoring of multiple semiotic fields can become quite intricate. In other words, what has been traditionally viewed as complex, even mysterious, and thus innate about language are its grammatical complexities; however, the true complexities of language reside not in its grammatical nature but in its dependence on interactionally and contextually relevant semiotic fields.

---

48. We use *nonlinguistic* in the traditional sense, meaning nearly everything other than syntax and perhaps phonology and morphology; we would argue that all of these systems and resources should be an inherent part of what we study when we study *language*.

Competence Is Performance

The claim that processing limitations are not a factor for formal grammatical theory began, of course, with Chomsky. The famous example was some variant of *The cat the rat the dog chased bit ran* presented earlier, where the multiple embeddings are considered perfectly acceptable and well formed by the language faculty unimpeded by nonlinguistic cognitive/psychological limitations, which linguists claim interfere with our performance. In short, *competence* is the psychological capacity with which all native speakers of a language are innately equipped, while *performance* is the sort of language that is produced in real language use. This dichotomy is interesting but useless to the students of inter-action. If one is to accept that spoken language, such as that seen in conversation, is what needs to be explained for an evolutionary and neurobiological account of language (precisely because it is the sort of grammar and language that most closely reflects our interactional tendencies), then these processing limitations are clearly important and necessary to the ways in which language evolved and developed to be understood by the brain.

In fact, when examining interaction, we find that the ways in which one employs grammar, typically regarded as one's performance, actually demonstrate one's competence (Schumann, personal communication). In this way, competence should be regarded as what one can accomplish with language in ordinary settings and ordinary circumstances, while performance should be seen as the ways we can manipulate language in nonordinary settings and nonordinary circumstances. For instance, the sort of refined and practiced language that is used by poets, musicians, and academics should more rightly be regarded as performance, since these varieties of language use require preparation, skill, and training of a whole different sort (an artificial sort) from that required to use language in natural interaction. Again, we see how linguistics, in beginning with the wrong sort of data to support its claims, has progressed in a "backward" fashion.

Understanding these terms by essentially reversing their definitions is per-haps best illustrated by what have been regarded as speech "errors" or "disfluen-cies" in linguistics. Lerner (1996) notes that "the possibility of opportunistic completion provides a systematic 'motivation' or basis for speakers to produce their turn without extended pauses and as fluently as possible" (p. 267). This observation may suggest that when perturbations and other such disfluencies occur, they have interactional import. Disfluencies may not be disfluencies at all; they are often systematically employed by speakers with interactional conse-quences. This, in turn, demonstrates that not only are such hitches and perturba-tions[49] in interaction not *performance errors* or merely the result of processing

---

49. Hitches can be seen as "momentary arrests in the continuity or 'progressivity' of the talk's production" and perturbations as "marked departures from the prosodic character of the talk's articulation to that point" (Schegloff, 2000b, p. 11).

limitations (although they may be as well), but they are reflections of one's interactional competence. In one of Jefferson's early papers (1974) on error correction as an interactional resource, she discusses error corrections "as matters of competence, both in the production of coherent speech and the conduct of meaningful interaction" (p. 181).

Jefferson's paper suggests that *uh* is not a disfluency or a result of some processing limitation employed to buy more time to think of what one wants to say but is rather a (semi)-planned element of interaction. She is able to show this in an analysis of *uh* when it occurs after a definite article. The definite article in Standard North American English follows phonological rules. When *the* is produced before a word that begins with a consonant, it is pronounced *thuh* (*thuh car*); however, it is pronounced *thee* when occurring before a word beginning with a vowel (*thee example*). The article, therefore, is capable of projecting for the recipient this characteristic of the word that is to follow. Because North American English works this way, Jefferson was able to examine how *the* was phonologically realized when it was followed by *uh*. She found that *uh* is often projected by the article that precedes it; her data show that speakers produced *thee uh jeweler's shop* and *thee uh drum corps*. She argues that *uh* should not be treated as "haphazard" but as "a rule-governed phenomenon" and can be seen as "a projectable syntactic unit with the article selected by reference to *uh*'s forthcomingness," indicating that *uh* may be characterized as a word in American English (p. 184).

However, Jefferson also documents cases in interaction where *uh* is preceded not by the *thee* variant of *the* but by the *thuh* variant, which generally occurs before a word beginning with a consonant. She argues that such cases merely prove the rule and that when this occurs, it indicates a type of error correction in which the speaker projects a word beginning with a consonant and produces *thuh* but is able to correct the word before it is uttered. For instance, in example 3.35, Jefferson argues that the speaker did not project the word *officer* but perhaps projected the word *cop* to follow the article *thuh*. The speaker then corrects the projected word before it is uttered in order to produce *officer*.

(3.35) PTC Materials: I:71 (Jefferson, 1974)
Parnelli: I told that to THUH- UH- officer.

She offers additional cases in which the projected word is partially or fully realized by the speaker to demonstrate more convincingly that *uh* is an indicator of error correction.

(3.36) PTC Materials: I:41 (Jefferson, 1974)
Wiggens: I wz- made my left, uh my right signal . . .

(3.37) SFD Materials: IV:71 (Jefferson, 1974)
Desk: He was here lay- uh earlier, but 'e left.

Jefferson argues that *thuh- uh* is a "feature of speech"; specifically, she claims that it is "an indicator of error correction" and that this is a practice, "a device," that can be interactionally significant for participants (p. 185).

Goodwin (1980) also examines disfluencies in speech; he shows that both restarts and pauses, which he calls phrasal breaks, can be used as devices for achieving mutual gaze at turn beginnings, something that is negotiated and important for participants, especially the speaker. He claims that speakers must have an attending recipient (a recipient attends to a speaker with eye gaze) when they begin a turn. When an attending recipient is not available to the speaker, the speaker will, in the majority of circumstances, deploy various practices to secure a gazing addressee. These practices include restarts, pauses, and cutoffs in which speakers can restart, pause, and/or abruptly cut off an utterance that is not brought to completion. Precisely at the point of restarting the utterance, an addressed recipient overwhelmingly turns his or her attention and gaze toward the speaker, as in example 3.38.

(3.38) (Goodwin, 1980)
Debbie: Anyway, (0.2) uh:, (0.2) we went [t- I went ta bed
Chuck: [X_____

The start of Debbie's utterance is produced with several so-called performance errors; there are two short pauses, an *uh*, and a cutoff after /t/ (indicated in the transcript by the dash). If linguists were to extract this utterance from its context to examine the syntax, they would surely ignore all of these features of Debbie's utterance as irrelevant to the production of the talk, leaving them with the complete sentential TCU *I went to bed*. However, examining this utterance in its natural context, Goodwin shows that while Debbie produces these "performance errors," her addressee is not attending to her as the speaker; Chuck is not looking at Debbie. Just at the moment of the cutoff on /t/, Chuck turns his eye gaze toward Debbie (marked in the transcript by the X) and continues to attend to Debbie until the end of her TCU (marked in the transcript by the continuous line). Once Debbie secures an attending recipient, she continues her turn unimpeded.

(3.39) (Goodwin, 1980)
Lee: Can ya bring?- (0.2) Can you bring me here that nylo[n?
Ray: .... [X

In example 3.39, we see a similar situation; however, Ray's eye gaze does not meet Lee, the speaker, until the tail end of his utterance. While a listener's eye gaze is preferred by a speaker, it is enough for the speaker to see an attempt by the hearer to look at them. That is, if the speaker can see the recipient orient his or her body and/or head position, this is enough for the speaker to understand that the listener is attempting to attend to his or her talk. Here, Lee begins his utterance, abruptly cuts it off, and follows it with a short pause. At this point, Ray begins to turn himself physically toward Lee to demonstrate that he is attending to him (marked in the transcript by the series of dots). Lee can see Ray's attempt to reposition himself, and at that point, Lee continues the utterance without any hitches or perturbations.

In all of Goodwin's examples, he deals with sentential TCUs and argues that speakers, by employing restarts, can have an attending addressee for the entirety of the complete sentence being uttered. He notes that the sentences being constructed are thus done specifically for the hearers. Goodwin shows that single restarts, as well as multiple restarts and other types of disfluencies, commonly regarded as noise and thus disregarded, are not performance errors but are interactionally deployed by participants.[50] He demonstrates this as well for pauses, also considered a performance error (see Schegloff, 1987, for an analysis of recycled turn beginnings).

Hitches and perturbations can also be strategically deployed to "win the floor" in a conversation. Schegloff (2000b) shows in a range of instances how speakers will use practices that diverge from the normal progression of an utterance in order to beat out another speaker who is currently in overlap. There are various sorts of divergences from the smooth progression of talk that are systematically employed to complete or secure a turn at talk. "The talk can get suddenly (i) louder in volume, (ii) higher in pitch, or (iii) faster or slower in pace, depending on where in the overlapping talk the change in pace occurs. The talk-in-progress may be (iv) suddenly cut off, most commonly with what linguists call a glottal, labial, dental, or some other oral stop; or (v) some next sound may be markedly prolonged or stretched out; or (vi) a just prior element may be repeated" (Schegloff, 2000b, p. 12). Again, he shows how such delays of speech are strategic practices and not a result of cognitive overload, short-term memory limitations, nervousness or anxiety about speaking, or having to speak too quickly, as has been previously assumed.

(3.40) TG, 14:36–43 (Schegloff, 2007, p. 285)

```
1        Bee:   t! We:ll, uhd-yihknow I-I don' wanna make any- thing
2               definite because I-yihknow I jis:: I jis::t thinkin:g
3               tihday all day riding on th'trai:ns hhuh-uh
4               .hh[h!
5        Ava:      [Well there's nothing else t'do.<I wz
6               thingin[g of  taking the  car  anyway. ] .hh
7   →   Bee:          [that I would go into the ss-uh-]= I would go
8               into the city but I don't know,
```

50. In a later paper, Goodwin (2000b) also notes the importance of restarts for language acquisition: "if the party attempting to learn the language did not have to deal with ungrammatical possibilities, if for example she was exposed to only well-formed sentences, she might not have the data necessary to determine the boundaries, or even the structure of the system" (p. 159). Thus, *when we went t-* is repaired by a speaker to *I went to*, the replacement makes it clear to a language learner that certain forms of words occur in certain slots; the pronouns *we* and *I* can be seen to belong to the same word class.

In example 3.40, Bee produces a sound stretch on *city* that, as Schegloff puts it, "'absorbs' the remainder of Ava's overlapping talk, allowing Bee to emerge 'into the clear'" (p. 13). The overlapping talk having been "absorbed" allows Bee's talk to be heard without any danger or impediment of ongoing talk. Schegloff points out that it is at just this moment when Bee's talk is free of overlap that she stops producing the sound stretch and redoes her turn. Therefore, "we can see the sound stretch not as a toll exacted by overloaded speech production and reception systems, but rather as a deployable resource, mobilized to do a determinate job at a determinate place in an ongoing positional conflict" (p. 14).

Just as "elisions" and "irregularities" in syntactic structure are not performance errors but interactionally useful, even necessary, for participants, Schegloff (1996b) also reminds us that "contingency—interactional contingency—is not a blemish on the smooth surface of discourse, or of talk-in-interaction more generally. It is endemic to it. It is its glory. It is what allows talk-in-interaction the flexibility and the robustness to serve as the enabling mechanism for the institutions of social life" (p. 22).

Conclusions

If our goal is to understand grammar and/or language in evolutionary or neurobiological terms, especially as a social phenomenon, we must begin with the sort of language the brain most likely evolved to use and manipulate (language in interactional contexts). This requires an examination of context, of real language use, of real grammatical usages, and even of the contingencies of ordinary spoken discourse, ideally in face-to-face interaction and casual conversation. Unfortunately, formal theory has had such a hold over all language-related research that nonlinguists interested in language have now turned to formal linguists to gain the answers to the fundamental question: How does language work? Hopper (1999) claims that "the larger educated public remains unaware of the accomplishments within social interaction studies" (p. 77). The majority of nonlinguists (and even linguists) remain unaware of what spontaneous spoken grammar looks like in natural settings. For instance, neuroscience has taken to studying aspects of language that have been put forth by formal theory, however doubtful it is that the answer to the question of how language works can be found by resolving what part of the brain "understands" sentences or "does" c-commanding. Rather, answers will be more adequately resolved by understanding how the brain accomplishes social action, using the traditional notion of grammar as one of its many tools. The blind acceptance of formal linguistic theory by nonlinguists has also thrown us off course, and while these questions may be worth asking and investigating, we must be aware of their narrow applications. Wong (2005) reviews the neurobiological approaches of both Pulvermuller (2002) and Calvin and Bickerton (2000) and questions whether their neurobiology of syntax is an appropriate target for uncovering the neurobiology of language.

She suggests that "grammatical sentences out of context do not represent language. Instead, emergent language structure from language use in oral interaction better represents the phenomenon" that needs to be explained (p. 56).

Neuroscience is not the only field that has adopted the tenets of formal syntax. Both conversation analysts and functional linguists, who often explicitly couch their approaches so as to avoid the assumptions of a formal view of language, have also (presumably unknowingly) assumed beliefs of formal theory. For example, Fox, Hayashi, and Jasperson (1996) mention that "English is somewhat odd cross-linguistically in requiring the presence of a subject in all utterances.... it is rare, even in fast conversation, for speakers to produce a main clause without explicit mention of the subject" (p. 200). The examination of argument structure above, while not documenting the frequency of null subjects, demonstrates that utterances are indeed produced without explicit mention of a subject. In fact, Carter and McCarthy (2002) note that "ellipsis is *pervasive* in spoken discourse" and *"frequently* involves the omission of personal subjects" (p. 14, emphasis added).

Such phenomena in conversation are not syntactic anomalies but are regularly employed by language users where language exists in its most natural state. Unfortunately, linguists have neglected this sort of grammar and language or have imposed inappropriate categories from writing. While it is generally true that subjects of main clauses occur explicitly in writing in English, there is no such prescriptive rule for speech. We must conclude, then, that the "omission" of subjects (and other arguments) is not an omission at all but a natural and ordinary practice in English grammar that has simply been overlooked because of our reliance on artificially manipulated grammar. If anything, overt subjects are "additions" to English grammar. To quote Ong (2002) once more in his discussion of oral literature:

> Thinking of oral tradition or a heritage of oral performance, genres and styles as "oral literature" is rather like thinking of horses as automobiles without wheels. You can, of course, undertake to do this. Imagine writing a treatise on horses (for people who have never seen a horse) which starts with the concept not of horse but of "automobile," built on the readers' direct experience of automobiles. It proceeds to discourse on horses by always referring to them as "wheelless automobiles," explaining to highly automobilized readers who have never seen a horse all the points of difference in an effort to excise all idea of "automobile" out of the concept "wheelless automobile" so as to invest the term with a purely equine meaning. Instead of wheels, the wheelless automobiles have enlarged toenails called hooves; instead of headlights or perhaps rear-vision mirrors, eyes; instead of a coat of lacquer, something called hair; instead of gasoline for fuel, hay, and so on. In the end, horses are only what they are not. No matter how accurate and thorough such apophatic description, automobile-driving readers who have never seen a horse and who hear only of "wheelless automobiles" would be

sure to come away with a strange concept of a horse. The same is true of those who deal in terms of "oral literature," that is, "oral writing." You cannot without serious and disabling distortion describe a primary phenomenon by starting with a subsequent secondary phenomenon and paring away the differences. Indeed, starting backwards in this way—putting the car before the horse—you can never become aware of the real differences at all. (pp. 12–13)

It is only after we take seriously the nature of grammar and language of ordinary, casual conversation that we can begin to reflect adequately on the evolutionary motivations of grammar and language. And only then can we understand what needs to be accounted for in terms of neurobiology.

Appendix

Transcription Symbols (Jefferson, 1985)

[ ]	overlap boundaries
=	single, continuous utterance or break between speakers with no recognizable pause
(0.3)	length of silence in tenths of a second
(.)	micropause
.	falling intonation
?	rising intonation
,	continuing intonation
::	lengthening
word/WORD/<u>word</u>	increased amplitude or stress
<>	markedly slow speech
><	rushed speech
hh	hearable aspiration
(word)	indicates transcriber's uncertainty

FOUR

Interactional Readiness:
Infant-Caregiver Interaction and the
Ubiquity of Language Acquisition

As we described in chapters 1 and 2, language structure emerges when an aggregate of agents attempt to communicate with one another. In the interactions, individuals create a lexicon and organize it into structures. Then, if the words and structures are efficiently producible, comprehensible, and learnable, their use will spread as a cultural artifact. Language is neither in nor of the brain but is rather an interactional artifact that may develop with each succeeding generation or may lock in structure to form a grammar for the language. The interaction generates the structure and ensures that the forms that ultimately become part of the grammar are those that fit the capacities of the brain (Kirby, 1998). Therefore, the brain does not require a genetically based mechanism or module to specify the structures of a language.

If languages are interactional artifacts, what ensures the interaction? Lee and Schumann (2005) argue that there are two fundamental developmental precursors that ensure the ubiquity of language acquisition among typically developing children. The first is an innate drive to attune to, imitate, and seek out interaction with potential interlocutors in their social environment. We call this drive the *interactional instinct*. It drives human beings, beginning from infancy, to interact with others, leading to social attachment and affiliation and ultimately to conformity with conspecifics. Once attachment and affiliation are achieved, a typically developing newborn will continue to interact with his[1] caregivers in his environment, leading to reciprocal emotional interactions, the emotional entrainment of objects associated with words in their environment, and the ability to form symbols. At the same time, other developmental abilities provide a means by which children can

---

1. In this chapter, for purposes of clarity and ease of reading, we will use male pronouns to refer to infants and female pronouns to refer to mothers and caregivers.

detect and learn the structure of the language in their social environment. These abilities are general learning strategies such as joint attention, pattern finding, and statistical learning (Tomasello, 2003).

Since the 1960s, developmental psychologists have photographed, video-taped, and described the world of the infant. Using methods that allow them to see and analyze the split-second actions between infants and caregivers, it became clear that although infants appear to be extremely fragile and helpless, they are social, and they both respond to and elicit interaction with conspecifics. This chapter, in part, reflects on what the past four decades of research reveal about what human newborns do and why. It focuses the phenomena of human neonate behavior with parents and caregivers as behavioral manifestations of the interactional instinct. Throughout the chapter, we specify what researchers have shown to be human endowments, and through behavioral studies, we report how these might be deployed to facilitate interaction with conspecifics and achieve social attachment and affiliation. The second part of the chapter contains what may be considered behavioral manifestations of a human being's innate capacity to interact with conspecifics. The capacity consists of five broad categories: imitation, infant-initiatedness, emotional perception and expression, human-specificity, and an understanding of the organization of interpersonal interaction. Although other social animals may exhibit the same manifestations, following Lee and Schumann (2005), we contend that the instinct is much more powerful and consequential in humans. The third part of the chapter provides evidence that infants do, in fact, have abilities that allow them to detect patterns in the language input of their social environment. Thus, the focus here is to examine the behaviors and abilities that infants display and to suggest some of the neurobiological processes that might serve the interactional instinct.

Biological Adaptations: Some Preliminaries

In the 1950s and 1960s, Freud protégés Rene Spitz (1949) and John Bowlby (1969) shocked the world with haunting images of children who were listless, unnaturally passive, developmentally slow, linguistically deficient, less spontaneous, and with fewer emotional expressions, laughter, and tears as a result of maternal or caregiver neglect. Spitz even reported that mortality increased in institutions where children were not exposed to sufficient emotional interchanges. Harlow's studies (Harlow, Dodsworth, and Harlow, 1965) that compared isolated monkeys with neglected children from orphanages further showed that children subjected to these conditions exhibited autisticlike behaviors. It was assumed that social interactions were essential for normal development and were, in fact, necessary for survival. Interaction in all of its forms, including emotional interchanges, touching, eye gaze, and so on, was seen as a central force powerful enough to shape a person while he was still an infant. Thus, the infant's social environment was destiny with respect to a child's development. From this perspective, the child was perceived to be a passive participant molded and shaped by his social environment. However, studies of early infant behavior over the past four decades have dramatically altered this view and have allowed us to see infants not as blank slates waiting to be written on but rather as organisms born with innate social-stimulus feature detectors and perceptual abilities that are precursors to allowing them to be active participants in interaction with caregivers.

Sensory Abilities

Studies have shown that immediately after birth, newborns have remarkably developed visual and auditory abilities, allowing them to see and hear potential interlocutors in their social environment. In his controversial report on 40 newborns with a median age of nine minutes old, Goren observed that neonates turned their heads to follow moving stimuli (Goren, Sarty, and Wu, 1975). His studies found that not only will babies fix their eyes on a drawing that resembles a human face, but given that the face is moved at a reasonable speed, newborns will follow the face for 180 degrees with their eyes and will continue to turn their heads to keep it in view. Furthermore, he reported that newborns will follow an adultlike face back and forth and up and down the delivery room. Fifteen years later, Goren's study was replicated with 24 newborns in the first hour of life (Johnson, Dziurawiec, Ellis, and Morton, 1991). The infants were presented with three head-shaped stimuli. One stimulus was a face, another was a scrambled face, and the third was blank. The results replicated Goren's findings; the neonates were able to track the images visually and appeared to track the moving facelike pattern farther than the other stimuli.

Other studies show that two-to-five-day-olds and four-month-olds have the ability to discriminate between direct and averted gaze and have a preference for faces that engage them in mutual gaze (Farroni, Csibra, Simion, and Johnson, 2002; Farroni, Massaccesi, Pividori, and Johnson, 2004). In addition, studies show that infants less than six months old can discriminate between normal and abnormal face configurations (Fantz, 1963; Carpenter, Tecce, Stechler, and Freidmann, 1970) and are also able to discriminate between faces of different individuals (Carpenter, 1973; Field, 1985).

Regarding a newborn's capacity to hear stimuli, studies of infant musicality show that six-month-olds discriminate features of tempo, rhythm, melody, and key in the structures of both song and instrumental sound (Trehub, Trainor, and Unyk, 1993). Studies also show that human speech is salient to a neonate among an array of auditory stimuli in the environment (Eisenberg, 1975), and infants seem to make a distinction between human and nonhuman sounds and behave accordingly. For example, when newborns are given auditory stimuli of various sounds, there is a qualitative difference in their sucking patterns. With nonhuman sounds, babies stop sucking to attend to them but then resume sucking. On the other hand, when they hear a human sound, newborns also stop sucking as if to attend to it but then resume sucking "in a pronounced burst-pause pattern—as if waiting for more human signals" (Cairns and Butterfield, 1975, p. 59). There is much evidence for an infant's auditory abilities, showing that infants are able to decompose the stream of speech in their environment when they are as young as four days old (Bijeljac-Babic, Bertocini, and Mehler, 1991; Ramus, 2001; Saffran, 2001; Saffran and Thiessen, 2003; Kuhl, 2004). They are able to notice the differences between languages that are prosodically different (Mehler et al., 1988; Mehler and Christophe, 1995), and even preterms, around 26 to 28 weeks gestational age, react to sounds by rotating their heads and trunks in a startled way. Furthermore, studies have shown that the fetus in the last trimester responds to visual, auditory, and kinesthetic stimulation (Tanaka and Arayama, 1969; Brazelton, 1981).

In addition, studies show that just hours after birth, human beings have a well-developed ability to smell. Steiner (1979) held swabs with "rotten" or "foul" odors as well as "pleasant" odors under the noses of babies in the first hours of life, before they had any contact with food or odors of food. The odors were first tested with adults. Babies grimaced when they were given the foul swabs and smiled when smelling the pleasant swabs, which was consistent with the adult controls. In another study, MacFarlane (1975) tested to see whether an infant would discriminate between the smell of his mother and her milk and the smell of another mother and her milk. His study showed that six-day-olds had a preference for their mothers' odor and milk, having not only the ability to smell but also the ability to discriminate between odors.

To elaborate further on the capacity of newborns, studies have also shown that the ability to sense touch begins very early in human ontogeny. A preterm in the third month of gestation will respond to the touch of a hair around its mouth. This shows a newborn's remarkable sensitivity to touch, which is greater than an adult's, in part because of thinner skin and a greater number of nerve endings (Barlow and Mollon, 1982).

Facial Expressions, Gestures, and Vocalizations

Newborns seem also to be born with an inventory of distinctive expressions and vocalizations that can be interpreted as communicative and can lead to interpersonal communication as well. The most familiar early expressions are cooing and smiling, which seem to be based on a motor pattern formed before birth. Cooing is described as positive, noncrying vocalization that adults often find pleasurable. And although the vocalizations are not clear and strong until the second month of life, the appropriate mouth opening and shaping for cooing is often made by infants less than two months old (Trevarthen, 1977). Cooing apparently also develops partly independently of auditory feedback from self and others. At the same time, smiling develops. Both normal and premature infants display recognizable smiles just minutes after birth. Even completely blind infants smile to a voice, although this response eventually diminishes because of lack of visual support. Thus, smiling does not seem to be an imitative response to seeing the smile of others (Fraiberg, 1974).

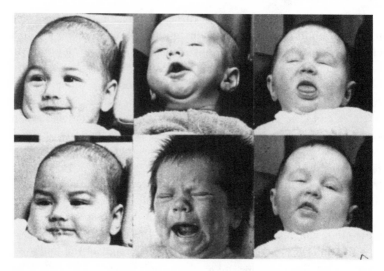

Figure 4.1. Infant expressions. *Left:* smile and jaw set (boy, 12 weeks). *Center:* above, coo (boy, 6 weeks); below, crying (girl, 6 weeks). *Right:* simulations of disgust and sneer (girl, 6 weeks). From Trevarthen (1979, p. 325). © Cambridge University Press 1979. Reprinted with the permission of Cambridge University Press.

In addition, all adult facial expressions with gestures can be found in photographs of neonates, which change very little in morphology throughout life (Charlesworth and Kreutzer, 1973). Izard (1978) has identified facial expressions of interest, joy, disgust, surprise, and distress in young infants. Figure 4.1 is a photographic sample that captures some infant facial expressions (Trevarthen, 1979).

Trevarthen also argues that the posturing of the head during many forms of facial expression (fig. 4.2) seems to be systematically related to particular facial expressions and suggests that a full pattern of body expressions is present in infants at birth, because the gesticulations of infants (hand-waving, index-finger-pointing, and fingertip-clasping movements near the face when they are vocalizing) are clearly not imitations of adult partners.

Although infants are born before they can control and articulate speech and sounds, infants show movements that resemble adult articulation, which Trevarthen calls prespeech. The image in figure 4.3 shows a comparison of the prespeech of infants to that of adults.

Selective Attention

Evidence for an infant's capacity for attunement can be found in a series of studies by Condon and Sander (Condon and Sander, 1974a, 1974b; Condon, 1977), who demonstrate that newborns ranging in age from 12 hours to two days old respond organizationally to an adult's speech regardless of whether

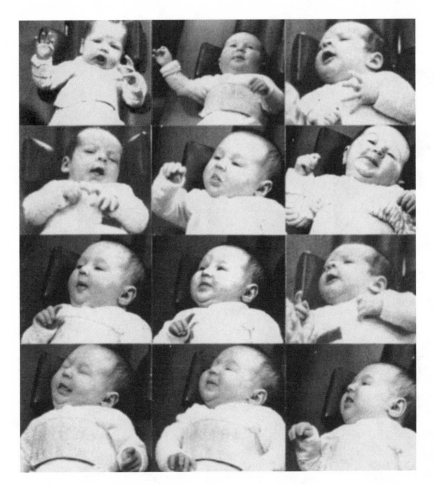

Figure 4.2. Gestures in communication. *Top:* large, waving hand above shoulder, extending fingers wide while vocalizing (6–7 weeks). *Upper center:* touching two index fingers and thumb (7 weeks). *Lower center:* pointing index finger with prespeech, pursed lips (7 weeks). *Bottom:* "disdain" or "disgust," hand held to side, flexed down (7 weeks). From Trevarthen (1979, p. 329). © Cambridge University Press 1979. Reprinted with the permission of Cambridge University Press.

the adult speaker is present or whether the voice comes from a tape recorder. By analyzing the micro-body movements of 16 newborns in response to an adult's speech, they find that infants in the first hours of life synchronize their movements to the rhythms of their mothers' voices. This behavioral attunement with human speech is observed to occur in word stretches of up to 180 words. Eye contact is ruled out as a contributor to the synchronicity, because the infant is not looking at the adult. Furthermore, when Chinese is presented to American

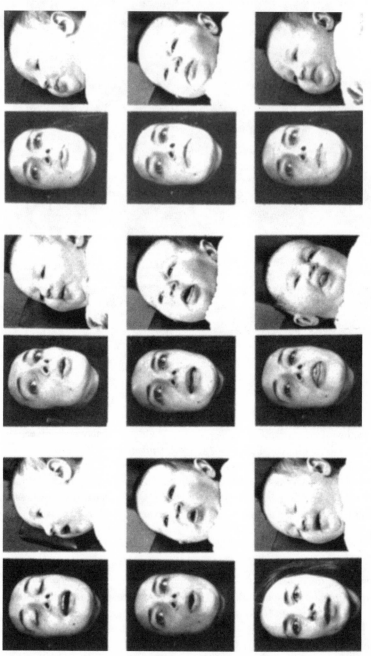

Figure 4.3. Prespeech compared to adult speech. Normal speaking of an adult, not the mother, reading a word list. Photographed with a motor-driven Nikon at 4 frames per second. Girl, 7 weeks, during a period of excited communication in front of mother but with averted gaze. Only climax postures shown. From Trevarthen (1979, p. 328). © Cambridge University Press 1979. Reprinted with the permission of Cambridge University Press.

neonates, there is as clear a correspondence and attunement as there is with American English (Condon, 1980).

Other studies have shown that preterm infants seem already equipped with the capacity to sustain attention to the sights and sounds of people around them. In one study, preterm babies, at 33 weeks postconceptional age with very low birth weight, if in an awake and nondistressed state, responded to motherese in a way that would resemble what is considered attention in healthy full-term newborns. Even when interacting with strangers, the infants also maintained high levels of attention, particularly exhibiting eye opening and low-limb activity (Eckerman, Oehler, Medvin, and Hannan, 1994). In addition, an interesting auditory stimulus, such as a rattle or a soft voice, will move an infant from a sleepy to an alert state in which breathing becomes irregular, the face brightens, and the eyes become wider. If the infant is completely awake, the eyes and head will turn toward the sound, which is often followed by a searching look and a scanning motion of the eyes as if trying to find the source of the sound. Furthermore, infants seem to orient their gazes and bodies to attend to social stimuli that arouse interest. In these studies, an experimenter tries to capture the interest of a newborn by first moving a stimulus up and down slowly until the baby becomes alert. Then the examiner moves the stimulus slowly from side to side, waiting for the newborn to follow it. Although this shows that a newborn does not visually adjust immediately to a moving object, it is clear that sight in a newborn is not a passive ability, because an infant actively tries to prolong attention to an attractive object. When a bright object is brought into a newborn's line of vision and is moved slowly up and down to attract the infant's attention, the baby's pupils contract slightly. Then, when the object is moved from side to side, the baby's eyes begin to widen, the limbs become still, and the baby stares at the object and begins slowly to track the object and its movements (Brazelton and Cramer, 1990).

In sum, this section has provided evidence that preterms, newborns, and very young infants have the following:

1. Developed sensory systems that allow them to see, hear, smell, and touch social stimuli.
2. A repertoire of adultlike facial expressions, gestures, and movements.
3. The kinesic development to attend and attune to social stimuli in their environment

These seemingly inborn abilities are demonstrated in human newborns long before a child utters his first word. Below, we explore the import of these abilities for the infant and infant-caregiver interaction. Although these abilities are not traditionally categorized as linguistic, they provide a newborn with communicative equipment and behaviors that are powerful enough to elicit and engage in rewarding interactions with the mother or caregiver.

Behavioral Manifestations of the Interactional Instinct

As demonstrated above, typically developing human beings are endowed with a number of capabilities from and before birth. These abilities are part of the interactional instinct and enable the infant to achieve innate goals of social affiliation and attachment. Therefore, early in life, tendencies that demonstrate an infant's motivation leading to the satisfaction of the interactional instinct are observable. These behaviors consist of the abilities in the repertoire of the infant described above and are deployed to communicate desire for social engagement. They fall under five broad categories: imitation, infant-initiatedness, emotional perception and expression, human specificity, and an understanding of the organization of interpersonal interaction. Furthermore, these behaviors are distinct from those that show an infant's curiosity to explore the social environment and accumulate information from it (Jones, 1996), such that an infant's behaviors make an interactional response relevant from the infant's interlocutors and can be consequential for the trajectory of the interaction. In this way, an infant's actions can signal desire for communication, as well as the potential to achieve and prolong interaction with the mother or caregiver.

Imitation

Imitation can be roughly defined as the coordination of visually perceived movements of other people with one's own movements. However, recent research seems to suggest strongly that infant imitation is more than just chance congruence. Researchers propose that neonatal imitation is "non-reflexive, volitional and intentional" (Meltzoff, 1998). If neonatal imitation is more than just the chance mirroring of actions of another and is intentional, then we might ask what infants intend to achieve through imitation. Here, we provide evidence that human neonates do, in fact, imitate and that they do so purposively, and we suggest that one objective may be to achieve attachment and affiliation with conspecifics.

The first observations of infant facial imitation were recorded as early as 1908, when a four-month-old infant was observed to be imitating the tongue protrusions of her parent (McDougall, 1908). Then, in a series of experimental studies, Maratos (1973) showed that four-week-olds were able to imitate tongue protrusions and mouth openings. Meltzoff and Moore (1983, 1989), in two more controlled experiments, supported Maratos's and McDougall's findings and demonstrated that newborns imitate two facial gestures: mouth opening and tongue protrusion. The mean age of these infants was 32 hours, and the youngest was a mere 42 minutes old at the time of the test. Furthermore, the person eliciting the imitation was not the mother but rather an experimenter. Similarly, Reissland (1988), who studied neonatal imitative responses during the first hour postpartum in rural Nepal, observed neonates imitating various mouth gestures. Again, as in Meltzoff and Moore's study, the experimenter was the first person the baby saw and the first person with whom the baby interacted. (See fig. 4.4.)

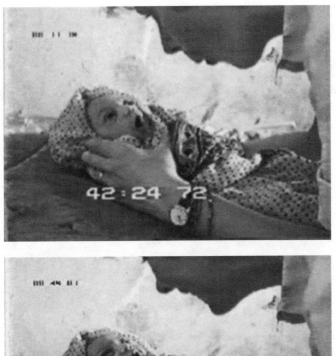

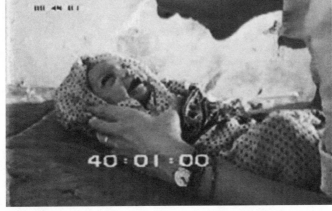

Figure 4.4. Examples of neonatal imitation with *(top)* vertically pursed lips and *(bottom)* lips laterally widened. From Reissland (1988, p. 4). Reprinted with the permission of the author.

Further studies reported tendencies to imitate mouth openings and tongue protrusions by infants only 35 to 68 hours old (Ullstadius, 1998). An infant's ability to imitate tongue movements was further confirmed by research showing that infants differentially imitate two different kinds of movement with the tongue (Meltzoff and Moore, 1994, 1997). In another group of infants, ranging in age from 12 to 21 days, imitation of four different gestures was observed: lip protrusion, tongue protrusion, mouth opening, and finger movement (Meltzoff and Moore, 1977; see fig. 4.5).

Although the evidence is substantial, partial failures by some researchers to replicate the studies of Meltzoff and Moore raised the possibility that neonatal

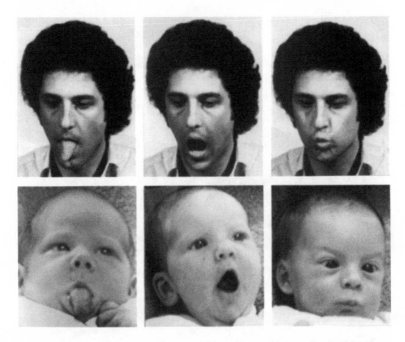

Figure 4.5. Photographs from videotaped recordings of 2-to-3-week-old infants imitating *(left)* tongue protrusion, *(center)* mouth opening, and *(right)* lip protrusion demonstrated by an adult experimenter. From Meltzoff and Moore (1977). Reprinted with the permission of AAAS.

imitation was not a genuine phenomenon (Koepke, Hamm, Legerstee, and Russell, 1983; McKenzie and Over, 1983). However, these are merely a fraction of the studies on infant imitation that have been conducted in separate laboratories and research institutions. Numerous studies have demonstrated that there is a broad range of rudimentary behaviors that infants imitate, such as mouth openings (Fontaine, 1984; Heimann, 1989, 2002; Legerstee, 1991), hand movements (Locke, 1986; Vinter, 1986), emotional expressions (Field, Woodson, Greenberg, and Cohen, 1982; Field et al., 1983), head movements (Meltzoff and Moore, 1989), lip and cheek movements (Fontaine, 1984; Kugiumutzakis, 1999), and eye blinking (Kugiumutzakis, 1999).

Four other studies by Kugiumutzakis (1998) show that neonatal imitation occurs right after birth, which eliminates the possibility that imitation is based on learning and socialization. Kugiumutzakis was able to observe 170 newborns immediately after delivery. The mean age of the newborns was approximately 26 minutes. After a 40-to-100-second adaptation period until the infant was entirely calm, four models for imitation were presented at a distance of 20 to 23 centimeters from the baby's face: tongue protrusion, mouth opening, eye blinking, and some vocalizations (/a/, /m/, /ang/). Kugiumutzakis's studies demonstrate that infants clearly try to imitate and succeed. Seventy-five percent of the newborns imitated with precision on the first attempt, and when they reproduced the model several times, they converged toward a more precise match each time. With regard to the vocal imitations, which were only presented to infants in the fourth study, the newborns tried—"with clear observable effort—to direct their attention to the mouth part of the experimenter's face. The attention intensifies from a relatively fixed gaze to selective visual exploration" (p. 72). Kugiumutzakis and Meltzoff and Moore suggest that these subsequent attempts to match the experimenters demonstrate that imitative behavior is not just a reflex but show that infants are intentionally and volitionally trying to imitate their interlocutors.

Some imitation has also been observed in premature babies. One video observation of a preterm at 29 weeks gestational age with her father showed that the preterm mirrored facial expressions and vocalizations (Van Rees and de Leeuw, 1987). Preterm infants with an average gestational age of approximately 35 weeks also demonstrate an ability to discriminate and imitate three facial expressions (Field, 1985; see fig. 4.6).

The innateness of imitation is also supported by observations that an infant's first response to seeing a facial gesture is to activate the corresponding body part. This is known as organ identification (Meltzoff and Moore, 1997). When an infant

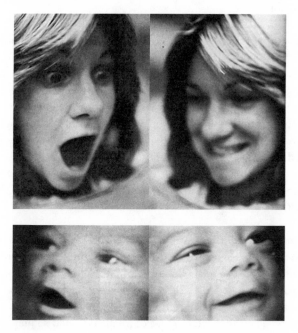

Figure 4.6. Examples of a model's happy and surprised faces and a preterm's imitation (gestational age 34 weeks). From Field (1985). Copyright 1985 by Ablex Publishing Corporation.

sees an adult protrude the tongue, there is a quieting of other body parts (lips or fingers) and an activation of the tongue in the oral cavity. The infant elevates or moves the tongue. Although the infant may not protrude his tongue at first, he seems to isolate that body part, before even knowing how to move it. Kugiumutzakis (1998) also reported this observation in his study of newborns. Organ identification and observable attempts by newborns to correct their efforts to match an interlocutor's behavior also show that imitation is an intentional activity.

We have seen that infants have innate facial and gestural imitative tendencies that are observable within the first hours of interaction. One possible explanation for this would be that human beings have an innate propensity to be like other conspecifics and thus have an underlying motivation to engage in imitative interactional activity.

Infant-Initiatedness

In studies of infant behavior, a number of observations find interaction not elicited by a caregiver but rather by the infant. In other words, an infant actively initiates social engagement through the use of abilities that are inborn (cooing, vocalizations, gestures, smiling, etc.) or are learned early through experience. These behaviors may collectively display infant-initiatedness and provide some evidence for an innate drive for interaction. Consider the following narrative of a dyadic interaction:

> F (a newborn) is sitting in her seat holding a rubber toy which is tied to the side of the chair. Mother has her back to F as she reaches for a dish. F squeaks the rubber toy making a noise. As a "consequence" F kicks her feet and squeals with apparent delight. Mother turns toward F smiling. F looks at mother and vocalizes. Mother walks toward F smiling and vocalizing. F quiets, eyes fixed on mother. Mother touches F's face. F vocalizes and moves her hands toward mother. Mother sits in front of F and vocalizes to her. (Talking about the toy which mother now holds.) F watches mother and listens. Mother pauses. F vocalizes. Mother touches F and vocalizes to her. F vocalizes. (Lewis and Freedle, 1972, p. 3)

In this sequence, the newborn is the initiator of the interaction with her mother. By squeaking a rubber toy, squealing, and kicking, the infant successfully gets her mother's attention and elicits a smile from her, which is followed by a period of vocal exchange. One study, which observed the interaction between eight mothers and typically developing infants from 17 weeks old until they were 43 weeks old, revealed that the number of infant-initiated sequences was much greater than the number of mother-initiated sequences (Pawlby, 1977). Out of a total 1,651 imitative sequences observed for all dyads, 1,308 (79 percent) were reported to be infant-initiated. Studies of infant imitation also seem to provide evidence for an infant using the behaviors in his repertoire to elicit gratifying behaviors from an interlocutor. In one study, infants observing an adult were given pacifiers so that they could not imitate during the adult's demonstration (Meltzoff and Moore, 1977). When the pacifiers were withdrawn, the infants initiated their imitative responses in the subsequent 2.5-minute period when they were met with a passive-faced interlocutor. In another study, several six-week-olds performed deferred imitation after a 24-hour delay. On day one, an infant during a play interaction saw a gesture; the next day, the infant met the same adult, who displayed a blank face. In response to the familiar yet blank face, the infant initially stared and then imitated the gesture from long-term memory to initiate interaction with the adult (Meltzoff and Moore, 1994).

Still-face studies also seem to show that infants make repeated attempts to elicit their mothers' response (Tronick et al., 1978; Als, Tronick, and Brazelton, 1980; Als and Brazelton, 1981; Dixon et al., 1981; Adamson and Frick, 2003). In these studies, a mother is instructed to play with her baby (about three months old) for approximately three minutes, just as she would at home, and then to withdraw briefly. After a minute, the mother returns for another three-minute period and maintains an *en face* position with her infant. However, this time, the mother is asked to present a perfectly still face and not to respond to her baby. This study was repeated with a number of variations: with mothers, fathers, blind infants with sighted parents, sighted infants with blind parents, brain-damaged infants, and premature infants. A typical observation of a still-face study is as follows; descriptions of what may be interpreted as infant initiation are emphasized:

> Before the second 3-minute period, while still alone, the baby might look contemplatively down at her hands, fingering the fingers of one hand with another. *As the mother enters, her hand movements stop. She looks up at her mother, makes eye-to-eye contact, and smiles.* The mother's masklike expression does not change. The baby looks quickly to one side and remains quiet, her facial expression serious. Her gaze remains averted for twenty seconds. *Then she looks back at her mother's face, her eyebrows and lids raised, hands and arms stretching slightly out toward the mother.* Finding no response, she quickly looks down again at her hands, plays with them for about eight seconds, and then checks her mother's face once more. . . . She turns her face to the side but keeps her mother in peripheral vision. (Brazelton and Cramer, 1990, p. 108; emphasis added)

Tronick (1989) reports that when confronted with the still face, most three-month-olds "initially signal to their mothers using facial expressions, vocalizations, and gestures in an attempt to get their mothers to resume their normal behavior" (p. 114). Throughout experimental periods, infants remain intensely fixated on their mothers. Similarly, when the mother is not in *en face* position but is in profile view, the infant coos, vocalizes, and often leans forward in his seat. The infant may also pretend to cry and intersperse his vocalizations with long

periods of looking at his mother. These activities may be interpreted to be eliciting behaviors from his mother. Mothers report that a similar type of performance
often occurs when they are driving their cars and are unable to maintain an *en
face* position with their babies (Tronick, Als, and Adamson, 1979).

Emotional Perception and Expression

The third type of behavior that engages the innate abilities of infants and through
which the interactional instinct is manifest consists of actions that show an
infant's sensitivity to the emotional signals of his interlocutor, the signal's
value, and the infant's ability to communicate his emotional state. Gianino and
Tronick (1988) labeled these affective displays made by infants as "other-directed
regulatory behaviors." We must keep in mind that infants are active, not passive,
participants in an interaction and, in fact, are part of an "active communication
system in which the infant's goal directed strivings are aided and supplemented
by the capacities of the caretaker" (Tronick, 1989, p. 113). Within this system,
Tronick notes that infants have specific internal goals, which include meeting
their homeostatic and sociostatic needs. To accomplish these goals, infants
process information about their current state and the state of those in their social
environment. They evaluate whether they are succeeding or failing in meeting
those goals, at times by "reading" the messages given by caregivers through their
emotional expressions, and they will modify their behaviors, at times communicating their emotional state to reach their goals. Thus, we see infants regulating
interaction to achieve a desired interaction.

In the still-face studies mentioned earlier, when the mother continues to
display a blank face, her infant's response seems to express distress, which
increases as the mother walks away. In an example of a second three-minute
period, we can see the infant displaying an emotional stance when confronted
with a still face through the use of facial expressions and entire body posture
(emotional displays are emphasized): "She [the infant] *grimaces* briefly, and her
facial expression becomes more *serious, her eyebrows furrowing.* Finally the baby
completely withdraws, *her body curls over, her head falls.* She does not look
again at her mother. . . . She looks *wary,* helpless, and withdrawn. As the mother
leaves the alcove at the end of the three minutes, she looks halfway up in her
direction, but her *somber* facial expression and *curled over body position* do not
change" (Brazelton and Cramer, 1990, p. 108).

Figure 4.7 is an illustration of a typical still-face response pattern of a 74-day-
old infant. The 30-second sequence begins with the infant "greeting" his mother.
When responded to with a still face, the infant becomes still and then warily
looks away. He again checks back toward his mother. Finally, the infant withdraws from the interaction.

In addition to the still-face studies, other research has examined the sensitivity and expressive capacities of infants less than three months old (Murray and
Trevarthen, 1985). In one study of six-to-12-week olds, infants experience two

Figure 4.7. A time series of photos taken from the recorded video image of a still-face condition (infant 74 days old). From Tronick, Als, and Adamson (1979, p. 365). © Cambridge University Press 1979. Reprinted with the permission of Cambridge University Press.

different interactional situations. In the first, a mother talks to her baby, and then an experimenter enters the room and asks the mother a few questions, causing the mother to turn away and break the interaction between her and the infant. Prior to this, the infant displays behaviors that are typical in positive interactions. He looks at his mother's face most of the time, actively moving his tongue and mouth, and smiles frequently. The expression of the brows is also fairly relaxed, with very few frownlike expressions. When the mother is interrupted, the baby's attention to her decreases, and the baby turns his attention to the experimenter. Efforts to communicate, such as mouthing and tonguing, decrease, as do the signs of positive affect. Smiling and brow raising are also no longer sustained. However, the infant does not seem to be withdrawn or distressed, and a relaxed expression is maintained. The second situation is similar to still-face studies, in that the mother is directed to become unresponsive and give a blank, expressionless face for 45 seconds while continuing to look at her baby. Within a few seconds, the infant shows signs of distress, by grimacing, increased handling of clothes, touching the face, sucking the fingers, and frowning. Efforts to communicate are also intensified at first, and mouthing and tonguing postures are maintained and accompanied by active gesturing. The researchers interpret the infant's actions as protesting or straining to reinstate interaction with the mother. Eventually, the infant withdraws and averts his gaze downward from the mother's face. The relaxed expression fades, and the infant almost never smiles.

Tronick (1989) finds even more evidence of an infant's ability to perceive emotions. He reports on a study showing that infants have a preference for facial expressions of joy rather than anger (Malatesta and Izard, 1984). He also notes studies in which different maternal emotional expressions lead to different infant emotions. If newborns are in a quiet and alert state, looking at them and gently talking to them can produce a smile. However, 10-week-old infants react to facial displays of anger with anger and have fewer angry responses when their mothers display sadness (Lewica and Haviland, 1983).

The responses and actions of infants in these studies seem to indicate that newborns have an inborn ability to communicate their emotional states and the capacity to perceive emotional states, which they employ to elicit, reinstate, and enhance interaction and to communicate evaluations of the interaction. Infants seem to take into account the visible emotional stances of their interlocutors and use that understanding to deploy their next actions. Infants also seem to have an innate ability to communicate their affective states when desired and anticipated interactions occur or fail.

Human Specificity

This category of behaviors manifesting the interactional instinct is related to the specificity of the motivation of the instinct, which is to achieve social affiliation and attachment with a conspecific and to become like conspecifics. We demonstrate here that infants make a distinction between human and nonhuman acts, they prefer animate entities to inanimate ones, and they can distinguish between and among conspecifics.

Studies show that by the second week of life, infants are able to use their ability to smile discriminately, such that infants smile more often in the presence of people. In addition, the human voice elicits more smiling in infants than the sound of an inanimate object such as a bell or a rattle (Bower, 1977). Other evidence of human specificity comes from studies of infants' perception of faces. Three studies reported by Maurer and Barrera (1981) suggest that infants have a preference for the human face. In the first study, 24 two-month-olds are shown a naturally drawn face and two faces with selected features deleted. The results show that infants look less than half as long at the face in which the features are omitted than at the naturally drawn face. In the second study, the same infants are shown a naturally drawn face, two faces with the mouth and nose deleted, faces with eyes that are either properly or improperly located, and a face in which the eyes and eyebrows are arranged "unfacelike." Infants again show a preference for the naturally drawn face. In the third study, 24 two-month-olds are shown a naturally drawn face, a face with a design in the bottom half, a face with a single eye, and a face in which the eyes and eyebrows are omitted. As in the previous studies, infants attend longer to the naturally drawn face than to the other faces. Subsequent studies report that four-month-old infants also show a preference for a natural drawing of a human face over distorted drawings of faces (Maurer, 1985). Also, if presented with a flat face after a humanlike one, a newborn will look worried and turn away. Although these studies seem to indicate that human beings are born with a preference for the human face, the fact that the "unfacelike" faces are distorted makes it unclear whether infants are simply showing a preference for something with good form and not for facedness.

Another series of experiments demonstrates that neonates ranging in age from 12 to 17 days have a preference for breast odors, including from unfamiliar and unrelated lactating females (Makin and Porter, 1989). In the experiment, neonates who have no breast-feeding experience and have only been bottle-fed are exposed to gauze pads soiled with an unfamiliar lactating female's breast odor and clean pads. The infants spend significantly more time turned toward the breast pads than toward the clean ones. Follow-up experiments demonstrate that the infants are not simply responding to an odor versus no odor at all or to the strength of the odor.

Other studies seem to support the notion of human specificity such that infants are able to distinguish between social and nonsocial contexts and respond accordingly. One study shows that when a newborn watches a human face, the infant's involvement and attention are more prolonged than when he is shown an object (Brazelton and Cramer, 1990). Tronick (1989) also reports on Brazelton, Koslowski, and Main's (1974) observations that infants show a fundamental distinction between people and objects. When presented with an object, "[infants] look intently at it, sit up straight, remain relatively still, and punctuate their fixed gaze with swiping movements and brief glances away. Presented with people, infants' posture is more relaxed, and their movements are smoother. They become active at a slower pace and then look away for longer periods of time than they do with objects. Furthermore, infants give full greeting responses to people but not to objects. Simply stated, infants communicate with people and act instrumentally with objects" (p. 114).

Trevarthen (1974) observes the distinction in one- and two-month-olds' responses to a physical object (a dangling toy) versus a person. Infants look, listen to, or touch objects. They also seek and interact with physical objects as sources of interest and as potentially graspable, chewable, and kickable, whereas human beings are perceived as communicatable and are communicated with through expressive movements that are distinct from those used with objects. Trevarthen (1977) notes that the "responses of the infants to persons were different in kind from those of objects, and they were pre-adaptive to reception and reply by persons" (p. 114). Similarly, other researchers show that two-month-olds smile, vocalize, and alternate their gazes with an adult, but if presented with an object that moves and sounds contingently, infants will engage in intense arm activity while staring at the object (Legerstee, Pomerleau, Malcuir, and Feider, 1987).

In another study, a face-sensitive ERP recorded from the scalp surface using electroencephalography showed that infants N170 were affected only when shown a face, and the response was even larger for human faces than for monkey faces (De Haan, Pascalis, and Johnson, 2002). The researchers suggested that the larger response for human faces than for monkey faces might have occurred because the infants processed the monkey faces more like objects.

Neonatal imitation is also specific to people, as attempts using inanimate objects to elicit imitative responses from infants fail. In one study, 27 infants between five and eight weeks old were divided into two groups. Twelve infants were presented with tongue protrusions and mouth openings modeled by an adult, and 15 were presented with these gestures simulated by two objects. Infants imitated the adults but not the objects (Legerstee, 1991). In another study, two sets of infants, one with a median age of five weeks and another with a median age of 12 weeks, were presented with two inanimate models, one demonstrating tongue movements and another demonstrating mouth openings and closings. Infants were also presented with a human model who made the same facial gestures. In neither group did the inanimate models elicit imitations. Live human models, however, did increase the tongue protrusions among infants (Avranel and De Yong, 1991).

The studies of Meltzoff and Moore also suggest that infants attempt to distinguish among individuals and pay attention to unique identity. In their study of delayed imitation (1994), they suggest that the delayed gesture is deployed to see whether the person is the same person seen the day before. In other words, infants use gestures to reidentify people, to see if the person is the same one who did that thing before. In another study, they explore whether infants as young as six weeks could differentiate individuals from one another (Meltzoff and Moore, 1992). In their studies, infants are presented with two individuals who appear and then disappear. The mother appears and shows one gesture. She exits and is replaced by a stranger who shows a different gesture. The infants are able to switch their actions to play two different gestural games depending on whom they are interacting with. Meltzoff and Moore suggest that "early interactive behaviour is directed toward *human individuals*" (Meltzoff, 1998).

Understanding the Organization of Interpersonal Interaction

With his studies of mother-infant interaction with five two-month-olds, Trevarthen (1974) claims that "the foundation for interpersonal communication between humans is 'there' at birth" (p. 230) when cognitive processes are just beginning, because he observes that the interaction between a mother and an infant show signs of coordination that resemble conversation among adults. He describes sequences in which the infant moves his mouth, hands, and eyes in a turn-taking format with an adult (Trevarthen, 1979). Bateson (1979) similarly looks at newborns 49 to 105 days old and also notices mothers and infants "in a pattern of more or less alternating, non-overlapping vocalization, the mother speaking brief sentences and the infant responding with coos and murmurs, together producing a brief joint performance similar to conversation" (p. 65). Bateson calls this collaboration "protoconversation." Jaffe et al. (2001) also shows that four-month-old infants are highly proficient in vocal turn-taking. Another study finds that as early as six weeks of age, coordinated timing occurs between an infant gaze and adult vocal behavior (Crown et al., 2002). Jaffe et al. (2001) also find that the way an interaction unfolds between an infant and an adult is akin to the interaction between adults. The rhythms, turn-taking, and vocalizations are more tightly coordinated in the beginning, and the coordination eventually decreases as comfort with a stranger increases, which seems to occur in adult interactions as well (Kendon, 1970).

Beebe, Stern, and Jaffe (1979) conducted a frame-by-frame analysis of a continuous interaction between a mother and her four-month-old infant. They examined two kinds of kinesic patterns: "coactive episodes," periods in which mother and infant are simultaneously engaged in kinesic behavior, and "non-coactive episodes," in which behaviors do not overlap. They also looked at behavioral pauses, which end with the initiation of a behavior, and onset-to-onset times, which mark the beginning of a behavior of either the mother or the infant. The temporal analysis of the kinesic behavior showed patterns that were similar to the temporal patterns of the vocal interactions of mothers and infants. In noncoactive episodes, the pair had a tendency to match the duration of their kinesic rhythms. The researchers suggest that both coactive and noncoactive vocal and kinesic patterns can be seen as the temporal precursors of later adult conversational patterns. Furthermore, the infant seemed to be predicting maternal initiations of behavior. These protoconversational interactions may be seen as precursors to adult conversation patterns. A behavioral pause is comparable to a possible turn transition or point of recognizable completion, and onset time is similar to uptaking a turn in conversation. These elements are central to the systematic organization in adult conversation (Sacks, Schegloff, and Jefferson, 1974; Schegloff, 2000b). Coactive episodes are similar to overlapping speech and may be a precursor to systematic overlapping in adult dialogue, which the field of conversation analysis has demonstrated to have an extremely fine order of precision in the organization of interactive speech (Jefferson, 1973, 1983).

Thus, infants, on a basic level, seem to be born with an understanding of how interpersonal communication is systematically organized. From birth, we are already participating and anticipating dialogic practices in multiple ways. The still-face studies of Tronick et al. (1978) mentioned above also demonstrate that infants are attuned to and detect the responses of caregivers. Trevarthen (1979) suggests that the behaviors of infants are manifestations of "a specifically human system for person-to-person communication" (p. 321). In 1985, Murray and

Trevarthen demonstrated that infants were sensitive to the social behavior that is contingent on their own actions. They had mothers and six-to-12-year-olds interact via video so that each dyad saw and heard the other on video monitors. Then the researchers rewound the videos of the mothers and played them back for the infants, with the mothers' facial expressions, vocalizations, and gazes exactly the same as they were moments before, except that the mothers' actions were not contingent on the infants' behavior. The infants showed a marked sensitivity to the lack of contingency with a loss of positive affect and attention. The same phenomenon occurs with infants of depressed mothers who are characterized as less responsive, less spontaneous, and more constrained in their interactions when compared with nondepressed mothers (Field, 1984). In their study of infants' reactions to simulated maternal depression, Cohn and Tronick (1983) suggest that "infants have a specific, appropriate, negative reaction to simulated depression in their mothers" (p. 185). In another study that was similar to Murray and Trevarthen's (Nadel, Guerini, Peze, and Rivet, 1999), with 10 two month old infants, a double teleprompter device allowed researchers to offer an infant a continuous image and voice of the mother while they alternated 30 seconds of live video, 30 seconds of replay video, and return to 30 seconds of live video seamlessly. The results produced the same responses from the infants as in Murray and Trevarthen's study; only noncontingent interaction induced a negative change in the infant's affect. In addition, some of the infants recovered a positive state when the video returned to the live contingent interaction. Thus, early in development, infants demonstrate that they are highly attuned and sensitive to the actions and responses of interlocutors.

Behavioral Manifestations in Sum

Infants show imitation, initiatedness, human specificity, an ability to perceive and convey emotional states, and an understanding of interpersonal organization. These seem to be inborn abilities, all of which are useful for eliciting and sustaining interaction, the means through which attachment and affiliation are achieved. The five general categories of infant behaviors through which the interactional instinct is manifest are not mutually exclusive. Emotional perception may lead to infant-initiatedness, which may lead to sequences of imitation. One example is Meltzoff and Moore's (1997) study, in which infants deployed an act that was imitated 24 hours earlier to initiate an interaction with a familiar conspecific who was showing an expressionless face. Another example from the still-face studies shows that an infant may communicate emotional distress at his mother's unresponsiveness in an attempt to reinstate or to solicit a positive interaction, or an infant may look distressed and turn away and begin to suck his thumb to signal that he would like the interaction to end.

As these behaviors are ubiquitous in very young, typically developing infants, with mothers as well as strangers, and are believed not to have been learned, they show that human beings enter their social world with an "effective interpersonal intelligence" (Trevarthen, 1979, p. 15) that instantiates an innate "drive" for interaction in human beings. Next, we provide some evidence that the motivation underlying these infant behaviors is the sociostatic value of interaction.

Some Motivations for Interaction

In this chapter, we argue that the interactional instinct is motivated by the sociostatic value of attachment and affiliation. Human beings are born with an appraisal system to determine the emotional relevance and motivational significance of stimuli received through the sensory systems. The appraisal system determines three kinds of value: homeostatic, sociostatic, and somatic (Schumann, 1997). Depending on the value, the appraisal system directs the appropriate action vis-à-vis motor systems. Homeostatic regulation guides organisms in ways that maintain homeostasis and ensure survival (to feed, to breathe, to seek light or darkness, to get warmth or coolness). Sociostats are the innate tendencies of a human organism to seek out interaction leading to attachment and social affiliation with conspecifics. Thus, sociostatic value is what underlies the interactional instinct, as the instinct motivates human beings to actively pursue and achieve attachment and social affiliation with others. Some of the support for this claim comes from behavioral and biological studies, which show that interaction with the mother is a rewarding achievement and may be separate from other goals that an infant pursues.

Studies indicate that contact with the mother is the goal of infant vocalizations. In one study of 24 mother-infant dyads, infants were found to have spent more time vocalizing during maternal absence than while being held, and infants vocalized significantly more when mothers were within arms' reach than while they were being held (Anderson, Vietze, and Dokecki, 1978). The vocalizations were apparently seeking interaction with the mother because they remained significantly less when the mother was absent and because the mother did not provide any other form of reward (e.g., food or ease of discomfort). Researchers have suggested that infant vocal behaviors function to maintain close proximity between mother and infant before the infant is mobile (Bowlby, 1969). Crying seems to promote close contact by signaling distress and bringing the mother to the infant, and vocalizations, in general, elicit visual attention. Nondistress sounds, such as cooing and grunting, also bring the mother to the infant and elicit attention. But during visual attention, infant vocalizations predictably elicit reciprocal vocalizations. Studies of mother-infant dyads report that when an infant vocalizes, the mother is most likely to respond with a vocalization of her own. Her next most likely response is to smile at, look at, or touch the infant (Freedle and Lewis, 1977; Stevenson, Ver Hoeve, Roach, and Leavitt, 1986), which are all gratifying responses to the infant. Transcriptions of mothers' responses to infants during imitation also show that when an infant imitates an interlocutor, he is automatically rewarded in several ways. First, the interlocutor continues to pay attention to him. Second, the interlocutor will react with excessive pride and pleasure at the infant's abilities. This is seen in the following account of a mother's reaction when imitated (Pawlby, 1977): " 'Go . . . ,' as mother demonstrates. 'You do that!' Child imitates action. Mother continues, 'Ooo! There's a good boy, there's a good boy! That's quite clever'" (p. 221). As in the studies regarding infant behavior during maternal absence mentioned above, the mother's responses seem to be sufficiently rewarding and seem to have been the goal of the infant's behavior. At the same time, the infant increases his social affiliation and attachment with his mother.

Biological evidence also provides backing for the motivation underlying the interactional instinct. Observational studies show that mutual gaze is a powerful interpersonal event, "which greatly increases general arousal and evokes strong feelings and potential actions of some kind, depending on the interactants and the situation. It rarely lasts more than several seconds. In fact, two people do not gaze into each other's eyes without speech for over ten or so seconds . . . " However, a mother and an infant can remain locked in mutual gaze for 30 seconds or more (Stern, 2002, p. 34). Studies indicate that the intimate contact between a mother and her infant is regulated by the reciprocal release of dopamine, oxytocin, and beta-endorphins. Beta-endorphins are endogenous opiates produced by the pituitary gland; when released, they produce a feeling of quiescence. As mothers and infants spend time gazing into each other's faces, they stimulate each other's opiate systems such that they mutually feel pleasure. Mutual-gaze transactions release increased levels of beta-endorphins, causing increased states of pleasure in both participants (Kalin, Shelton, and Lynn, 1995), which is expressed in the reciprocal dilation of pupils in both mother and infant. In addition, the mother's face induces regulated levels of dopamine in the infant's brain, which causes high levels of arousal and elation. At the same time, a mother's gaze is often accompanied by soothing and calming vocalizations, as well as manual grooming, which are stimuli that regulate the child's level of oxytocin, which facilitates bonding between mother and child (Schore, 2000).

The neuropeptides oxytocin (OT) and vasopressin (AVP) have also been associated with the emergence of social bonding and social communication. Studies with nonhuman animals show that animals increase their positive social interactions as the levels of OT and AVP rise, which leads to social bonds. Furthermore, AVP appears to be involved in forming the memories of these social interactions (Popik and Van Ree, 1992) and is critical for recognizing familiar individuals (Bielsky and Young, 2004). The release of beta-endorphins, dopamine, oxytocin, and vasopressin makes social interactions rewarding and promotes bonding between mother and infant, which, in turn, may motivate the interactional instinct causing an infant to initiate, reinstate, and work to prolong the interaction resulting in rewarding consequences. The infant's attempts result in a close coordination of behavior between caregiver and infant, leading to a circle of emotional communication, which Stern (2002) calls "an elaborate dance

choreographed by nature" (p. 3). This dance between infant and caregiver promotes and motivates affiliative and social bonding. A detailed account of the
neurobiology of the interactional instinct is presented in chapter 5.

Learning Strategies: Pattern Perception and Statistical Learning

It is the thesis of this book that the drive for language development and acquisition is motivated by an interactional instinct, but language acquisition and
development are not contingent solely on reward experiences or sociostatic
value. Although these motivate infants toward achieving interaction, interaction
alone does not guarantee acquisition, because it does not specify how infants are
able to make the critical units of language available to the infant. This chapter
argues that it is within the local interaction of caregiver-infant dyads that language is transmitted through other developmental precursors: pattern finding
and statistical learning. As Condon and Sander (1974a) suggest: "If the infant,
from the beginning, moves in precise, shared rhythm with the organization of the
speech structures of his culture, then he participates developmentally through
complex, sociobiological entrainment processes in millions of repetitions of
linguistic forms long before he later uses them in speaking and communicating.
By the time he begins to speak, he may have already laid down within himself the
form and structure of the language system of his culture" (p. 104).

According to Tomasello (2003), pattern finding is a set of skills that human
beings use to find perceptual and conceptual categories, perform distributional
analysis of sequences, learn recurrent patterns from the utterances they hear, and
learn how conspecifics use language across different utterances. Although pattern finding isn't linguistic per se and is not a specific adaptation for language
(Conway and Christiansen, 2002; Fisher and Aslin, 2002), it seems to be a
necessary cognitive skill for language acquisition, as some longitudinal studies
suggest that the ability to perceive speech in infancy (six months) predicts
language competency later in life (two years) (Tsao, Liu, and Kuhl, 2004).
Below we attempt to condense 30 years of research that indicates that by simply
listening to language, infants can acquire sophisticated information about a
language.[2]

The early studies of Eimas, Siqueland, Jusczyk, and Vigorito (1971) use the
high-amplitude sucking technique (HAS) to show that infants one to four months
old are able to discriminate a 20-millisecond difference in voice-onset time
(VOT), which is an acoustic difference sufficient to distinguish between the
voiced /b,d,g/ and the voiceless /p,t,k/ stop consonants in English. Other studies

2. For a broader discussion of the field of infant speech perception and language
development, see Jusczyk (1997, 2001).

show that infants are sensitive to the subtle acoustic differences among vowel sounds (Trehub, 1973; Aldridge, Stillman, and Bower, 2001). And further studies show that infants are able to perceive a number of contrasts: stops versus nasals (Eimas and Miller, 1980), /r/ versus /l/ contrast (Eimas, 1975), and changes in pitch contour (rising versus falling) (Morse, 1972).

In addition, two-month-old infants can perceive the differences between allophones (Hohne and Jusczyk, 1994), and nine-month-olds are sensitive to the phonotactics of their native language (Friederici and Wessels, 1993). Another set of studies, in which the high frequencies of speech are eliminated from the stimuli while the prosody is preserved, suggests that newborns are sensitive to the rhythms of languages, such that they can use prosody to discriminate between languages: French-Russian and English-Italian (Mehler et al., 1988); English-Japanese (Nazzi, Bertoncini, and Mehler, 1998); English-Spanish (Moon, Cooper, and Fifer, 1993); Dutch-Japanese (Ramus, 2002).

Two other studies demonstrate that infants are sensitive to the prosodic boundaries of a language. In the first, 48 French neonates with an average age of 2.6 days are presented with Spanish stimuli. The French newborns discriminate between bisyllabic stimuli that differ within a sentence regardless of whether they contained a phonological phrase boundary. The researchers conclude that French newborns can perceive local acoustic correlates of phonological phrase boundaries in Spanish (Christophe, Mehler, and Sebastian-Galles, 2001). In the second study, 13-month-old American infants perceive phonological phrase boundaries as well (Christophe, Gout, Peperkamp, and Morgan, 2003).

The groundbreaking research of Saffran, Aslin, and Newport (1996) demonstrated that eight-month-old infants can extract wordlike strings of phonemes from the statistical properties of the input after only two minutes of exposure. Specifically, the researchers provide evidence that infants can distinguish syllables that regularly appear together from those that are randomly juxtaposed. This study was supported by subsequent researchers with seven-month-olds (Marcus, Vijaya, Bandi Rao, and Vishton, 1999), eight-month-olds (Johnson and Jusczyk, 2001), and 12-month-olds (Gomez and Gerken, 1999). Although researchers agree that no single word-boundary, prosodic, or phonotactic cue is sufficient to provide lexical access, they do suggest that taken together, they may allow infants to start acquiring a lexicon. Christophe, Gout, Peperkamp, and Morgan (2003) claim that "infants recover words by relying on phonological properties of the speech stream, that is readily available in the input" (p. 587).

While Condon and Sander's postulation is an attractive, even sensible, solution to how children acquire language, given their remarkable discriminating and pattern-finding abilities, it may be erroneous, because pattern finding is not a linguistic adaptation per se, as other animals (cotton-top tamarin monkeys and chinchillas) also have this ability (Kuhl and Miller, 1978; Ramus et al., 2000). Furthermore, infants may not simply be passively entrained into the language system, as we have seen that infants, from birth, are active participants in "an elaborate dance" in which they attune to, initiate, engage, and imitate conspecifics. Thus, although pattern finding may be a cognitive skill necessary for children to find patterns across different utterances, it alone is not sufficient for language acquisition.

The Caregiver's Instinct

In the interactions described above, the focus has been on the behaviors of the infant, but it is important to note that the infants' behaviors are directed toward conspecifics in their social environment, whose responses and behaviors may have import for the action the infant will do next. Therefore, it is important not to overlook the abilities and behaviors of caregivers, because their actions are relevant information for the infant. In this section, we show that caregivers have interactional abilities enabling them to behave differently with infants from how they do with adults. We also suggest that one reason these behaviors are deployed is to achieve social affiliation and attachment, and they perhaps represent another manifestation of the interactional instinct.

Early in life, infants exhibit the full range of facial expressions that are also seen in adults. However, despite the repertoire that is available to the caregivers, they rarely, if ever, use the full range of expressions with infants. Stern (2002) observes that only a limited set of expressions is needed in early communication to regulate the general flow of interaction. These "basic" expressions are the mock-surprise expression, the smile, the concerned face, the frown, and the neutral face (p. 27). The mock-surprise expression is the most commonly observed and is typically used to signal readiness for or invitation to a potential interaction, as well as to motivate it. A mother uses this expression nearly every time the infant focuses his vision on her. Stern notes that the smile and the expression for concern function to maintain and modulate an ongoing interaction. The smile is a signal that the interaction is going well, while the concerned face is made when the interaction is ongoing but is slowing down. It is an attempt to reengage, and thereby maintain the interaction. The frown, combined with a head aversion and a break of gaze, is a signal to stop the interaction momentarily or completely. The neutral or blank face, especially when combined with a gaze aversion, is a clear signal of the mother's intent not to interact. Furthermore, when the caregiver displays these expressions, they are often exaggerated, usually marked by slow formation but elongated duration.

Studies have also shown that parents are acutely sensitive to their infants' emotional expressions and behavior. Mothers of one-month-old infants have been found to be able to discriminate the discrete emotional expressions of anger, fear, surprise, joy, interest, and sadness. Parents are also attuned to their infants' direction of gaze and modify their behavior accordingly, such that they maintain a certain observational distance (about 40 centimeters) when the infant is looking at something other than them, but they move to a "dialogic" distance (about 22.5 centimeters) when the infant is focusing on them (Papousek and

Papousek, 1987). In addition, when parents give an initial greeting, they usually tilt the head slightly back, raise the eyebrows, and open the eyes and mouth wide.

A caregiver's use of gaze with an infant is also qualitatively different from her gaze transactions with other adults (Papousek and Papousek, 1987, p. 34). During play interactions, mothers spend up to 70 percent of the play time gazing at their infants, with an average gaze duration of 20 seconds. While feeding, caregivers also gaze at infants about 70 percent of the time. Furthermore, mothers have an innate ability that makes them very sensitive to the babies' cries. There are four identifiable types of crying—pain, hunger, boredom, and discomfort—which are apparently distinguishable by the mother by the end of the second week, and by the third day, a mother can distinguish her baby's cry from that of other newborns (Boukydis, 1979; Lester, Hoffman, and Brazelton, 1985). An infant's expressions of sadness and anger produce the same affective responses in their mothers (Tronick, 1989).

In addition to the use of gaze, body distancing, and recognition of expressions, caregivers often have a distinctive way of speaking to infants. This infant-directed speech (IDS) is simpler, slower, clearer, higher in pitch, more regular in tempo, repetitive, and so on. The exaggerated stress and increased pitch appear to assist infants in discriminating phonetic units. In one study, women in Russia, the United States, and Sweden were recorded while speaking to their two-month-old infants and to another adult (Kuhl et al., 1997). Mothers used the vowels /i/, /a/, and /u/ in both settings, and their speech was analyzed using a spectograph. The results demonstrated that the phonetic units of IDS are exaggerated. The same exaggeration was observed in Mandarin-speaking mother-infant pairs (Liu, Kuhl, and Tsao, 2003). Caregivers also make other adjustments when addressing infants that aid in learning. Kuhl (2000) reports that parents often repeat a word in stereotyped "frames" (where's the _____, see the _____, that's a _____) (p. 11855), which highlights items in sentence-final position. There is also some evidence that these production universals in IDS seem to be recognized reliably by infants (Bryant and Barrett, 2007, 2008).

These behaviors may also serve to facilitate and increase affiliation and attachment with an infant. Thus, they might be considered to be manifestations of the interactional instinct as well. In addition, experiments show that the unconscious modifications made by caregivers aid in highlighting the critical parameters of the language, which facilitates the discovery of patterns and regularities in the input.

The Role of Mirror Neurons

More than a decade ago, a new class of premotor neurons was discovered in the ventral premotor cortex or F5 region of the macaque monkey brain. These neurons were observed to discharge not only when the monkey executed actions but also when observing similar actions executed by others. These neurons came to be known as the mechanism that subserve action-recognition, because the observation of an action causes in the observer an automatic activation of the same neural mechanism. They were called mirror neurons.

Several studies have indicated that mirror neurons exist in humans. Specifically, support comes from the study of reactivity of the cerebral rhythms during movement observation. Traditional EEG studies distinguished two types of rhythms, both in the alpha range: a posterior alpha rhythm and a central mu rhythm. These two rhythms have different functional significances. The posterior alpha rhythm is present when the sensory systems, the visual one in particular, are not activated, and it disappears at the presence of sensory stimuli. The mu rhythm, on the other hand, is present during motor rest and disappears during active movements. Cochin, Barthelemy, Roux, and Martineau (1998) show that the observation of an action made by a human being blocks the mu rhythm of observers. They demonstrate that during observation of an actor performing leg movements, there is a desynchronization of the mu rhythm, as well as of beta rhythms of the central parietal regions. In control experiments in which nonbiological motion, such as a waterfall, is shown to the subjects, the rhythms are not desynchronized. Thus, the rhythms that are blocked or desynchronized by movements are desynchronized by action observation. Another experiment by Cochin, Barthelemy, Roux, and Martineau (1999) involves observing and executing finger movements. The results show that the mu rhythm is blocked while participants are observing or executing the same movement.

Other neurophysiological studies with humans have supported the idea that action observation causes activation of cortical areas involved in motor control. Fadiga, Fogassi, Pavesi, and Rizzolatti (1995) show that when the premotor cortex is stimulated with transcranial magnetic stimulation while a subject is observing an action, there are increases in motor-evoked potentials in the muscles that are usually used for performing the same action.

Research on mirror neurons indicates their central role not only in understanding actions but also in understanding the intentions, emotions, and language of others. During infant-caregiver interactions, behaviors and interpretations are inextricably intertwined. Through vocalizations, gaze, emotional expressions, and other abilities in the infant's and caregiver's repertoire, both interactants are communicating something about their emotional stances and their intentions to initiate, engage, and reinstate interaction that each participant interprets. Therefore, we suggest that the mirror-neuron system may be another mechanism underlying the interactional instinct that facilitates understanding intentions, experiences, emotions, interaction, and language between infants and caregivers and that it optimizes social interactions to facilitate affiliation.

Understanding Intentions and Prediction

When an individual starts a movement in which he or she intends to achieve a specific goal, such as picking up a cup, the individual usually has a clear intention of what to do with the cup. The intent of the action precedes the movement of picking up. However, the observed actions or even the start of actions can actually be interpreted to have a number of intentions, such that picking up a cup can be seen as an intention to drink, to throw it away, to share, and so on. Some mirror-neuron studies show that mirror neurons seem to code the intentions of actions. Using event-related neuromagnetic recordings, Nishitani and Hari (2000) studied normal human participants under three conditions. They were asked to grasp an object, to observe the same grasping action performed by an experimenter, and to observe and simultaneously imitate the observed action. During execution, there was an early activation in the left inferior frontal cortex with a response appearing approximately 250 ms before the touch of the object. The activation was followed by activation of the left precentral motor area and later that of the right one. This study suggests that the participants were anticipating the motor actions before completion.

Umilta et al. (2001) show that F5 mirror neurons are also activated when the final critical part of an observed action is hidden, indicating that the goal of the observed action is predicted. In this study, mirror neurons were tested in two conditions. In one test, the monkey saw the hand approaching, grasping, and holding an object. Then the monkey saw the same action but with the final part (the grasping and holding of an object) hidden behind a screen. The neuron was discharged during the observation of the full and completed action as well as when only the hand approaching the object was observed without completing the action. The researchers conclude that it was the understanding of the intention of an observed action that determined the discharge and that the monkey predicted the type of action that would follow.

More recently, Fogassi et al. (2005) showed that neurons in the rostral sector of the inferior parietal lobule of monkeys code the same motor act differently depending on the intention of the action. Two monkeys were tested in three different conditions. First, a monkey reached for and grasped a piece of food in front of it and brought the food to its mouth. Next, the monkey reached and grasped an object and placed it in a container. In the third condition, the monkey was trained to grasp a piece of food or an object and place it near a container near the monkey's mouth (this condition was to account for the possibility that any differences may be caused by the arm flexing). All of the neurons that discharged more strongly during the grasping-to-eat condition also discharged less strongly in both grasping-to-place conditions. Furthermore, neurons that discharged most strongly during the first grasping-to-place condition also discharged when the placing was done in the container near the mouth. Thus, neurons in the monkey's inferior parietal lobule discriminated between the intentions of actions, and the main factor that determined the discharge intensity was the intention of the action and not the arm flexion. In the same area, some neurons have been found to have mirror properties. Although some neurons discharged with the same intensity regardless of the intention of the grasp (for eating or placing), the majority of the neurons were differentially activated depending on the movement following the grasp, such that some neurons discharged with more intensity when the monkey observed an experimenter grasping a piece of food and then placing the food in his mouth. The same neurons also had a weaker activation when the activity following the grasping was placing the food or object in a container. In comparison, other neurons were found to have the opposite behavior, while other neurons did not show any significant difference in discharge. Furthermore, the neurons discharged before the monkey observed the experimenter starting the second motor act (bringing the food to the mouth or placing it in a container). Fogassi et al. found that 75.6 percent of the neurons in that area were influenced by the final goal of the action. Together, these studies demonstrate that neurons code the same act of grasping in a different way according to the intention.

In another fMRI study (Iacoboni et al., 2005), human subjects watched three kinds of video clips. The first was of a hand grasping a cup without a context. The second was context only without a hand grasping (a scene before tea or a scene after tea). The third clip was a hand grasping in a context suggesting the intention associated with the grasping action (either drinking tea or cleaning up). The researchers found an increased activity in the right inferior frontal cortex when participants observed hand-grasping actions embedded in a context, in comparison with the activity in the same area when observing only hand-grasping actions without a context. These findings suggest that mirror neurons in the right inferior frontal cortex participate in understanding the intentions underlying the observed actions.

The role of mirror neurons in understanding and predicting intention has led researchers to ask the basic question of how such associations can be formed. How can one know that action X mostly likely leads to Y and not A or B? Gallese (2006) speculates that at present, "it can be hypothesized that the statistical detection of what actions most frequently follow other actions, as they are habitually performed or observed in the social environment, can constrain preferential paths chaining together different motor schemata" (p. 5). In other words, the ability to find patterns through experiences of different social contexts and observations may contribute to understanding the intentions of others and constrain the possibilities of what follows. We know that some actions of caregivers and infants will predictably elicit particular behaviors (e.g., vocalizations elicit visual attention; during visual attention, infant vocalizations elicit reciprocal vocalizations, which are most likely followed by a smile, a gaze, or touching the infant). Studies have also shown that neonates two to 48 hours old have the capacity to perceive regularities of social events (Blass, Ganchrow, and Steiner, 1984; Nadel, Prepin, and Okanda, 2005). The mirror-neuron system, along with pattern-finding abilities, may allow an infant to understand a caregiver's intended trajectory of interactions.

Imitation

The human neonate and infant studies discussed above provide evidence that human beings have a remarkable capacity to imitate conspecifics. In fact,

Rizzolatti (2005) suggests that perhaps "the main purpose of these behaviors [imitation] is to create a link between individuals by facilitating affiliative behaviors and inhibiting aggressive behaviors" (p. 75), which is consistent with the goals of the interactional instinct proposed in this chapter. Given the research showing that mirror neurons seem to be involved in understanding actions and directly matching the observed actions to their corresponding motor representations, it is likely that the mirror-neuron system may be a human mechanism for imitation, which has prompted researchers to find the specific neural substrates in humans that are activated during imitation.

Iacoboni et al. (1999) used fMRI technology to study neural responses of humans under two conditions. The first was observation only, in which the subjects were required only to observe a finger that was lifted (index or middle), a static hand with a cross on the index or middle finger, or a cross on an empty background. The second condition was observation-execution. The first part involved imitation, in which participants were instructed to lift their index or middle fingers on their right hands as fast as possible in response to the stimuli of a hand with a finger lifting. The second part was symbolic instruction, during which a static hand was displayed on a screen, a cross appeared on either the index or the middle finger, and the subjects were to lift the corresponding fingers of their right hands in response to the cross. The third part was spatial instruction, in which a gray rectangle was presented, and a cross randomly appeared on the left or the right side. Participants were instructed to lift their right index fingers when a cross appeared in the left side of the rectangle and their right middle fingers when a cross appeared in the right side. The imitation task produced stronger activation in the left frontal operculum (BA44), the right anterior parietal region, and the right parietal operculum. However, during all observation tasks, there was greater activation in BA44 and the right anterior parietal region. This strongly suggested to the researchers that a direct mapping, or a mechanism for imitation, between the observed and the executed act occurs in these areas. It also suggested that BA44 codes the motor goal of the observed action, while the parietal area codes the precise kinesthetic aspects of the movement.

In a follow-up study using the same experimental paradigm as in their first experiment, Iacoboni et al. (2001) studied whether the superior temporal sulcus (STS) region is part of the cortical network for imitation. This seemed to be reasonable, as the STS is known to have reciprocal connections with parietal regions and is a visual region in which there are a large number of neurons that respond to the observation of biological actions. In results similar to those of the first study, there was a greater overall activity in observation-execution conditions than for observation only. Furthermore, there was greater activity in the STS during imitation conditions than in other execution conditions.

Taken together, these studies suggest that a mirror-neuron network, consisting of the STS, BA44, and parietal areas plays a central role in the imitation of actions. The researchers also suggest that the STS may provide the early description of the action to the parietal neurons, which then add additional somatosensory information to the movement to be imitated, which is then sent to BA44, where the goal of the action to be imitated is coded and then sent back to the STS for monitoring purposes.

Speech Perception

The speech-perception studies described earlier in this chapter demonstrated that human beings are born with remarkable auditory discriminating abilities that do not seem to be specialized for the acquisition of human language. However, mirror-neuron studies using a variety of methodologies suggest that the mirror-neuron system in humans is, in part, employed to code some aspects of language.

One study instructed participants to observe mouth actions (Buccino et al., 2001). The results confirmed the speculation that mirror neurons in the premotor cortex also code actions made by the mouth. Brodmann premotor areas 6, 44, and 45 were also active during observations of mouth actions. The activation of these areas in viewing speech has been confirmed by another study that found the identical areas used during lip-reading (Santi et al., 2003). Ferrari, Gallese, Rizzolatti, and Fogassi (2003) studied the properties of neurons located in F5 of the macaque monkey, where activity has been mostly related to mouth actions. The researchers found that 25 percent of mouth neurons had mirror properties.

The motor theory of speech perception suggests that the objects of speech perception are the speaker's articulatory gestures (Liberman and Mattingly, 1985). The discovery of mouth neurons increases the probability that the mirror-neuron system might play a specific role in speech communication by aiding in the recognition of other people's articulatory gestures. From this perspective, observed articulations are coded in the same motor structures that are used during speech production.

There is increasing evidence for a system that motorically resonates when the individual listens to specific phonological material. Fadiga, Buccino, and Rizzolatti (2002) recorded the motor-evoked potentials (MEPs) from tongue muscles in normal participants who were instructed to listen carefully to verbal and nonverbal stimuli. The stimuli were words, pseudo-words, and bitonal sounds. Either a double *f* or a double *r* was embedded in the middle of words and pseudo-words. *R*, a linguopalatal fricative, in contrast to *f*, a labiodental fricative, requires more tongue-muscle movement. During the experiment, the participants' left motor cortices were stimulated. The results showed that listening to words and pseudo-words containing double *r* created a significant increase in MEPs recorded from the tongue muscles compared with the stimuli with *f*.

Watkins, Strafella, and Paus (2002), used transcranial magnetic stimulation to record MEPs from specified lip and hand muscles. Subjects were exposed to four stimuli: continuous prose, nonverbal sounds, speech-related lip movements, and eye and brow movements. Compared with control conditions, listening to speech enhanced the MEPs recorded from the specific lip muscles.

Furthermore, MEPs did not increase from a specific hand muscle when listening to speech. Similarly, Sundara, Namasivayam, and Chen (2001) found that visual observation of speech movement enhanced the MEP amplitude specifically in muscles involved in the production of the observed speech.

In another fMRI study, subjects passively listened to meaningless monosyllables and produced the same speech sounds to examine whether motor areas involved in producing speech would be activated (Wilson, Saygun, Sereno, and Iacoboni, 2004). The research found that listening to speech bilaterally activated a superior portion of the ventral premotor cortex that largely overlapped with a speech production motor area centered just posteriorly on the border of Brodmann areas 4a and 6. A more recent magnetoencephalographic study showed that viewing another person's articulatory mouth movements enhances activity in the left primary somatosensory cortex. This effect was not seen in the corresponding region in the right hemisphere or in the somatosensory hand area of either hemisphere. Thus, action viewing of articulatory gestures activates the primary somatosensory cortex in a somatotopic manner and is consistent with other research (Mottonen, Jarvelainen, Sams, and Hari, 2004).

Buccino et al. (2004) also conducted a study that posits that action observation is the basis for our capacity to form a new motor pattern. They suggest that during learning of new motor patterns by imitation, the observed actions are broken down into bits of motor acts that activate, via mirror mechanism, the corresponding motor representations in the motor region. They propose that once these motor representations are activated, they are recombined, according to the model of the observed action in the prefrontal cortex, in the ventrolateral part of Brodmann area 6 (Pmv), and in the pars opercularis of the inferior frontal gyrus. The main task of their study was the imitation of guitar chords played by an expert guitarist. Cortical activation was mapped during four events: action observation, pause (during which a new pattern was formed), chord execution, and rest. There were three control conditions: observation, observation followed by execution of nonrelated action (scratching the guitar neck), and free play of the guitar chords. The study found that the centers for new-motor-pattern formation coincided with centers for the mirror-neuron system, Brodmann area 6, with area 46 of the prefrontal cortex playing a fundamental role. Although the study was of imitative learning of a new motor pattern, playing guitar chords, a similar system might be involved in learning motor patterns for speech as mothers and infants engage in interaction.[3]

Understanding and Perceiving Emotions

In previous sections, we described how human beings are born with a repertoire of emotional displays, but it is not until the infant engages with a conspecific that

---

3. Rizzolatti (2005) notes that another possible neural substrate for sequence learning is the basal ganglia.

the import of facial expressions, vocalizations, and gestures is realized. Although studies have shown that gestures with emotional meaning do not activate the mirror neuron system, its apparent connectivity to the limbic system, an area critical for emotional processing, provides further insight into how the symbolic meaning of facial expressions, vocalizations, and gestures may be entrained in an infant. This system may also, in part, subserve how words and behaviors become imbued with an affective value.

Anatomical data suggest that the mirror-neuron network consisting of the superior temporal cortex, the parietal cortex, and the inferior frontal cortex may be connected to the limbic system, particularly the amygdala and the anterior cingulate, via the disgranular field of the insular lobe. To test this connectivity, Carr et al. (2003) used fMRI to observe activations while subjects were imitating and observing six basic emotional facial expressions: happy, sad, angry, surprised, afraid, and disgusted. They demonstrated that the anterior insula was activated during the observation and imitation of facial expressions, with greater activation during imitation. Furthermore, as predicted, they observed activity in premotor areas, the superior temporal cortex, the inferior frontal cortex, and limbic areas, particularly in the amygdala, and to a lesser degree in the anterior cingulate cortex. This study provides support for the possibility that the insula might be the link between understanding actions and processing their emotional content. Although the anterior insula and the amygdala were active during imitation and observation, imitation does not necessarily mean that subjects *experienced* the imitated emotion. Thus, the study only suggests that the insula is involved in imitation but not in the experience of emotions.

Research had already shown that the amygdala and the insula are activated during the observation of disgusted facial expressions and exposure to disgusting odors or tastes, so following Carr et al.'s study, researchers aimed at determining whether the same areas of the insula are activated during the experience of disgust and the observation of a disgusted facial expression (Wicker et al., 2003). Using fMRI, the findings showed that the anterior insula and the right anterior cingulate are activated both during the observation of disgusted facial expressions and during the emotion of disgust evoked by unpleasant odors. The study provides evidence for the possible involvement of the insula and the anterior cingulate in the experience of emotions during imitation and observation.

Because the insula has connections to the limbic system, an infant's experience, both positive and negative, of facial expressions and vocalizations from a caregiver may then be perceived in the limbic system by the amygdala, which is operating from birth. Thus, as Schumann (1997) reports, citing Shore (1994), through vocalizations and facial expressions, the mother and the infant are communicating information about their emotional states, which modulates interaction. Following Schore, Schumann states that an infant's perception of the positive affect of touch, vocalizations, and facial expressions, perceived by the amygdala, leads to the release of beta-endorphins and adrenocorticotropic hormone (ACTH) into the bloodstream from the anterior pituitary, which travels to the ventral tegmental area (VTA) of the midbrain. The release of the endorphins promotes the growth of axons of dopamine neurons in the VTA to extend to and release dopamine in the orbitofrontal cortex, creating a circuit between the VTA of the midbrain and the orbitofrontal cortex, where the pleasurable affect is eventually registered and imprinted.

As the child continues to grow and the orbitofrontal cortex develops, the child's actions require that the mother and/or caregivers discipline the child. The discipline is accompanied by negative affect from facial expressions, vocalizations, and touch. The negative affect leads to a state of low arousal, and through the connections from the midbrain to the orbitofrontal cortex, the behaviors that engender the negative affect are imprinted in the orbitofrontal cortex as well (Schumann, 1997). Thus, a stimulus-appraisal system consisting of the mirror-neuron network, the insula, the amygdala, and the orbitofrontal cortex is formed, and the child associates the positive and negative affects with their behaviors.

Symbol Formation

Greenspan and Shanker (2004) argue that when words, objects, or intentions become imbued with an emotional valence in an experiential context, they will then exist as free-standing images or as symbols. In addition, specific to action-related words, one hypothesis suggests that understanding such words depends on the motor structures involved in the execution of the very same actions (Pulvermuller, 2002). Thus, we may understand the acoustic signal of an action-related word or symbolic reference because it manages to activate our own inner representation of the action that we've gained through experience. As mirror neurons seem to code actions, there is increasing evidence that they also code the meaning of actions with the sound related to the action, and that increased experience reinforces the association of the acoustic signal to the action.

Researchers showed that neurons in the prefrontal cortex (F5) of a monkey discharge when the animal performs a specific action and when it hears the corresponding action-related sound (Kohler et al., 2002). Neurons were found to activate when monkeys saw a hand dropping a stick. The same activation was also present when the monkeys only heard the sound of the stick hitting the floor. These neurons were called audiovisual neurons, and they were found for seven different actions: peanut breaking, paper ripping, plastic crumpling, metal hitting metal, paper shaking, dry-food manipulating, and stick dropping. In a follow-up, the same researchers showed that activation of these audiovisual mirror neurons does not differ significantly whether the action is heard, seen, or both heard and seen, because the sound of an action in the dark activates the neurons (Keysers et al., 2003). These studies demonstrate that audiovisual neurons may be a link to how inner representations of actions could be connected to hearing spoken language.

The evidence that mirror neurons subserve the understanding of actions and code meaning has led to a test of whether the same network is also activated during the processing of action-related sentences (Tettamanti et al., 2005). The study looked at whether the comprehension of action might rely on the mirror-neuron system when the actions are auditorily *described* using language. In this fMRI study, participants passively listened to sentences describing actions performed with the mouth, hand, or legs (*I am biting an apple; I grasp a knife; I kick the ball*). For control, participants also passively listened to syntactically comparable sentences with abstract content (*I appreciate sincerity*). The results showed that listening to the action-related sentences activates a network that overlaps with the areas that are activated during action execution and action observation, and the activations seem to be somatotopically organized. Furthermore, the activations associated with abstract sentences are distinct from the action-related sentences and have activations in the posterior cingulate gyrus. This study provides further evidence for how the acoustic signal of an action and its inner representation gained through experience become an embodied signal early in life.

Role of Mirror Neurons in Sum

Since their discovery, research has shown that mirror neurons are involved in prediction, coding, and understanding the intentions of actions, imitation, articulatory gestures, and the verbal representation of a sound and/or actions. This mirror-neuron system may be a neural system subserving the preverbal and verbal acquisition during vocal and behavioral interaction between infants and caregivers. Furthermore, through the mirror-neuron system's connection to the limbic system via the insular lobe, the affective value associated with the experience of an action or a behavior is coded. Mirror neurons combined with an infant's pattern-finding abilities may be yet another part of the interactional instinct leading to social affiliation and attachment with caregivers and the acquisition of language for typically developing humans.

The Interactional Instinct in Autistics

Many researchers believe that the onset of autism occurs from before birth through the first two to three years of life. Although the symptoms of autism can vary from person to person, autism's primary manifestation is an impaired ability to relate socially with other people, which could conceivably be caused by deficits in social recognition, lost positive and rewarding qualities of social contact, and a dysfunction in the ability to form social attachments (Baird, Cass, and Slonims, 2003). Other symptoms of autism include deficits in imitative behaviors and in the ability to read emotions in others through facial and vocal cues. In addition, autism almost always occurs with other debilitating symptoms that vary in severity, such as pathological imitation of both sounds (echolalia) and gestures (echopraxia), as well as delayed or abnormal language development. Thus, the manifestations of autism would also have implications for the interactional instinct. Is the interactional instinct "dysfunctional," or is it constrained by biological deficiencies in autistics? In either case, given our claim that the interactional instinct is a powerful developmental precursor to language acquisition, if the instinct is impaired, how do some autistic children access and acquire language?

Although the exact causes of autism are still unknown, researchers seem to have made some progress in understanding some of the biological processes connected with the condition. As mentioned earlier, the neuropeptides oxytocin and vasopressin appear to be connected to the rewarding nature of social interactions and have implicated in social attachment and social recognition. One study compared the level of oxytocin in the blood of 30 typically developing children and 29 autistic children. Autistic children had significantly less oxytocin in their blood (Modahl et al., 1998). Furthermore, oxytocin levels increased with age in the normal children but not in the autistic children. Other studies created knockout mice that lacked oxytocin (Ferguson et al., 2000; Ferguson, Aldag, Insel, and Young, 2001). The mice in these studies behaved normally, except that they could not recognize other mice, even after repeated social exposure. They also could not recognize their mothers' scent, even though their sense of smell was normal. However, when a single dose of oxytocin was injected into the brain before interaction, the mice were cured. Other studies have shown that injecting a synthetic form of oxytocin (pitocin) into the bloodstream of adults with autism rapidly and significantly reduces repetitive behaviors (Hollander et al., 2003). Hollander et al. (2006) have also looked at the effects of oxytocin on the ability of autistics to read affective cues in speech (anger, sadness, and happiness). That study found that participants injected with pitocin demonstrated an improvement in their ability to retain and assign affective significance to speech even after two weeks passed, whereas the control group given placebo injections did not show the same ability.

Vasopressin, another social-behavior modulator, is reported to stimulate social communication in birds, frogs, and hamsters (Young, 1999), as well as to increase affiliative and paternal behaviors in voles (Young et al., 1999). Studies of vasopressin in mice with a mutation in a vasopressin gene (V1aR) reveal that they lack the ability to recognize familiar conspecifics despite repeated exposures (Bielsky et al., 2004). In humans, one experiment examined the effects of vasopressin intranasally administered to adult autistics (Thompson et al., 2004). This experiment reported that vasopressin enhanced responses toward emotionally expressive facial expressions. Although research explaining the possibility of defective oxytocin and vasopressin systems in autistics is still inconclusive, it seems plausible from these studies to suggest that impairments in these systems may impair the interactional instinct.

Research on mirror neurons in autistics also suggests that a dysfunction in the mirror-neuron system may have a role in impeding observation and imitation.

Recall that the observation of an action made by a human blocks the mu rhythm of observers (Cochin, Barthelemy, Roux, and Martineau, 1998). In one study, mu-wave suppression was observed in 10 high-functioning individuals with autism and 10 controls while watching a video of a moving hand or moving their own hands (Oberman et al., 2005). Control subjects showed significant mu suppression when observing both their own hand movements and the movements of others. However, autistics showed significant mu suppression to self-performed hand movements but not to observed hand movements. The researchers concluded that there was evidence for a dysfunctional mirror-neuron system in high-functioning autistics. Other studies have implicated a dysfunctional mirror-neuron system for an autistic's inability to perceive emotions. In one study (Dapretto et al., 2006), 10 high-functioning autistics and 10 typically developing children underwent fMRI while imitating and observing 80 photos of emotional expressions such as anger, fear, happiness, or sadness. Both groups showed activations in the fusiform gyrus and the amygdala, areas associated with face processing. Thus, both groups seemed to have been attending to the face stimuli. But the study also revealed that the autistics had virtually no activity in the pars opercularis of the inferior frontal gyrus, a central part of the mirror-neuron system. Furthermore, the high-functioning autistics showed reduced activity in the insula and limbic structures, areas associated with understanding emotion (Carr et al., 2003), providing a possible explanation for why autistics generally show an inability to perceive emotions. In another study, cortical thickness in 14 high-functioning autistic adults and a group of controls was examined (Hadjikhani, Joseph, Snyder, and Tager-Flusberg, 2006). Several areas central to the mirror-neuron system, including the pars opercularis, the IPL and the STS, were significantly thinner in autistics. The study also showed that severity of cortical thinning of the mirror-neuron system correlated with the severity of autism-spectrum-disorder (ASD) symptoms.

There is also some evidence that an impaired mirror-neuron system may be related to the imitative deficits that also characterize autistics. Using fMRI and an experimental design previously used to determine the neural substrate for imitation (Iacoboni et al., 1999), Williams et al. (2006) compared activity in the mirror-neuron network in 16 males with ASD with a control group. Activity in areas associated with mirror neurons were less extensive in autistics. In addition, McIntosh, Reichmann-Decker, Winkielman, and Wilbarger (2006), through EMG readings, found that autistics appear to have an inability to "automatically" mimic emotional faces, although the same subjects also demonstrated an ability to voluntarily imitate emotional expressions. They suggest that perhaps the deficit is caused by a dysfunctional mirror-neuron system. Therefore, as the instinct to attune to the other is biologically subserved, dysfunctions in these systems may constrain the behavioral manifestations of the instinct, including imitation, emotional perception, and expression.

Autism raises another question: If the instinct is obstructed by dysfunctions in biological systems, and therefore obstructs the interaction that is necessary to acquire language, then how do some autistics acquire language? Autistics may rely heavily on other learning strategies of pattern finding and statistical learning. They are generally reported to be very detail-oriented, such that when they look at a room, they see not a room but every detail of a room. Perhaps it is the same with language. Autistics may hear and see language but in doing so attend to the details or patterns of the language. Some severely low-functioning autistics appear to be savants in areas that require highly complex calculations, statistical probabilities, and precision. In fact, a majority of calculating prodigies suffer from autism (DeHaene, 1997). Consider the case of Dave, a 14-year-old autistic, who knows nothing about math, reads at the level of a six-year-old, hardly speaks, and has an IQ of less than 50. In an instant, Dave can give the day of the week corresponding to any past or future date, because he spends hours of his day studying the kitchen calendar. Another example is Jedediah Buxton, who, after watching a performance of *Richard III*, could only comment that he had focused on the number of steps the actors took during the dances and the number of words the actors spoke. He calculated that the actors took 5,202 steps and spoke 12,445 words—which was found to be exactly correct. Considering the reported talents of some autistics, although the interactional instinct is impeded, they may be able to acquire enough language—its lexicon and structure—from the ambient language through the use of other general learning abilities.

Autism is an extremely heterogeneous affliction. Some autistics acquire language, and others do not. Because of the heterogeneity, the relevance of the syndrome to the interactional instinct can be worked out only on a case-by-case basis. In order to use autism as either a support or counterevidence for the interactional instinct, one would have to know the etiology of the disease (age of onset and the child's linguistic ability prior to onset). Additionally, one would want to know the child's attachment profile (his or her performance on tests of attachment, such as the Strange Situation), his or her ability to hypothesize about the intentions and dispositions of others (Theory of Minds tests), and his or her current ability to communicate.

Manifestations of the Interactional Instinct in Nonhuman Primates

It is clear that human beings are born to seek out social engagement. However, sociality is not distinct to human beings. Studies comparing the behaviors of adult nonhuman primates with humans have shown similarities in face-to-face interaction behavior. Adult chimpanzees have been observed to take turns in communication (de Waal, 1989), to communicate with gestures (Gardner and Gardner, 1989), to use natural and artificial sign systems, and to follow the gaze and other interactional behaviors of conspecifics (Savage-Rumbaugh, Rumbaugh, and Boysen, 1978; Tomasello, Call, and Hare, 1998). The social behaviors of adult nonhuman primates make it seem even more logical to assume that they may have similar neonate behavior and perhaps an interactional instinct that manifests itself similarly.

It seems that nonhuman primates parallel human development in significant ways. Bard (1998) reports that at least newborn chimpanzees exhibit the same kind of "helplessness" and dependency on the mother as human newborns. Both are unable to support their own weight by clinging (Plooij, 1984; Bard, 1995), and both are unable to survive without active cradling and nurturing (Rijt-Plooij and Plooij, 1987; Bard, 1994). Like human neonates, neonatal chimpanzees also have a capacity for sustained attention to visual and auditory stimuli and have been found to respond significantly more to social stimuli than to nonsocial stimuli throughout their neonatal period (Bard, Platzman, Lester, and Suomi, 1992).

With regard to their communicative abilities, infant nonhuman primates exhibit a repertoire of communicative tools within the first days of life. Neonate chimpanzees have been reported to show emotional expressions in appropriate interactional contexts. Infant chimpanzees smile, fuss, show distress, and cry. They also greet, make a scream face without vocalization, vocalize effort grunts, pout, show anger, tongue click, and laugh when tickled and when playing games (Bard, 1998, 2003). In addition, infant gorillas seem to initiate interaction; they have been observed to encourage an otherwise nonengaged mother to share food, play, or follow them (Maestripieri, Ross, and Megna, 2002). Neonate chimpanzees also imitate facial gestures of tongue protrusion, mouth opening, and lip pursing as early as one week old (Myowa-Yamakoshi, Tomonaga, Tanaka, and Matsuzawa, 2004). In addition, as we have mentioned, cotton-top tamarin monkeys seem to have pattern-finding skills as well as mirror neurons (Ramus et al., 2000; Rizzolatti and Craighero, 2004). Indeed, research indicates that human beings may not be alone in their ability for cultural learning (Kawamura, 1959). A few findings, however, seem to suggest that early human dyadic interaction is qualitatively different from early nonhuman dyadic interaction. First, human beings are dependent on caregivers for a much longer period of time than nonhuman primates. Also, some communicative interactions, such as play dialogue with adults, which is found in human three-month-olds, have not been reported in nonhuman primates. In interaction, other social animals imitate far less than humans. Furthermore, nonhuman primate mothers seem to interact with their infants qualitatively differently from humans. For example, although neonatal chimpanzees have been found to engage in mutual eye gaze with their mothers, the mothers appear to encourage quick glances by the infant instead of prolonging mutual-gaze transactions (Rijt-Plooij and Plooij, 1987; Bard, 1994). Western lowland gorilla mothers also seem to show little encouragement to their infants (Maestripieri, Ross, and Megna, 2002). However, because there are only a few studies to date of infant nonhuman primates in comparison with the numerous studies of humans, the uniqueness of neonatal behaviors in both human and nonhuman species has yet to be established. Such striking similarities in early-infant primate behavior and abilities could be viewed as a challenge to the notions of unique human propensities and the interactional instinct as a significant developmental precursor that guarantees the acquisition of language for all typically developing children—an adaptation that sets human beings apart from other species.

Tomasello (1999) has argued that it is humans' ability to understand other humans as intentional beings like themselves that ultimately separates them from nonhuman primates. He also suggests that human infants are not just social as other primates are but that they are "ultra-social" (p. 59). Greenfield (2006) suggests another perspective based on the theoretical and evolutionary connections between ontogeny and phylogeny:

> First, earlier stages of development are more universal within a species than are later stages of development. Second, earlier stages of development are more similar among phylogenetically-related species than are later stages in development. In other words, as phylogenetic divergence progresses, the evolutionarily later developments are more likely to occur later than earlier in ontogenetic sequence. In that way phylogenetic changes interfere less with subsequent ontogenetic developments that may have depended on something that has disappeared through evolutionary modification. Note that this formulation is contrary to the evolutionary myth that adult chimpanzees resemble human children. The notion is simply that human and chimpanzee babies will be more alike than human and chimpanzee adults....Third, characteristics among groups that are phylogenetically related indicates that characteristic was likely a part of the common ancestor of those species. (p. 5)

Thus, because they are phylogenetically related, humans and chimpanzees may, at the earlier stages, display similar characteristics that exhibit an innate drive for interaction and pattern-finding abilities. This drive is part of the foundation of both species. The studies of chimpanzee imitation and observation, key components of primate cultural learning (Greenfield, Maynard, Boehm, and Yut Schmidtling, 2000) and the interactional instinct, suggest that these processes go back to the origins of humans and chimpanzees as well. However, as humans and primates diverged, the accumulation of ontogenetic changes within humans eventually also led to a disparity in language abilities. This can be supported by Greenfield (1991), who has argued that early in the ontogeny of humans, the neural mechanisms for language (including Broca's area) are not so distinct from the mechanisms underlying tool use and object combination, but with maturation and increased complexity of language and object combination abilities, each eventually generates its own specialized circuitry.

To answer the challenge raised by cross-species comparisons of the behavioral manifestations and underlying mechanisms, we make two points. First, the interactional instinct is phylogenetically and ontogenetically basic in both humans and nonhuman primates. Thus, it is not surprising that characteristics that show readiness for interaction are seen in both humans and nonhuman primates. Second, the innate readiness and drive for interaction is only argued to be necessary but not completely sufficient for the development and transmission of language. Perhaps the ways in which humans are "ultra-social" compared with nonhuman primates may provide the clues to the points of divergence between species. Our position is that all social animals have an interactional instinct commensurate with their socialization needs, but because humans have such prolonged infancy, childhood, juvenility, and adolescence (Locke and Bogin, 2006), their socialization demands are extended. For this reason, the interactional instinct may be much stronger and more elaborated than in other animals, even closely related primates.

Conclusions

In 1871, Darwin remarked that although language needs to be learned, "man has an instinctive tendency to speak as we see in the babble of our young children." Trevarthen (1974), a pioneer in the studies of mother-infant interaction, observed infants and their mothers and claimed that the foundation for interpersonal communication between humans is "there" when cognitive processes are just beginning. In the same vein, in this chapter, we have proposed that the vast amount of human neonate and infant research into what infants do indicates that human beings are born with an innate readiness to attune to, imitate, and interact with conspecifics. To review, the notion of an interactional instinct is supported by substantial behavioral research:

- Studies of neonate and delayed imitation reveal that infants may have an innate propensity to become like conspecifics and may have an underlying motivation to engage in interactional activity.
- Still-face and other experimental studies show that infants are active participants in interactions, and they show agency in the initiation of interaction.
- Infants show pleasure when an expected interaction occurs and show distress when it does not.
- Some studies also show that perhaps we are born with a bias or preference for other conspecifics who can reward and meet the infant's sociostatic goals.
- Studies of infant contingency expectations, turn-taking, and interaction show that infants are highly attuned to the responses and actions of adults and respond accordingly.

These behaviors, we suggest, not only reveal that human beings are born with a capacity and desire for interaction but also contribute to infants becoming attached to caregivers. The neonate entrains onto adults who are the source of the language the child is exposed to. Language acquisition is facilitated in part by domain-general pattern-finding abilities, by the mirror-neuron system, and by neurobiological systems of affiliation. However, what may impel all typically developing children toward this developmental course of first-language acquisition is a drive for interaction.

FIVE

A Neurobiology for the Interactional Instinct

When we examine infant needs and motoric abilities to meet those needs, we find that infant development is predicated on affiliation with conspecifics, particularly caregivers. Coinciding with a *need* to affiliate is the *ability* to affiliate. Initially, these are reflexes such as rooting, but the infant quickly learns to use the motoric capacities he has to summon a caregiver or respond to her. Coincident to the application and development of the maturing infant's motor system is a reward system that refines and motivates the infant's behaviors. This chapter presents a neurobiology for the consummatory and affiliative reward systems and the formation of affiliative memories that support infant affiliation.

An Instinct for Survival: Affiliative Behavior

Infant nervous systems are underdeveloped at birth and do not reach full capacity without social and environmental interaction. Cortical development is characterized by increased myelination and dendritic arborization (Sarnat, 2003). Myelin is the fatty sheath that surrounds axons, preserving and speeding up electrical impulses (action potentials) traveling from one neuron to the next. Kinney, Brody, Kloman, and Gilles (1988) reported that in 162 infants who were autopsied at ages ranging from full term to 33 postconceptional months, not one of the 62 cortical sites they tested exhibited mature myelination at birth. In fact, some did not exhibit mature myelination even at two years old, the upper age limit of the study. Dendritic arborization is the development of processes that project from the neuronal cell body, expanding in area, density, and complexity to increase synaptic contact with the surround (Mrzljak, Uylings, Van Eden, and Judas, 1990; see fig. 5.1). Both myelination and dendritic arborization are

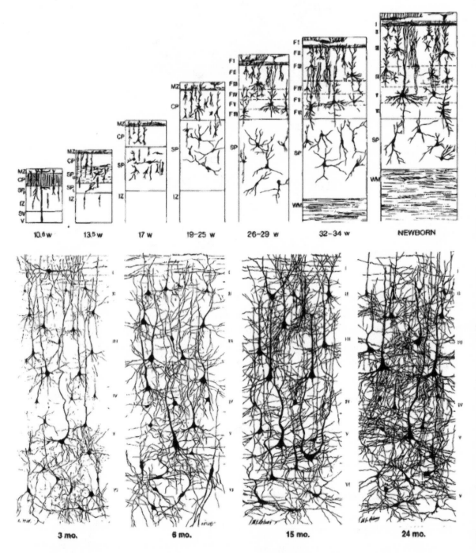

Figure 5.1. Dendritic arborization in the developing human cortex. *Top*: prenatal period from 10.5 weeks to birth. From Mrzljak, Uylings, Van Eden, and Judas (1990), with permission. *Bottom:* postnatal period from 2, 6, 15, and 24 months. From Conel (1963), with permission.

necessary for full function, and both are not yet mature at birth. Postconception, infants undergo a marked and rapid period of cortical development before reaching a period of dramatic tapering called pruning (Huttenlocher, 1979).

Maturity does not just come over time, although time is necessary, but is dependent on interaction with the environment. And while nonsocial stimuli are important (Sherman and Spear, 1982; Weisel, 1982), social stimuli are also important. This is apparent from the results of rearing infants in socially barren environments. Harlow's well-known monkey studies (1958), in which infant monkeys were fed from a wire mother and received no touch, showed that despite adequate food and water, the socially deprived infants developed psychotic behaviors. These deprived monkeys were so impaired that later in life, when the deprived females themselves become mothers, all ignored their young unless the young themselves were particularly persistent. The extent of impairment was such that some of the mothers killed their own offspring (Harlow, 1959). Socially isolated children in Romanian orphanages "exhibit disrupted physiological, sensory-motor, emotional, and cognitive development reminiscent of that observed in socially isolated rhesus monkeys" (Fleming, O'Day, and Kraemer, 1999). Without adequate interaction with caregivers, successful development of survival behavior, which is dependent on underlying neural development, is severely stunted.

Conversely, socially enhanced settings benefit the nervous system of the infant. Much of the literature on environmental enrichment comes from rodent studies. Environmental enrichment in the laboratory usually includes an increased number of conspecifics with which to interact, as well as more nonsocial stimuli. Chapillon et al. (2002) report that in this environment, rodents have shown increases in total brain weight (Rosenzweig, Bennett, and Diamond, 1972; Wainwright et al., 1993), the cerebral cortex is thicker (Uylings, Kuypers, Diamond, and Veltman, 1978), hippocampal neuron density is greater (Kempermann, Kuhn, and Gage, 1997), and synaptic contacts and the number of dendritic branches are greater (Greenough and Volkmar, 1973; Greenough, Whiters, and Wallace, 1990). Behavioral benefits from an enriched environment for rodents include protection from excessive anxiety in response to stressors in the immediate environment, as well as a reduction in the effects of past stressors (Fox, Merali, and Harrison, 2006). Cognitively, an enriched environment has a positive influence on learning and memory (Denenberg, Woodcock, and Rosenberg, 1968; Morgensen, 1991, in Chapillon et al., 2002; Escorihuela, Tobena, and Fernandez-Teruel, 1994; Janus, Koperwas, Janus, and Roder, 1995). In humans, randomized controlled studies have shown that preterm neonates who receive massage therapy gain more weight (Field, 2001; Ferber et al., 2002). Deigo, Field, and Hernandez-Reif (2005) designed a study to try to explain this phenomenon, and their results suggest that massage enhances vagal activity, which increases gastric motility, thus aiding in the food-absorption process.

If neural and thus behavioral development are necessary for survival but are dependent on environmental stimuli in general and social stimuli in particular, the next question is whether infants can, in fact, engage in interaction using the underdeveloped brains with which they are born. Infants do manage to make it out of their cortical immaturity, and they manage quite well, because the abilities they do have can be used to facilitate and promote interaction.

One of the first survival needs of the newborn infant is for sustenance. Several infant reflexes facilitate the successful amelioration of this need. First, even the immature vocal apparatus of the infant allows him to emit high-pitch, high-volume distress vocalizations, which garner caregiver attention. These vocalizations—crying—signal need, although they do not distinguish among different needs of which food is one (Karp, 2004). Second, infants are born with a rooting reflex, such that when the cheek is pressed with a finger or nipple, the infant will turn toward that finger or nipple (Zafeiriou, 2004). Third, a sucking reflex responds to the tapping on the roof of the mouth (Zafeiriou, 2004). All of these reflexes are immediately available at birth and facilitate nursing, which produces opiate rewards for both interactants. This is explored further below.

In addition to these basic, involuntary reflexes, some voluntary control is available to the infant through the corticobulbar system, which develops earlier than the corticospinal system (Porges, 2001). The corticospinal system is the pathway from the cortex, the brain's command center, to the spine, which controls the voluntary movement of arms and legs which are not well coordinated in newborn infants. Corticobulbar pathways connect the cortex to the brain stem, from which cranial nerves project. Of the 12 cranial nerves, Porges proposes that five (V, VII, IX, X, XI) regulate "muscles that provide important elements of social cueing" and "facilitate the social interaction with the caregiver and function collectively as an integrated social engagement system" by collectively controlling "facial expressions, eye gaze, vocalizations, and head orientation" (Porges, 2003, p. 34). While many of the descending motor tracts are not well developed in newborns, the corticobulbar tract is sufficient to support many of the infant behaviors described above in chapter 4.

Thus far, we have seen that interaction is necessary for infant survival and that even with their underdeveloped nervous systems, infants are capable of participating in interactions, particularly with a maternal caregiver. Now we present the work of Depue and Morrone-Strupinsky (2005) from the perspective of infant learning. Their synthesis on the neurobiology of affiliation suggests that infant social interaction is met with reward, which facilitates the process and provides further incentive to it. For nursing infants and for mothers, lactation stimulates opiate release in both, producing a sense of calmness and well-being. What the infant does reflexively out of physiological need induces a positive affective state marked by satiety and quiescence. As memory of this reward state develops, infants use what is under their voluntary control to return to that reward state. This is a development of affiliative memory. In the maturation process, the infant develops memories for reward, and another reward system begins to develop, one that rewards goal-seeking behavior. This reward for seeking pushes the infant along until he reaches that remembered consummatory reward state when the goal is achieved.

Being necessary from birth, affiliation begins at birth. The first reward received from affiliative behavior comes from reflexive behavior in response to caregiver stimulation, whether from touch or feeding. This is a "consummatory reward"(Depue and Morrone-Strupinsky, 2005) that comes with actually achieving interaction and affiliation. For the infant, it is tied to physiological quiescence and satiety. With time and continued cortical development, the infant remembers the situations and features of such reward, thereby building "affiliative memories" (Depue and Morrone-Strupinsky, 2005). From these affiliative memories, the infant can begin to build a repertoire of affiliative behaviors that will help him attain these consummatory rewards. This process of goal seeking involves its own set of "appetitive rewards" (Depue and Morrone-Strupinsky, 2005). Appetitive rewards, consummatory rewards, and affiliative memories become the frame on which, first, social affiliation and, ultimately, all forms of affiliation rest.

Affiliation: A Neurobiological Account

Knowing the behaviors that infants engage in, we turn to the neurobiological model Depue and Morrone-Strupinsky (2005) present based on their review of the past several decades of psychological and neuroscientific literature. Their model carefully delineates rewards in two phases: appetitive and consummatory. In other words, neurobiological rewards are produced in both a "seeking" phase and a "finding" phase. However, rewards in the here and now are not enough, particularly for social behaviors over time and long-term relationships. A neurobiology for building affiliative memories will also be necessary.

Two important realities must be remembered. First, the discussion here treats appetitive reward, consummatory reward, and affiliative memory as if they are distinct systems that operate along a linear trajectory or time course. The systems do not, in fact, operate in such a simplistic, linear manner. Our limited ability to tease out nonlinear systems and the linear time stream in which we live should not prevent us from recognizing that the reward systems are interactive. Second, by introducing these systems as reward systems, it is easy to fall into a deterministic mode of thinking in which humans become some kind of affiliative robots. While infant reflexes may be automatic, with the formation of memory in general and affiliative memory in particular, the infant world expands in complexity quickly and simple cause-and-effect relationships become multiple-causes-one-effect or single-cause-many-effects or multiple-causes-multiple-effects. Neuromodulators should be seen as physiological, emotional coloring that may render certain situations preferable. They are not causal or agentive.

As mentioned previously, there are affiliative behaviors that are inherently rewarding to the infant (and his mother). These behaviors include nursing, exposure to light touch, and certain facial, gestural, and vocal behaviors (Depue and Morrone-Strupinsky, 2005). Reward is encoded in the increased output of mu-opiates, such as beta-endorphins. In this way, the opiate system mediates the pleasure and physiological quiescence experienced (Depue and Morrone-Strupinsky, 2005).

Generally speaking, this system is sensitive both to the released opiate and to the opiate receptor. Thus, one way the opiate function has been studied has been through the application of an opiate receptor (OR) antagonist such as naltrexone or naloxone to block the receptor from uptaking the opiate in question. Morphine and heroin are probably the most well-known opiates that are exogenously made and bind to these ORs, but the body produces a variety of its own opiates for which those ORs were originally intended.

Beta-endorphins, better known for their pain-suppressant properties, are synthesized in the hypothalamus (Herbert, 1993) and are an opiate in the same family as morphine (Bear, Connors, and Paradiso, 2006). When beta-endorphins bind to mu-type opiate receptors (μORs), they facilitate a physiological response to a positive social interaction. Such chemical binding is associated with "*increased* interpersonal warmth, euphoria, well-being, and peaceful calmness, as well as *decreased* elation, energy, and incentive motivation" (Depue and Morrone-Strupinsky, 2005, p. 324). This system is available to not just infants and mothers. While infant-mother social interaction enhances both beta-endorphin production and μOR binding, this reward system continues to be available throughout life, responding to both social and sexual interactions.

Beta-endorphins are projected from the medial basal arcuate nucleus of the hypothalamus to a number of μOR-rich areas, which are listed in figure 5.2. These areas include the dorsal-medial and anterior nuclei of the hypothalamus; the nucleus accumbens shell (NAS); the central, medial, and basolateral nuclei of the amygdala; the bed nucleus of the stria terminalis (BNST); the medial preoptic area (mPOA); the septum; the diagonal band; the brain stem; and the periaqueductal gray (PAG), reticular formation, and nucleus solitarius through the pariventricular nucleus of the thalamus.

Beta-endorphin concentration has been shown to influence the frequency or intensity of social behavior displayed not only in rats and monkeys but in humans as well. Depue and Morrone-Strupinsky discuss Keverne's (1996) report that the influence is a modulation of anticipated reward. Vaginocervical stimulation, which occurs in parturition, triggers maternal behavior in part by rendering maternal behavior rewarding. The rewardingness of maternal behavior can be experimentally expanded or contracted by making beta-endorphin receptors more or less receptive. Depending on the experimental condition, mothers displayed increased or decreased levels of maternal behavior. Depue and Morrone-Strupinsky also present other experimental studies demonstrating the influence of beta-endorphins on amount of play in juvenile rats, grooming in rats and monkeys, and social interaction in human females.

While certain behaviors achieve consummatory reward, other behaviors also provide opportunity for reward before a goal is achieved. These rewards before the goal or rewards on the way are what Depue and Morrone-Strupinsky call appetitive rewards. Where consummatory rewards have been achieved by unconditioned proximal stimuli (light touch, grooming, mating, etc.), unconditioned appetitive rewards are associated with distal stimuli (smell, color, shape, temperature).

Following in the footsteps of the many studies on the neurobiology of reward and motivated behavior (Schultz, 2001), Depue and Morrone-Strupinsky also build their neurobiological explanation of "incentive motivated behaviors" (p. 323) on a

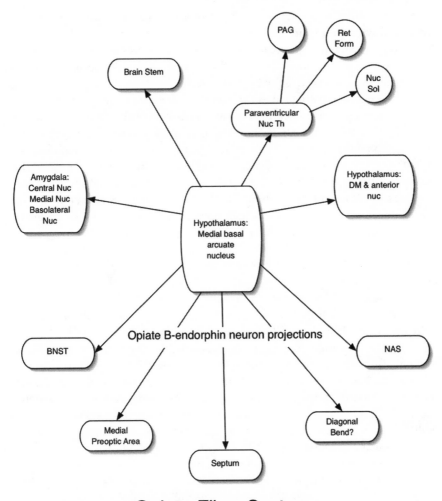

Opiate Fiber System

Figure 5.2. Beta-endorphin projections from the hypothalamus. PAG: periaque-ductal gray. Ret Form: reticular formation. Nuc Sol: nucleus solitarius. DM: dorsal medial. NAS: nucleus accumbens shell. BNST: bed nucleus of the stria terminalis.

dopamine-driven system. Dopamine (DA) synthesizing neurons are predominantly found in the ventroanterior midbrain consisting of the substantia nigra and ventral tegmental area[1] (Schultz, 2002). Different portions of this region play different behavioral roles. Lateral portions of the substantia nigra are tonically active, and

    1. The hypothalamus is also a site of DA production, but that system does not play a role in incentive motivated behavior (Schultz, 2002).

degeneration of this system is the cause of Parkinson's disease. The region is largely associated with the planning, initiation, and control of motor activity (Schultz, 2002). With our interest in explaining a reward system, we turn away from lateral midbrain to medial midbrain, from the substantia nigra to the ventral tegmental area (VTA), and from tonic activation to phasic activation.

Schultz (2002) distinguishes DA function across three different time scales in which elevated DA concentrations have been measured. The nigrostriatal DA pathways are tonically active, meaning that in the areas innervated by DA neurons, there is a "sustained, low extra cellular concentration" (Schultz, 2002, p. 247). In stark contrast, phasic activation produces spikes in DA concentration within as little as 100 to 300 milliseconds. While tonic and phasic activation are the two more researched contributors to DA concentration, Schultz cites a number of studies (Louilot, LeMoal, and Simon, 1982; Abercrombie, Keefe, Di-Frischia, and Zigmond, 1989; Young, Joseph, and Gray, 1992) that suggest that there is an intermediate time course of seconds to minutes that acts much in the same manner as hormones. Of the three time courses, research into DA's role in reward focuses on the shortest.

Spanagel and Weiss (1999), in their review of the DA hypothesis of reward, demonstrate that while the mesolimbic dopamine system has been described, its role remains unclear. Schultz (2001) summarizes a number of studies suggesting that phasic activation of VTA DA correlates with prediction error. He models DA response as a function of the occurrence and prediction of reward, such that *"Dopamine Response = Reward Occurrence − Reward Prediction"* (p. 296). Unpredicted reward brings about the greatest release of DA. As the predictive capacities develop such that reward occurrence is anticipated, DA release is reduced. This phenomenon is described as a component of the self-organization of goal-directed behavior, because trials will be repeated in response to DA until there is no error, thus no learning, and no change in DA concentration.

Interpreting the data differently, Redgrave, Prescott, and Gurney (1999) have suggested that short-latency DA response may indicate an attentional shift. They point out that many experiments have confounded novelty with reward, making it unclear whether the DA response is specifically to the rewarding nature of the stimuli or more generally to its novelty. They reinterpret two studies by Schultz et al. (Schultz et al., 1995; Schultz, Dayan, and Montague, 1997) that demonstrate phasic DA response to novel stimuli and argue that this would be problematic for a hypothesis that depends on the rewarding nature of a stimulus. Novel stimuli, in their novelty, cannot a priori be assessed as appetitive or aversive.

The phasic activation of VTA DA, also described as short-latency DA response (Redgrave, Prescott, and Gurney, 1999), released to the nucleus accumbens shell (NAS) is most often associated with expectation of reward, novelty, or deprivation (Schultz, 2002; Spanagel and Weiss, 1999). Additionally, the VTA is a site of high concentrations of μORs (Koob, 1992), bringing this DA-dependent site under the influence of opiates, which were previously implicated in consummatory reward.

The neurobiological system for appetitive reward focuses on DA produced in the VTA and projected to the NAS because of its functional association with "incentive motivated behaviors" (Depue and Morrone-Strupinsky, 2005, p. 323). Manipulating VTA DA concentrations influences activities that bring rats and monkeys closer to stimuli that might be consummatory reward. Depue and Morrone-Strupinsky list these as "locomotor activity to novelty and food; exploratory, aggressive, affiliative, and sexual behavior; food-hoarding, and motivational nursing behavior" (p. 323).

The neurobiology of incentive motivation (appetitive reward) and satiety or goal achievement (consummatory reward) is not a new area of inquiry, and the neuroscientific literature appears confident of their primary mechanisms and functions. Depue and Morrone-Strupinsky propose that a third key component is necessary for affiliation: affiliative memory, which results from an association between the predictive context and the affiliative reward.

In their affiliative-memory system, Depue and Morrone-Strupinsky focus on the NAS as the association site that integrates reward and context. They provide a dense figure (reproduced here as fig. 5.3), which we will unpack below.

As already discussed, the NAS is the site of DA projections from the VTA receiving appetitive-reward information. In addition to these projections, the NAS receives glutamatergic (Glu) projections from the hippocampus, the basolateral amygdala, the extended amygdala, and the medial orbital prefrontal cortex (MOC 13). The hippocampus brings information about the spatial organization of the contextual environment, which is perhaps more basic, critically necessary contextual information. The remaining three areas are implicated in the encoding of various aspects of context and reward.

Depue and Morrone-Strupinsky's review of the literature reveals that the basolateral amygdala is highly conditionable for explicit, discrete stimuli. It is made up of four nuclei: basal, accessory basal, mediobasal, and lateral. While the basolateral amygdala's NAS efferents can increase DA release and thus serve to add a contextual coloring to the reward stimuli, the prefrontal cortex is able to exert inhibitory control over them. Thus, even though the amygdala is more often associated with fear and aggression (Schumann, 1997), lesions of the whole amygdala show impairment in the performance of affiliative behaviors, perhaps resulting from the inability to make affiliative associations. Indeed, specific lesions of the basolateral amygdala have been the source of our understanding of its role in conditioning with discrete, explicit stimuli (Aggleton, 1992; Everitt and Robbins, 1992; Gaffan, 1992).

In contrast to the basolateral amygdala, the extended amygdala is highly conditionable for *non*explicit, *non*discrete stimuli (Depue and Morrone-Strupinsky, 2005). The extended amygdala sits over the central and medial amygdala, merging with the caudal and medial NAS across the sublenticular area and bed nucleus of the stria terminalis (BNST). Its functional literature is summarized as follows: "Pharmacological and lesion manipulations of all central extended amygdala structures modify incentive motivation to work for

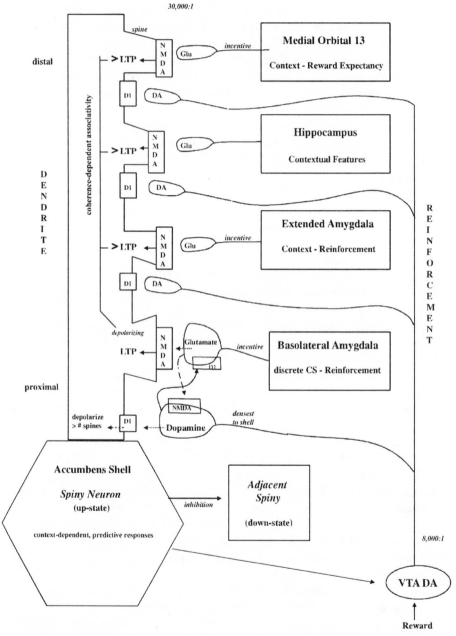

Figure 5.3. Affiliative memory, forming contextual ensembles. From Depue and Morrone-Strupinsky (2005), with permission.

rewards and initiation of locomotor activity as a means of obtaining rewards" (p. 327).

The extended amygdala is highly innervated by the previously mentioned basolateral amygdala, as well as the olfactory amygdala. This reminds us that the system under scrutiny is not linear. Discrete characteristics of the environment are simultaneously being fed to both the NAS and the extended amygdala. The extended amygdala, which associates the nondiscrete environmental features with reinforcement, is receiving the discrete features as it projects to the NAS. Thus, nondiscrete and discrete stimuli cannot be considered absolutely distinct bodies of information.

Finally, the NAS receives higher-order context-reward information in the form of prefrontal cortex innervation, particularly from the medial orbital prefrontal cortex area 13 (MOC 13). MOC 13, as Depue and Morrone-Strupinsky describe it, appears to be what others have described as the ventromedial prefrontal cortex or some subset thereof. Its dense connections with the neighboring orbital frontal cortex bring it in contact with "regions that process all sensory modalities of contemporaneous and stored information" (p. 328). At one point, the ventromedial prefrontal cortex was included in the orbital frontal cortex. It, too, has reciprocal connections with the basolateral and extended amygdala, with additional connections to the central nucleus of the amygdala. These connections provide the MOC 13 with the stimuli-reinforcement associations developed in those regions. With this input, MOC innervation of the NAS brings a macro-level synthesis of contextual information. In addition to conveying synthesized contextual information, Depue and Morrone-Strupinsky suggest that "MOC 13 may be capable of holding . . . representations of behavioral-reinforcement contingencies in working memory as motor strategies are selected over time" (p. 328). This will become important when we discuss the updating of the MOC 13 by the dorsomedial thalamus.

These three NAS input areas themselves receive input that is topographically arranged. This maps the outside world, its visual and auditory characteristics, in an organized pattern onto neural tissue. They receive input from the fusiform gyrus and the superior temporal gyrus and sulcus, regions associated with face processing and biological motion. This information would be clearly important in a model of social affiliation, as would the encoding of light, pleasant touch and the autonomic status that the insular cortex brings.

The NAS is said to be a site of integration because each NAS spiny neuron dendrite receives 30,000 efferents from the regions just described (p. 329). The high compression rate of contextual information leads Depue and Morrone-Strupinsky to propose that the NAS encodes incentive salience or value, which is passed along to the dorsomedial (DM) thalamus via the ventral pallidum. The DM thalamus connects back to the MOC 13 as an updating loop, providing the MOC with "not only incentive motivational intensity . . . but also of reinforcement priorities and behavioral outcome expectations constructed" there (p. 329).

Knowing that the NAS receives VTA DA projections as well as Glu projections from the previously described four areas, the next question is whether these two systems can be bound so that reward and context become part of one ensemble. Depue and Morrone-Strupinsky see two processes at work in building these reward-valenced, contextual ensembles. First is glutamate-induced long-term potentiation (LTP). LTP describes a facilitation of the connectivity between two synapses and is associated with learning and memory development at the neuronal level.

The second process is DA-glutamate interactions via NMDA and D1 receptors. In these interactions, each reciprocally increases the other's release. In fact, Depue and Morrone-Strupinsky cite further studies (Groenewegen et al., 1999; Groenewegen, Wright, Beijer, and Voorn, 1999; Malenka and Nicoll, 1999; Bissiere, Humeau, and Luthi, 2003; Li, Cullen, Anwyl, and Rowan, 2003; and others) that show that DA interaction is essential for glutamate-induced LTP to take place efficiently. Groenewegen et al. (1999) and Groenewegen, Wright, Beijer, and Voorn (1999) show that this DA-glutamate interaction, when it occurs at basolateral amygdala synapses proximal to the soma of NAS neurons, has a downstream effect on the synapses from other contextual inputs that are farther from the soma. This phenomenon leads Depue and Morrone-Strupinsky to conclude that "reward magnitude of *discrete, explicit* contextual stimuli carried by basolateral amygdala afferent to the NAS can facilitate the triggering of LTP in other contextual afferents to the NAS shell" (p. 330). Just as glutamate-induced LTP is facilitated by DA interaction, the effect of DA is modulated by the strength of the glutamate input from the previously discussed contextual afferents (Kalivas and Stewart, 1991; Dahlin, Hu, Xue, and Wolf, 1994; Kalivas, 1995; and others).

The DA-glutamate interactions summarized by Depue and Morrone-Strupinsky demonstrate that networks of neurons can indeed be formed that encode the relative rewardingness of a particular context. We mentioned briefly that VTA DA-driven systems are influenced by opiates because of the rich proliferation of μORs in the VTA. The NAS is also rich in μORs where NMDA1 receptors are expressed. When the ORs are agonized, these NMDA1 receptors facilitate glutamate-induced potentiation. Thus, we see that DA and its role in appetitive reward are not the only affiliative inputs to the NAS. Indeed, consummatory reward encoded in opiate release also projects to the medium spiny neurons of the NAS.

Clearly, all rewarding situations may not be affiliative interactions. That is not the argument here. Instead, we argue that affiliative behavior in both its seeking and finding phases is rewarding and, as such, may make use of the systems discussed above. These systems can be modulated or colored so that experiences may be valued as more or less rewarding and, therefore, memorable. Gonadal steroids and neuropeptides such as oxytocin and vasopressin are such modulators.

Gonadal steroids (most commonly, estrogen, testosterone, and progesterone), also commonly called sex steroids or sex hormones, are secreted by the gonads (ovaries and testes). Depue and Morrone-Strupinsky cite a wide array of research that has explored the role of gonadal steroids in behaviors that fall into the range of affiliative behaviors, such as sociosexual behavior. The concentration of gonadal steroids varies across differing time courses, such as pre- and postpubescent developmental periods, reproductive cycles, and circadian rhythms, to name a few. Additionally, affiliative experience also exerts influence back on gonadal steroid concentration (Depue and Morrone-Strupinsky, 2005). These shifts, in turn, appear to influence the perception of potentially affiliative stimuli as being affiliative. Research in sheep (Kendrick, Levy, and Keverne, 1992; Levy et al., 1992; Fabre-Nys, Ohkura, and Kendrick, 1997; Kendrick et al., 1997) shows that ewes in estrus respond to male faces and odors with high levels of mediobasal hypothalamus activity but not at other times. Likewise, lamb odors become salient to the adult ewe after she gives birth and not before (Kendrick, Levy, and Keverne, 1992). A similar phenomenon exists in rats (Agren, Olsson, Uvnas-Moberg, and Lundeberg, 1997). Research in humans does not provide evidence as compelling; nevertheless, gonadal steroids still appear to have a role in whether stimuli are perceived to be affiliative in the first place, thus influencing the development of contextual ensembles for future retrieval.

Oxytocin (OT) and vasopressin (VP) are neuropeptides found only in mammals (Insel, 1997). OT in the bloodstream is involved in lactation and parturition (Herbert, 1993), while VP is also known as the antidiuretic hormone (ADH) involved in kidney function (Bie, 1980). They can be found both peripherally in the bloodstream and centrally in the cerebral spinal fluid (Herbert, 1993) and play different roles in each system (Depue and Morrone-Strupinsky, 2005).

In their reading of the literature, Depue and Morrone-Strupinsky conclude that OT and VP do not mediate reward itself as much as they "facilitate" or "modulate" reward. This is their interpretation of studies of OT or VP knockout mice that were still able to perform a wide range of sociosexual behaviors, responding to them as being rewarding. The implication was that OT and VP have a role in initiation of sociosexual behavior more than the continuance or carrying out of the behavior. Therefore, if maternal behavior has been established, it will continue, but when an OT antagonist is introduced, the initiation of these behaviors is inhibited even though the animal has the ability to perform those behaviors (Ostrowski, 1998). While gonadal steroids play a role in many OT- and VP-induced social behaviors in the initial stages of interaction, we will not expand on the interactions between the two systems more here. For more information, see Depue and Morrone-Strupinsky's discussion.

Primarily, Depue and Morrone-Strupinsky present gonadal steroids, OT, and VP as internal milieu "tuners" or mood setters. They single out OT and foreground its influence on the formation of affiliative memories through its connection to hippocampal long-term potentiation (citing Tomizawa et al., 2003), opiate release in neurons in the arcuate nucleus, and DA release in the VTA and the NAS.

In addition to the memory systems already discussed, acetylcholine projections are also known to play a role in memory systems in the amygdala, hippocampus, and neocortex (Depue and Morrone-Strupinsky, 2005). These projections originate in the nucleus basalis of Meynert and the diagonal band of

Broca (Insel, 1997). Because the acetylcholine cell bodies of origin in these regions densely express OT receptors, we can infer that OT has an indirect effect on acetylcholine-facilitated memory formation.

Centrally, OT also influences opiate release in its projections from the paraventricular nucleus to the arcuate nucleus. Citing Csiffary, Ruttner, Toth, and Palkovits (1992), Depue and Morrone-Strupinsky present the claim that this projection can increase opiate release by 300 percent, which would make central OT a substantial player in all of the reward systems in which opiates participate. Peripherally, it has been observed that opiate release inhibits OT release, which supports the notion presented earlier that OT facilitates the initiation of behaviors because the opiate suppression coincides with consummatory reward. In other words, in order to achieve the quiescence of consummatory reward, initiating systems need to be suppressed, such as the DA-facilitated seeking phase as well as the OT-initiating system.

Not to leave out the appetitive-reward system, Depue and Morrone-Strupinsky suggest that OT is also involved in this system. Both OT and NAS DA play roles in establishing partner preference in female prairie voles (Gingrich et al., 2000). This, in conjunction with the high concentration of OT receptors in the NAS, which doesn't exist in promiscuous montane voles (Insel and Shapiro, 1992), forms the crux of Depue and Morrone-Strupinsky's argument that OT also plays a role in appetitive reward.

In the process of connecting systems back to other systems previously described, it is useful to describe another system implicated in affiliative behavior. Porges (2003) proposes that the inhibition of the central nucleus of the amygdala is necessary to prevent fight, flight, or freeze responses (fig. 5.4) and to allow social-engagement activities to take place that result in physiological quiescence. In Porges's "social engagement system," the first step is unconscious "neuroception," which he defines as an evaluation of the stimuli as either safe, dangerous, or life-threatening. If the environment is not safe for interaction, the central nucleus of the amygdala is activated, resulting in a fight, flight, or freeze response. None of these responses is thought to be conducive to affiliation. (Porges does suggest that the freeze mechanism has been evolutionarily co-opted for certain "intense" affiliative behaviors such as nursing and mating. He calls it an immobilization without fear.) In order for affiliative behavior to be enacted, this system, from amygdala down, must be inhibited. In Porges's model, the fusiform gyrus and the superior temporal sulcus and gyrus, parts of the temporal lobe that have been implicated in face recognition, do just that, inhibiting the amygdala's fear response when the environment is considered to be safe. Meanwhile, the motor cortex is activated for affiliative behaviors, such as open gestures and body position, physical and eye contact, and so on.

In infants, it may be that the mother-infant interactions, which were first described as triggers of opiate-mediated, consummatory reward, result in or are facilitated by the inhibition of the amygdala through a pathway of beta-endorphins

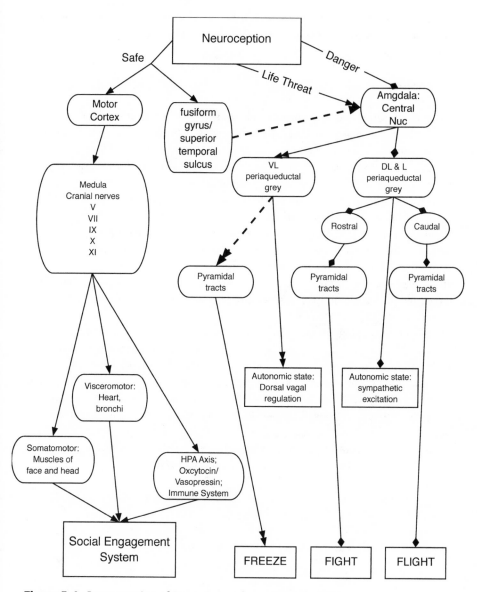

Figure 5.4. Interpretation of Porges's social engagement system.

to the amygdala system. This system is further developed and co-opted as the infant matures, developing into Porges's social engagement system.

Conclusions

We have presented here a neurobiological reward system that is active in affiliation. It is first engaged in infancy, moments after birth, as the infant is fed or tenderly touched. This experience elicits a consummatory reward from the opiate system. As a nonlinear course of development begins in the infant, memory systems build on experience built on encounters with appetitive, goal-seeking, dopamine-mediated reward. In the background, gonadal steroids, oxytocin, and vasopressin make affiliative stimuli more or less salient at a given moment. Oxytocin in particular has been shown to play a role in the opiate and dopaminergic systems, giving it an indirect role in reward experiences. Finally, Porges's social engagement system proposed an inhibitory mechanism that had to precede affiliative behaviors. Through his focus on the amygdala, we are reminded that a move toward affiliation may first require the shutting down of a fight, flight, or freeze system.

This neurobiology has not maximally described the potential system. From a behavioral standpoint, in observing children, one sees that they may engage in these fight-or-flight activities such as games of tag and consider them affiliative and often behave afterwards as if a deeper bond is formed. This would seem to contradict Porges's model. Additionally, as mentioned above, other researchers have noted that not all disaffiliative behaviors (e.g. a marital spat) result in a loss of affiliation and that, in fact, the contrary may be true (e.g. positive resolution; "make up sex") (Itoh and Izumi, 2005). Nevertheless, for the time being this review should shed some light on a significant part of the neurobiological mechanism at work for affiliation.

SIX

The Interactional Instinct in Primary- and Second-Language Acquisition

Chapter 5 presented a neurobiology of infants at birth that drives them toward interaction with conspecifics, initially for the maintenance of a stable body state, homeostasis. The interactions in which they participate facilitate social affiliation and are mediated by neurobiological processes of reward. Because the affiliation and the maintenance of homeostasis are so closely tied to one another, we are calling this biological imperative an interactional instinct. What we discuss next is language's role as social behavior and affiliation's role in its acquisition. Our basic claim is that insofar as language facilitates social affiliation, it will also be mediated by the same neural systems presented earlier.

The Role of Affiliation in Primary-Language Acquisition

Social behaviors and social bonds exist in reciprocal relationship (fig. 6.1). Social behaviors help to form social bonds, and social bonds often motivate social behaviors. Language is a social behavior. It may not be the only possible social behavior, but it holds a place of prestige in social life (Pinker, 2000). As an infant begins his interactive, affiliative life, he is surrounded by a world of language.

Working within the social bond-behavior feedback loop, the social bond that develops early between a child and a mother (facilitated by oxytocin and other hormones) rewards and thus motivates social behavior. In his development, the infant gains abilities that usher him into new worlds of social behavior. In chapter 5, we discussed the development of the infant brain in terms of myelination and density of dendritic arborization, showing that interaction and stimulation are necessary for these processes to occur. With ongoing interaction, infants

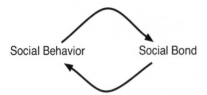

Social Behavior   Social Bond

Figure 6.1. Behavior-bond feedback loop.

develop enhanced cognitive skills, some of which are crucially also social and affiliative.

Cognitive Developments Necessary for PLA Are Social

Tomasello (2003) proposes a series of cognitive developments in the first year of life that he claims are fundamental to primary-language acquisition (PLA). These developments are not only cognitive, but they are also social. Insofar as they are social, the neurobiology outlined above should be an underlying process.

Joint Attention

The first of three important cognitive abilities Tomasello proposes for the facilitation of language acquisition is joint attention. This is a triadic interaction among the infant, an adult, and some third object or situation. This ability develops somewhere within the ninth to twelfth month and is by definition not only a cognitive ability but also a social ability, involving both the infant and another. We see here that affiliation and cognitive development have intertwined trajectories. The powerful neurochemical system that supports mother-infant bonding is still at work in the year-old infant who laughs with a caregiver about some other object under their joint attention.

Communicative Intention Reading

Communicative intention reading develops within the joint-attentional frame. There have been a number of studies on intention reading *simpliciter*, in which an infant might observe an adult fail at an activity such as flipping a switch and when presented with an opportunity to imitate the adult, the infant performs the intended action (flipping the switch).[1] Communicative intention reading is a more complex form of intention reading in which the infant develops and demonstrates the ability to recognize that an adult's action is calling for the infant's "intentional state" to attend to the adult's

---

1. For a review, see Tomasello et al. (2005).

"intentional state." This is a shift from an inert object to another agent with his or her own intentional state. Tomasello's argument is that without communicative intention reading, an infant will perceive adult speech as nonsense babbling, with no more bearing on the infant's world than sounds of running water that may signal a bath to come. However, once communicative intention reading is attained, adult speech becomes recognized as an activity that directs the attention of the infant somewhere. This is critical for PLA and develops in a social, interactive locus.

Role-Reversal Imitation

The third and final cognitive development necessary for PLA is a specific kind of cultural learning that Tomasello calls role-reversal imitation. Once a child has joint-attentional and communicative-intention-reading capacities, the cognitive tools are in place for the child to observe how another achieves goals. The ability to perform role-reversal imitation suggests that a child will attempt to apply his observations of others' behavior to achieve similar goals. Goals can be achieved via physical or symbolic tools. Just as a key may be used to unlock and open a door, a verbal request may also accomplish that intention. Language is a tool used for accomplishing any number of goals. Insofar as a child understands this and is able to imitate this behavior for the sake of accomplishing similar goals, we will see strides toward language acquisition.

Sociocognitive Development Guarantees PLA

PLA is virtually guaranteed because of the interrelationship that a child's pattern-detection abilities (Tomasello's cognitive precursors to PLA) have with the neurobiology of affiliation. In examining Tomasello's proposal that three cognitive abilities precede PLA, we see that these are in fact sociocognitive abilities. All of the cognitive abilities are developed in an interactional milieu. As such, their development depends on the neurobiological system laid out above in chapter 5.

That neurobiological system focuses on the enormous reward for affiliative behavior between conspecifics, but we can see that the distinction between behavior motivated toward conspecifics and nonconspecifics is difficult to make. Positive social relationships are rewarding, but we do many activities that are not intended for social-bond formation. Nevertheless, these nonconspecific-oriented behaviors often still require social interaction. One may go to a bar with the goal of meeting people, but going to a bar for the purpose of getting dinner still requires human interaction. Because of this, we argue that goal-directed behavior and affiliation are built on a common neurobiology.

The capacity for role-reversal imitation is the one most overtly dependent on the neurobiology presented here, because it supposes that the child has goals. With a goal in hand, the child accesses the appetitive-reward system as he moves toward that consummatory reward. All the while, memories are being laid down matching context to reward. Whether the child's goals are directly affiliative (wanting positive feedback or touch from a caregiver) or situationally interactive (requesting food), a child with these cognitive abilities will be motivated to make the best attempts to use language. The child's affiliative drive brings him into intimate emotional contact with the sources of language input, adults, and serves as an innate motivational and attentional system that allows his domain-general learning mechanisms to acquire language. It will bias the child to devote tremendous resources to PLA.

Accounting for Variability in SLA

Whereas primary-language acquisition is inevitable in all normal children, adult second-language acquisition (SLA) is never guaranteed. We examine SLA here by taking the variability claims of the acculturation model (Schumann, 1976, 1978) and matching them with later work on the neurobiology of stimulus appraisal and then extending the claim from individual variation to include neurobiological variation in the very systems that have been presented.

The Acculturation Model

Schumann (1976, 1978) proposed that a "major causal variable" in SLA was acculturation, defined as "social and psychological integration . . . with the target language (TL) group" (1978, p. 29). Social integration, as described by the model, reflected attitudes of the TL and second-language (SL) learning communities toward each other. Psychological integration, on the other hand, was characterized as a function of individual experiences and traits such as language shock, cultural shock, ego permeability, and motivation.

Variables for Social Integration

According to Schumann's model, social integration would be facilitated or inhibited by variables that increased or decreased social distance, the concrete or subjective separation between the two language groups. These variables include *social dominance, patterns of integration, degree of enclosure, cohesiveness, community size, cultural congruence, attitude,* and *intended length of stay.* *Social dominance* can involve a number of areas, such as technological advancement, economic development, or military strength. Learners might belong to communities with varying dominance patterns relative to the TL culture. Social equality between the two would facilitate integration, whereas dominance (the SL learners perceive the TL group as weaker or lesser) or subordination (the SL learners perceive the TL group as more powerful or better) would create distance and make integration more difficult.

Four of the variables are interrelated: *pattern of integration, enclosure, attitude,* and *cohesiveness.* First, a language community can have different patterns of integration. It may be more or less oriented toward preserving its own identity or may even purposefully desire assimilation into the host culture. *Assimilation* would facilitate social integration by reducing social distance; *preservation* would increase social distance and inhibit social integration by efforts to maintain native language, lifestyle, and values while avoiding those of the TL community. *Accommodation/adaptation* strategies have varying degrees of social integration and intragroup lifestyle and value maintenance and thus have varying degrees of social-distance reduction or increase. A second, related variable, *enclosure*, describes the structures and geography of the group. Schumann's model describes social entities such as group-specific churches, clubs, associations, and newspapers as indexes of a heightened degree of enclosure. It is easy to see that a preservation-oriented community might allocate resources to these features. A third variable, *attitude*, refers to the positive or negative assessment of the TL community by the SL learners. A final, related factor is *group cohesiveness*, how bonded the learners are within their native-language community versus the TL community. High enclosure and a pattern of integration that is preservationist would aid in developing a cohesive group. Likewise, the cohesiveness of a group might be facilitated by a negative attitude of the group toward the TL culture. An attitude of open hostility toward the TL culture would probably exert unifying pressure on the community. Interacting on one another, these four variables—*patterns of integration, enclosure, attitude*, and *cohesiveness*—can shift the community along a continuum of relative social distance with respect to the TL culture, thereby influencing the degree of social integration, which Schumann argued was a major causal variable in SLA in this model.

The other variables in the model are *group size, cultural congruence*, and *intended length of stay*. Size can be seen as a proxy for contact, in the sense that a large community would offer more opportunity for intragroup contact and diminish the opportunity or desire for intergroup contact. More contact would facilitate social integration. *Cultural congruence* refers to dimensions of similarity between the learning community and the TL community, which may include cultural institutions such as religion or degree of industrialization. The last variable is *intended length of residence*. Different communities may or may not see themselves as permanently residing in the TL area. A longer intended length of residence would lead to more commitment to acquire the TL.

Variables for Psychological Integration

Having described the social, group variables, we now turn to the affective, individual variables. The psychological variables are *language shock, cultural shock, ego permeability*, and *motivation*.

Language shock results from the distress that learners experience when they receive a negative response to their TL use. At its worst, their TL use may garner laughter instead of praise, social distance instead of bonding. This is in contrast to child learners, who may be more fearless and often "see language as a method of play and find communication a source of pleasure" (Schumann, 1978, p. 29). It is possible repeated lack of expected rewards in attempts at engagement in the TL forms the basis of language shock. From a neurobiological perspective, which will be elaborated on below, there may be dopamine depression that results from not receiving a reward when one was expected. Additionally, preliminary studies show anterior cingulate activation in sites for physical pain when people experience social isolation (Eisenberger and Lieberman, 2004). The more intense the experience of language shock, the more the learner will avoid interaction with TL users, and the more negatively affected SLA will be.

Where language shock may result from feedback from TL users, *cultural shock* results from the whole experience of living in a different environment. This often requires tremendous energy to accomplish what were formerly mundane activities. Keep in mind that Schumann's acculturation model was developed with one setting in mind: language learning outside the classroom in its environment of use. Language learners working in the TL culture experience repeated asymmetries between their remembered experiences of how the world works and the situation in which they now find themselves. How people should greet one another, cross the street, and buy groceries must be relearned. This experience of stress may have a snowballing effect, which leaves learners essentially paralyzed unless they encounter intervening positively rewarding experiences. Because of the negative effects of language shock and cultural shock, the acculturation model argues that they must be circumvented in order for SLA to proceed.

Two other affective factors must also be adequately tuned: *ego permeability* and *motivation*. The affiliative neurobiology subserving the two is largely the same. *Ego permeability* is the extent to which one's "language ego" (Guiora et al., 1972) will respond to the identity-threatening TL. It is a concept derived from Freud's "body ego." Where a developing body ego learns the physical boundaries of one's physical existence, a language ego learns the phonemic, morphemic, and syntactic boundaries of the language. Guiora et al. (1972) also proposed that elevated inhibition would diminish the permeability of language ego.

Schumann's 1978 model has one last variable for acculturation: motivation, which "involves the learner's reasons for attempting to acquire the second language" (p. 32). In the social-psychological literature, Gardner and Lambert (1972) characterized motivation for second-language learning as having two dimensions: integrative and instrumental. Integratively motivated learners learn the TL in order to get to know or perhaps even to become like the TL-speaking community. Instrumentally motivated TL learners are interested in the results that SLA will afford, such as improved job opportunities, the adulation of peers, and so on.

Stimulus Appraisals Underlie Psychological Variables

Within the framework of the interactional instinct, our focus is on the individual and not the complex milieu in which he or she lives. Therefore, with regard to the acculturation model described above, we will focus on psychological distance. Schumann (personal communication), in considering individual variation, would now eliminate from his model the four variables of psychological distance and replace them with the five domains of stimulus appraisal he describes in *The Neurobiology of Affect in Language* (1997). Having surveyed the literature on stimulus appraisal, Schumann adopts Scherer's (1984) five dimensions of stimulus appraisal: novelty, pleasantness, goal/need significance, coping potential, and self/norm compatibility.

Novelty and Pleasantness

Novelty is fairly straightforward. It assesses whether a stimulus has been encountered before, its degree of familiarity. Novelty is usually a positive attribution of a stimulus, with routine stimuli attracting little attention. Pleasantness, according to Scherer, is an intrinsic property of a stimulus that might cover what Frijda (1986) terms "valence" and Ortony, Clore, and Collins (1988) term "appealingness" (aggregated in a chart by Scherer, 1988, in Schumann 1997, p. 22).

Goal/Need Significance

This dimension evaluates how a stimulus situation will affect an individual's attempts to satisfy his or her needs or achieve his or her goals and can be viewed from four perspectives: relevance, outcome probability, conduciveness, and urgency. Relevance covers the relationship of a stimulus to one's goals or needs where the outcome probability is associated with the likelihood of achieving a desired outcome. The conduciveness of a stimulus to goal/need achievement involves whether a stimulus will aid or hinder an individual's attainment of his or her goals or needs. Urgency refers to the amount of time an individual believes is available to respond to the stimulus (Scherer, 1984).

Coping Potential

Assessment of coping potential evaluates the cause of the stimulus, the coping ability of the individual, the possibility of the individual changing or avoiding the stimulus, and the ability of the individual to adjust to whatever outcome arises from the stimulus. In short, coping potential appraises stimuli by asking why something happened, what one can do about it, and whether one can live with it. In SLA, it would involve an assessment by the learner of his or her language-learning aptitude.

Self/Norm Compatibility

To determine self/norm compatibility, stimuli are assessed with respect to how well they match one's self-image, expectations, or the expectations of one's valued others.

The appraisals reviewed above are built on an individual's experiences in navigating the world, and each individual's experience is unique. Therefore, individual stimulus-appraisal systems will contain a unique combination of preferences and aversions. Ultimately, the stimulus-appraisal paradigm is an idiosyncratic rubric for assigning approach-or-avoid assessments of stimuli. This conceptual reduction to approach-or-avoid makes the construct more amenable to a possible neurobiological account. The social factors in the acculturation model are both causes and products of appraisals that eventually come to characterize the group as a whole. For example, choices of integration strategy (assimilation, accommodation, preservation) or enclosure patterns are the net result of appraisals made by individuals that become shared by their immigrant group with respect to the TL group, and vice versa.

A Neurobiological Account of Stimulus Appraisal

Schumann's (1997) neurobiology of stimulus appraisal focuses on a tripartite complex of the amygdala, the orbitofrontal cortex (OFC), and the body proper. We summarize his neurobiological framework here before moving on to extensions of the framework.

The Amygdala

The amygdala is often associated with fear responses. Monkeys with lesioned amygdalas appear unable to connect familiar stimuli with corresponding emotional responses. They do not exhibit the innate fear that other monkeys have of snakes; they become extremely aggressive and overexplore objects, such as their own feces, with their mouths. It is generally thought that emotion does not reside in the amygdala but that it is part of a larger emotional system (Schumann, 1997).

The amygdala is located bilaterally in the anterior temporal lobes and receives pre- and postcortical transmissions from the thalamus. The amygdala can be said to receive a precortical, "unprocessed" and a postcortical, "processed" copy of external stimuli. Le Doux's (1986) research demonstrates that the pathway to the amygdala via the cortex (postcortical) assigns emotional significance to complex or highly discriminated perceptual information. The direct path (precortical) from the thalamus to the amygdala also assigns emotional significance to stimuli but to simpler and cruder representations. Information following the postcortical path, having an extra "stop," would arrive at the amygdala after the precortical path. Le Doux describes the amygdala as receiving a quick, crude, direct assessment of a stimulus, and then a more complicated, nuanced assessment arrives from several synapses away. Thus, a snakelike object would quickly trigger the amygdala and cause one to jump away (via precortical pathway signals), only to realize a moment later that the object was really a piece of rope (via postcortical pathway signals).

The amygdala is involved in the emotional understanding of the surrounding environment based on sensory perceptions and memories of past perceptions of similar stimuli. It sends projections distributing information on the emotional valence of stimuli back to the cortex and the thalamus, to other nuclei within itself, and to the basal forebrain, the hypothalamus, the midbrain, the pons, and the medulla.

The Orbitofrontal Cortex

Another important amygdala-emotion connection is the OFC, which is anatomically situated near the amygdala but in the prefrontal cortex, just above the orbits in which the eyes rest. Covered extensively in Damasio's book *Descartes's Error* (1994), it receives sensory input via the sensory-association cortex and reciprocally innervates the amygdala. Citing brain-damage studies, Damasio (1994; see also Schumann, 1997) paints a picture of OFC-mediated social skills. OFC-damaged patients, when tested, had normal intelligence but were unable to maintain socially acceptable behaviors; emotion was blunted, and they exhibited poor decision-making skills in relation to personal and social issues. In tests, they could describe possible choices in a given situation but did not prefer one over another, as if all options were equally appropriate. Without the OFC intact, these patients were able to describe and make inferences about the world around them but lacked emotional coloring to render one potential choice more desirable or less desirable.

The Body Proper via the Brain Stem and the Hypothalamus

Not only are the amygdala and the OFC reciprocally innervated, but they also both have reciprocal projections with the brain stem and the hypothalamus (Damasio, 1994). These two areas, in turn, connect to the body via the autonomic nervous system, the endocrine system, and the musculoskeletal system. Stimulus appraisal is not an "experience" or a mental classification in the brain, but through cortical connections to the brain stem and the hypothalamus, the appraisals change bodily states. In short, the body feels; it is an equal participant in stimulus appraisal.

The engagement of the body involves a feedback system between the amygdala/OFC and the autonomic nervous system, which is regulated by the brain stem (Schumann, 1997). The autonomic nervous system is divided into a sympathetic system and a parasympathetic system. The sympathetic nervous system controls aroused physiological responses, such as an increase in respiration and heart rate and a decrease in digestion, responses that ready or maintain the body for fight or flight. Alternatively, the parasympathetic nervous system controls bodily states associated with rest and calmness.

In addition to their autonomic connections, the amygdala/OFC also innervates the hypothalamus, which regulates the endocrine system and the musculoskeletal system (Damasio, 1994). The endocrine system influences the body through regulation of hormones in the bloodstream. These hormones variously influence salt and water metabolism, metabolic rate, insulin and glucose levels, and sexual response. The musculoskeletal system influences the bodily state via muscle tension, body position, and movement.

The Role of Memory

We have described the online, present-time functions of the amygdala, assessing the relevance of stimuli for maintaining homeostasis; the OFC, connecting cognition with emotion; and the brain stem and the hypothalamus, altering bodily states related to emotional states. However, a neurobiological stimulus-appraisal system needs a memory component. Schumann (1997) uses Damasio's (1994) construct of dispositional representations, which appear to correlate with a concept more broadly described as neural networks. Neural networks are made up of interconnected neurons with connections strengthened by repeated simultaneous firings of member neurons in a process of Hebbian learning (Pulvermuller, 2002). Schumann proposes that the areas described above also contain neural networks that represent memories of past experiences with similar stimuli. Thus, an online appraisal includes reference to information from past experiences.

In summary, Schumann's stimulus-appraisal framework presents a set of systems that attach emotional valence to perception, compares that with memories of previous stimuli, and issues approach-or-avoid signals.

Initiating and Reassessing Goals in SLA

We have discussed the dimensions of individual variation in stimulus appraisal and a neurobiology of stimulus appraisal. This is in marked contrast to the stability of the infant's interactional instinct. The stakes and motivations for language learning in SLA are much more varied than in PLA. We now move from appraisal to activity.

Learning as Foraging—Appraise and Reappraise

In 1997, Schumann was developing an understanding of some key biological systems that connected motion, cognition, and affect. His argument was that the interconnectivity of these three processes constituted a stimulus-appraisal system that would prompt one to approach or avoid a stimulus. Using diary studies, language-learner autobiographies, and questionnaires, he demonstrated that self-reported appraisals of learning experiences and encounters did, indeed, shape the trajectory of language learners. In 2001, Schumann augmented the paradigm with a metaphor of "learning as foraging." In foraging, an internal change, such as a decrease in blood sugar associated with "hunger," creates an "incentive motive" that prompts the motor system to engage in food seeking. Following

Stephens and Krebs's (1986) classification of foraging stages, Schumann also divided the process into three stages of search, encounter, and decision.

The process begins with some incentive motive that moves the forager to seek food in a search phase. Based on previous experience, different strategies may be deployed to arrive at an encounter. Encounters are defined as Schultz's (2001) "stimuli predictive of reward," which elicit a dopamine response. At every encounter, the forager must decide what to do next in relation to the motivating goal. For instance, a hungry urban human might leave his office and move toward a food court. As he draws nearer, smells wafting in the air signal sustenance nearby. He has had an encounter and must decide whether to proceed. Conversely, if there are no smells and no sounds of people, successful acquisition of food is not predicted, and the hungry human may reevaluate his strategy for acquiring food, turning aside to continue his search elsewhere. On the other hand, a new goal or novelty may supersede hunger, leading him to explore why there are no smells and sounds predictive of the food court. In this way, the appraisal of hunger motivates behavior that follows a cycle of search-encounter-decide until the goal ceases to exist, either through achievement or reorientation.

Schumann's 1997 stimulus-appraisal model was more static and unitary. In the 2001 work, SLA variability is accounted for by a dynamic process of reassessments in parallel with the food forager. As with the food forager, the language learner is prompted by an internal state, which we argue here is an affiliative[2] desire, to learn a new language. This is the incentive motive. In the search phase, the learner may look up Internet sites about the language of interest, enroll in a course, attempt to make friends with speakers of the language, frequent markets and other common spaces where the TL is the language of transaction, and so on. In this process, the language learner is encountering stimuli that predict opportunities for language learning, and, as the food forager did, the language learner is constantly assessing the stimuli against the goal, and that relationship is dynamic. Just as a forager might exhaust the berries on a bush before he is sated, a learner might exhaust the information available in a given environment before achieving the goal. The urban human's food court might undergo a dusty, chaotic renovation motivating him to seek a new lunch location. Likewise, intolerable classmates or increased work demands may motivate the language learner to find a different learning environment.

---

2. It is necessary to point out that our symbolic capacity extends our affiliative prospects very broadly. People may affiliate with pets, supernatural deities, celebrities, ideologies, and so on. The claim that language learning emerges from affiliative need does not suggest that all learners have high regard for the TL community. Instead, we are suggesting that those without such high regard have affiliative goals elsewhere, which may include local goals of impressing classmates or social-status goals of being able to demonstrate proficiency, to name a few.

A Neurobiology of Appraisal to Activity

Schumann and Wood (2004) lay out a neurobiological framework that could support a foraging process from incipient goal generation to resulting motor activity. The 1997 neurobiological model for stimulus appraisal consisting of the workings of the amygdala, the OFC, and the body proper was preserved as a mechanism for goal generation. Schumann and Wood propose that goals are updated by convergent input to the nucleus accumbens shell (NAS) from both appraisal regions (OFC and amygdala), reward-predicting dopamine (DA) from the ventral tegmental area (VTA), and reciprocating innervation from the NAS back to the VTA. Functionally, this suggests that the NAS takes an appraisal that might form a goal and matches it with real-time experiences of reward expectancy. This would help one know whether steps are being taken toward achieving the goal. Not only does the NAS receive input from the VTA, but it also sends projections back. Because their model shows the NAS receiving appraisals of the current surround via the OFC and the amygdala, as well as memories of past experiences via the hippocampus (p. 30), NAS projections back to the VTA can modulate the effect of the reward expectancy derived from VTA DA. This neurobiological model overlaps extensively with Depue and Morrone-Strupinsky's model for appetitive reward (2005); however, it does not address the consummatory phase of goal-seeking behavior.

Goals result in motor activity via connections that ultimately terminate in the spinal cord. The model presents the process as follows: the NAS projects to the ventromedial ventral pallidum of the basal ganglia, which projects on to the mediodorsal thalamus and to the prelimbic or anterior cingulate region of the PFC (area 32), then it sweeps down to the nucleus accumbens core involved in initiating motor activity, before coming back to the basal ganglia in the dorsolateral ventral pallidum. The dorsolateral ventral pallidum projects to the midbrain in the brain stem, to a locomotor region, the pedunculopontine nucleus; from there, direct projections to brain-stem motor nuclei will send signals down the spine to produce motor activity.

The 2004 work provides a resource for understanding the mechanism that transforms stimulus appraisals into activity. For SLA, this advancement is important, first, because it is a biological connection between motivation and behaviors that facilitate or inhibit learning. Second, the model gives an account for changing appraisals of the situation, which work in conjunction with the different degrees of motivation that a learner may experience over the course of SLA. Returning to the acculturation model outlined above, language shock and cultural shock result from repeated instances of not receiving expected rewards. With a neurobiological system that updates appraisals through the convergence of input on the NAS, enough negative feedback may entirely dampen the appraisal and extinguish the goal.

There are many dimensions along which appraisals can be made for and against the course of action a second-language learner is taking. This is radically different from the experience of the infant and should be considered a major reason for SLA variability in the face of PLA ubiquity.

Individual Differences in Neurobiology

Up to this point, variation in SLA has been attributed to varying stimulus appraisals. However, besides individual differences in stimulus appraisals, there are also individual differences in aptitude. Schumann (2004) characterizes the neurobiology of aptitude as all brains being different through genetic and epigenetic influences. Resulting from these differences are idiosyncratic neural hypertrophies and hypotrophies. Hypertrophies might facilitate various types of learning, such as mathematical acuity, acoustic parsing and imitation, or visual-spatial representation. We raise this issue of aptitude not to give a full summary but to acknowledge that this factor will also account for variation in SLA outcome.

Genetic Variation

Genetic variation can be found in opiate function as well as in opiate-function modulators, DA, OT, and VP. Recent research is beginning to show that these differences have behavioral ramifications. In Depue and Morrone-Strupinsky's (2005) review of the literature, they note that OR densities in humans "show a range of up to 75% between the lower and upper thirds of the distribution" (p. 341). This wide range has a nontrivial effect on experimental subject pools under the placebo condition. With differing OR densities, the reward value of opiates is variable, and drugs of abuse, such as cocaine and morphine, will vary in rewardingness.

Genetic variation in DA has been shown to have effects on incentive-motivated behaviors, which Depue and Morrone-Strupinsky (2005) hypothesize will affect the appetitive phase of their model in terms of varying the weights of appetitive reward and the contextual stimuli. This would affect social-bond formation. On the other hand, OT, a modulator of the affiliative model, "could influence *the frequency and quality of expression* of opiate-modulated behaviors, and could modulate formation of affiliative memories" (p. 342). The authors use the role of OT and VP in vole mating behavior to support their contention that genetic variation in this area would create variability in affiliative behavior.

Experience-Dependent Variation

In addition to genetic variability, individuals face different experiences, which play a role in shaping the internal neurobiological substrate. Depue and Morrone-Strupinsky divide experiential variability into two categories: experience-expectant and experience-dependent. Experience-expectant processes await experience for proper development and produce "sensitive periods," which offer a neurobiological perspective on the topic of critical period in SLA. Much remains to be discovered about experience-expectant processes, but what is known that has bearing on the neurobiology of affiliation is that there is an overabundance of OTRs (oxytocin receptors) and VPRs (vasopressin receptors) in limbic regions of the brain. This overabundance is modified by an experiential pruning process. After pruning is completed, behaviors can be different in different individuals.

Experience-dependent processes are what are generally considered learning processes. The convergence of reward and contextual information in the NAS medium-spiny neurons is an experience-dependent process. In terms of individual variation, Depue and Morrone-Strupinsky are saying that the repeated experiences can enhance the rewardingness of the next experience. In other words, past experiences can vary the response of the affiliation system. For example, a mother who smells her infant early and often is more likely to find her infant's odor pleasant and be able to recognize her own child.

Individual Difference in Neurobiology and Its Role in SLA

All of this individual difference amounts to variation in what Depue and Morrone-Strupinsky call "trait affiliation." We could say simply that what varies individually is how strong an affiliative stimulus will have to be before a particular individual experiences an affiliative reward. For some people with a sensitive appetitive and a consummatory reward system, a relatively weak stimulus will deliver reward. Conversely, if dopamine levels are low and there are relatively few opiate receptors, an individual might need a strong stimulus or many stimuli in order to experience the same level of reward.

MacIntyre, Dornyei, Clement, and Noels (1998) define willingness to communicate (WTC) as "a readiness to enter into discourse at a particular time with a specific person or persons, using a L2" (p. 547). They build an elaborate system of both stable and situation-dependent variables that influence WTC. Stable variables include intergroup climate, personality, intergroup attitudes, social situation, communicative competence, interpersonal motivation, intergroup motivation, and second-language self-confidence. Situation-dependent variables include desire to communicate with a specific person at a specific time and to state communicative self-confidence. These variables are appraisals that an individual will make using the appraisal system described above.

For MacIntyre's construct, individual differences in neurobiology suggest that all appraisals being equal, two different individuals may still exhibit differing levels of WTC. If one learner has X degree of second-language self-confidence, which allows her to engage in use of the language, another learner may need X + 3 in order to experience the same sense of expected reward. Thus, if both have X self-confidence, only the first learner may be willing to open her mouth and communicate.

Porges's social engagement system (2003) may also be relevant to WTC. His system depends on an initial appraisal of the safety of the stimulus situation. If it is appraised as being safe, then the amygdala will be inhibited from causing fight, fright, or freeze responses, and the motor cortex is free to prepare the face and head for action while calming the nervous system and activating OT and VP. In SLA, a learner has to decide whether to engage in second-language discourse. Depending on the appraisals the learner makes of her potential interlocutor and the situational context in terms of safety and with regard to coping potential and self- and social image, the learner will engage in interaction in the second language or not.

Ontogenetic Changes

Since Lenneberg's seminal book was published in 1967, it has been generally accepted that there is a negative correlation between age of onset of language learning and ultimate proficiency in the language. If, as we argue, the interactional instinct is the critical biological substrate for language acquisition, there should be ontogenetic changes in the system for the instinct that explain the differences in language-acquisition behavior of children and adults. That is, the appetitive system and the consummatory system should go through changes with maturation that make them more effective in children than in adults. Although more research seems necessary to illuminate these changes clearly, tantalizing data do support that they occur.

Ontogenetic Changes in DA

As discussed in chapter 5, dopamine (DA) is a neurotransmitter whose function includes subserving the appetitive phase of interaction. Figure 6.2 shows that dopamine is produced in midbrain areas, especially in the ventral tegmental area (VTA) and the substantia nigra pars compacta (SNc). The former projects mainly to the ventral striatum, which is the nucleus accumbens (NAS), and the prefrontal cortex, in addition to other areas, such as the hippocampus and both the extended and the basolateral amygdala. DA in these systems subserves the appetitive phase of affiliation. Furthermore, DA from the SNc projects to the dorsal striatum, which consists of the caudate and the putamen and which modulates procedural learning, mediating the acquisition of phonology and grammar (Schumann et al., 2004).

The possibility that DA promotes learning has been supported by numerous studies. It was shown long ago that DA plays a key role in reinforcement learning in animals (Wise and Rompre, 1989). Pessiglione et al. (2006) demonstrate that DA-dependent modulation of the activity in the striatum explains how human brains use reward-prediction errors to acquire instrumental learning to improve future decision making. In addition, studies on Parkinson's disease patients show how DA is involved in learning. The disease is caused by

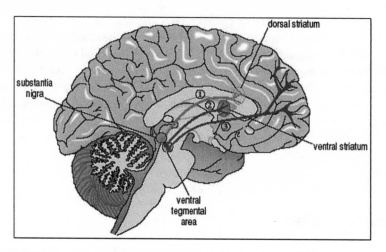

Figure 6.2. DA projections from the VTA to the PFC and the nucleus accumbens and from the substantia nigra to the dorsal striatum.

degeneration of dopaminergic neurons in the SNc, which leads to a DA deficiency in the dorsal striatum, resulting in a procedural learning deficit (Knowlton, Mangels, and Squire, 1996; Shohamy et al., 2004). When the patients are treated with DA-enhancer medication, their ability to learn from positive reinforcement improves (Swainson et al., 2000). The ventral striatum, to which DA neurons from the VTA project, also has been shown to be involved in procedural learning (Atallah, Lopez-Paniagua, Rudy, and O'Reilly, 2007).

Researchers who investigate ontogenetic changes of DA-receptor density have shown that DA from both VTA and SNc is high in children and decreases with age. Generally speaking, DA level increases until the onset of puberty and then tapers off throughout life. It has been discovered that in rats, DA receptors in the striatum are dramatically overproduced in neonates, peak at approximately 40 days of age (onset of puberty), and subsequently decline by 58 to 75 percent by 120 days (see fig. 6.3; Gelbard, Teicher, Faedda, and Baldessarini, 1989; Teicher, Andersen, and Hostetter, 1995). Andersen et al. (2000) also found the similar trend in rats. In the PFC, D1 peaked at 40 days, decreased 8 percent by 60 days, and declined by 50 to 66 percent by 120 days. D2 receptors increased until 60 days and declined by 27 to 41 percent from the peak by 120 days. In the NAS, they increased markedly until 40 days and maintained their level.

Similar trends were found in human subjects, according to Seeman et al. (1987; see fig. 6.4). The densities of D1 and D2 dopamine receptors in the striatum rise and reach the highest level at age three or four and then fall sharply until puberty for the D1 receptor and until age five for the D2 receptor. After age 20, D1 receptors disappear at 3.2 percent per decade, D2 at 2.2 percent. Generally speaking, in adults, the receptor density is 48 percent (D1) and 59 percent (D2) less than that of children.

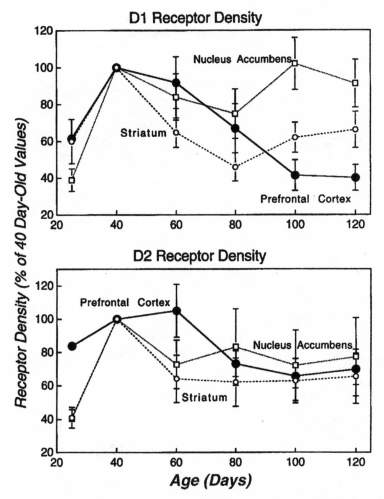

Figure 6.3. Ontogenetic changes of DA 1 and 2 receptor densities in the dorsal striatum, nucleus accumbens, and the PFC in rats. From Andersen et al. (2000, p.168). Reprinted with the permission of Wiley-Liss, Inc., a subsidiary of John Wiley & Sons, Inc.

The decrease in DA receptors in the NAS explains why adults may have a weaker drive for the appetitive phase of affiliation, and the decrease in the striatum may explain why adults are less effective at procedural learning. The process of receptor loss is called pruning because it reduces overexuberant synapses as a child matures. High synaptic density facilitates formation of new associations but may slow performance; pruning trades plasticity for speed

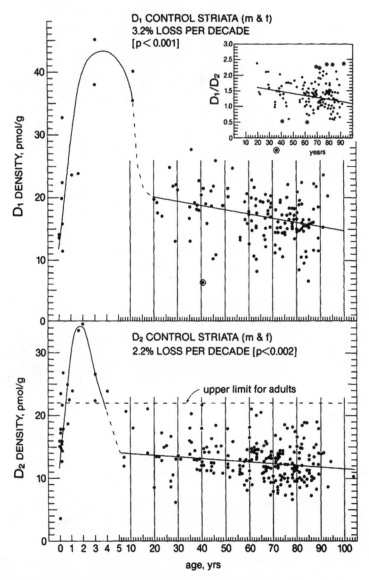

Figure 6.4. Ontogenetic changes of DA 1 and 2 receptor densities in the dorsal striatum, in humans. From Seeman et al. (1987, p. 401). Reprinted with the permission of Wiley-Liss, Inc., a subsidiary of John Wiley & Sons, Inc.

(Teicher, Andersen, and Hostetter, 1995). There is a general tradeoff in a neural system between processing speed and learning capacity.

Receptor elimination occurs during the transition to adulthood, in conjunction with a shift in primary developmental tasks from skill acquisition to performance.

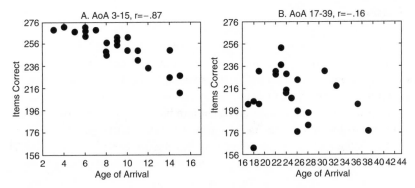

Figure 6.5. Age of arrival and ultimate proficiency in a language negatively correlate. From Johnson and Newport (1989, p. 80). Reprinted with the permission of Elsevier Limited.

Pruning occurs at the earliest age in the striatum, possibly because of the relatively early development of motor patterns. Protracted DA-receptor pruning in the PFC may have some relation to the delayed development of the PFC and later acquisition of higher-level abstract thinking.

The high density of DA receptors in the striatum and the PFC until puberty may be one of the reasons prepuberty learners acquire language better than their older counterparts. Comparison between the trajectory of language-acquisition ability and that of DA-level change is illuminating. Figure 6.5 is taken from Johnson and Newport (1989); it has a very close resemblance to Figure 6.4. An immediate implication of the comparison is that Johnson and Newport's Figure may be a behavioral manifestation of a biological substrate captured in Figure 6.4.

Ontogenetic Changes in Opiate Level

As discussed in chapter 5, μ-opiate (μO) is a neuromodulator that modulates the efficacy of other fast neurotransmitters, such as GABA and glutamate. It is critically involved in the process of interaction, especially at the phase of consummation. Unfortunately, there has not been much research on its maturational changes. However, it can be said that as DA receptors go through the overproduction and pruning, μO receptor (μOR) expression and density also undergo developmental changes. The μOR densities are high in the early postnatal period, when the infant spends most time with his caretaker (Pintar and Scott, 1993). Waterhouse, Fein, and Modahl (1996) also observed, "In normal infants brain levels of opiates at birth are 100 times greater than levels later in life" (p. 477). The μOR is modulated by neuropeptides such as vasopressin and oxytocin. The two are produced by the arcuate nucleus in the hypothalamus and project to the amygdala and the bed nucleus of the stria terminalis. According to Insel and Winslow (1998), both are also overproduced initially and then pruned later around weaning.

Conclusions

More research is needed on the developmental changes undergone by neural systems involved in interactional instinct. However, there are enough data to warrant our argument that children are better equipped with neural resources for interaction and, therefore, for language learning. Children are innately oriented to interaction with conspecifics and therefore have an advantage over adults in language learning. One of the major questions in the field of linguistics is why children inevitably become proficient language users when adults rarely do. This may be answered at least partly by the neural changes described above.

Conclusion: Broader Implications
of the Interactional Instinct

Several issues related to the notion of the interactional instinct have been raised as potential criticisms of the theory. Other issues reflect expansions on the theory and its relationship to other ideas.

Autonomous Grammar

Questions have been raised about how the theory of the interactional instinct handles the notion of autonomous grammar. In traditional linguistics, grammar is seen as the neural module that operates independently of intelligence and other aspects of cognition. Williams syndrome and certain cases of mental retardation have been viewed as evidence for this dissociation.

Williams Syndrome

Children with Williams syndrome have been reported to have a dissociation between mental ability and grammatical ability. These children are described as having normal language with severe mental retardation. Jones (2006) examined the language of Williams syndrome children and studied their grammatical abilities in narratives and conversations. In the narratives, she examined referential structures (determiners, pronouns, tense) as well as conjunctions. She compared her informants to both chronological-age-matched controls and to mental-age-matched controls. In Jones's research, as well as that of other investigators (Karmiloff-Smith et al., 1998; Krause and Penke, 2004), children with Williams syndrome performed on some aspects of grammar similarly to their age mates, but on other measures, they demonstrated language development that corresponded to controls who were chronologically much younger but equivalent in mental development. (For example, a child with Williams syndrome at the age of nine might perform similarly to a mental-age control at the age of five.) Both the number and the types of grammatical errors made by children with Williams syndrome were similar to those of the mental-age-matched controls but not to the chronological-age-matched controls. The children with Williams syndrome used complex structures in proportions that were equal to both the mental-age and the chronological-age controls. With respect to the cohesion elements, the performance of children with Williams syndrome was similar to that of the mental-age comparison group (on pronouns, determiners, and tense). On conjunctions, they performed similarly to chronological-age-matched controls. In general, the children appeared to reflect the linguistic abilities of mental-age mates rather than chronological-age mates. In the research literature, it is also argued that children with Williams syndrome acquire language in the same sequence as those without it but at a much slower rate.

Given these findings, language acquisition would seem to be governed not by UG but by general cognitive development, because the cognitive development of children with Williams syndrome apparently constrains their linguistic development. Therefore, they provide evidence that language and cognition are interdependent. In fact, these results indicate that in Williams syndrome, there is no clear dissociation between grammatical development and mental development. Jones concludes that children with Williams syndrome do not constitute a population that can be used to support the UG claim that grammar is constrained by a mental mechanism that is independent of general intelligence.

With respect to Williams syndrome, then, the simple story is that if grammatical development is delayed because of the children's reduced cognitive development, then we cannot argue that grammar is independent of cognition, intelligence, or mental ability.

In addition, Meyer-Lindenberg, Mervis, and Berman (2006) argue that recent research shows that "language abilities in WS, although a relative strength compared to visuospatial construction abilities, are not intact, and cognitive impairment in the WS is not severe. Emphasizing interdependence, and not modularity, in people with the WS, both vocabulary and grammatical abilities are strongly correlated with verbal working memory, nonverbal reasoning ability and the visuospatial constructive ability to an even greater degree than for the general population" (p. 388).

Mental Retardation

In exploring whether grammar is independent of cognition, Curtis (personal communication, 2005) argues that the best case can be made on certain mentally retarded children. She reports on three of them (Curtis, 1994). The etiology of the retardation is not known for two of the subjects. The third incurred developmental problems after he suffered anoxia during birth. The IQs of two of the subjects were reported; one was between 41 and 44, and the other was between 50 and 56. All three subjects had relatively preserved grammar, with extensive deficiencies in semantics and pragmatics. The assumption seems to be that the brains of these mentally retarded children were normal for grammar but deficient for general cognition and for the semantic and pragmatic aspects of language. But what is the justification for assuming that the neural mechanisms subserving language were normal? Schumann et al. (2004) have argued that because all brains are different at both the macro and micro levels, individuals can have different abilities, and sometimes the differences are substantial. In other words, certain individuals can have neural hypertrophies that provide them with mental or physical talents, and others can have neural hypotrophies that leave them with mental or physical deficits.

An example comes from research on Einstein's brain, which was preserved after his death. Diamond, Scheibel, Murphy, and Harvey (1985) have shown that Einstein had many more glial cells (support structures for neurons) than age-matched controls had. Witelson, Kigar, and Harvey (1999, as summarized in Schumann et al., 2004) showed that

> the posterior limbs of the Sylvian fissure do not exist and the fissure joins postcentral sulcus. This architecture eliminates the parietal operculum which, in normal brains, lies between the postcentral sulcus and the posterior segment of the lateral sulcus. In addition, Einstein's parietal lobes were symmetrical whereas those of most humans lack this symmetry. Each hemisphere of his brain was 15% larger than in controls, and his parietal lobes were wider and more spherical than normal. The elimination of the parietal operculum expanded the area of the inferior parietal lobule in which visual, somatosensory, and auditory stimuli are integrated and where visuospatial and mathematical cognition as well as movement imagery are processed. (Schumann et al., p. 12)

Witelson, Kigar, and Harvey suggest that this hypertrophy had functional consequences that allowed Einstein to cognize creatively in domains related to his scientific contributions.

Therefore, it is possible that the retarded individual brains were not normal with respect to grammar. They may have had neural hypertrophies that supported their grammatical performance. It is a priori belief in a neurally instantiated UG that forces generative linguists to assume that the neural substrate for language in retarded individuals is identical to that of normal individuals. If grammar is not linked to a specific universal substrate, then we can imagine that each of the three mentally retarded persons had a structurally different substrate that supported his or her grammatical abilities.

This possibility is seen to be even more probable in later research by Curtis and deBode (2003). They studied the acquisition of language (English) by eight children who had undergone left hemispherectomies. They focused on the manifestations of UG in the acquisition process: inflectional elements, determiner elements, null subjects, and complement phrases. Four of the children were at an early stage of language development (the root-infinitive stage), and four were at a more advanced point in learning. Both groups were compared with mean length of utterance-matched normal children. The researchers discovered that these children displayed normal language development (UG-constrained learning by the younger children and relearning by the older children). The authors concluded that language acquisition by the isolated right hemisphere is governed by UG constraints.

If we look at these results from the theoretical perspective of UG, the left hemisphere and the right hemisphere in children appear to be identically equipped to acquire language. It would appear that both hemispheres are capable of learning autonomous syntax, but in almost all cases, only the left hemisphere has to do it. From a biological perspective, however, this observation raises some questions. UG is supposed to be a genetically based neural module that is uniquely dedicated to grammar. Why would the module be available bilaterally? Another perhaps more plausible explanation is that language can be acquired in various neural tissue, and that tissue does not have to have domain-specific wiring for language.

The Anthropological Veto

The theory of interactional instinct is vulnerable to a potential anthropological veto. It is sometimes claimed that there are societies in which parents do not interact with children, or they interact very differently from parents in industrialized societies. Ethnographies of caregiver-infant interaction in such societies are not abundant, but where they have been undertaken, the reports indicate that there may be less face-to-face interaction between parents and children. However, the parents do not ignore their children. In the Kaluli population studied by Schieffelin (Ochs and Schieffelin, 1986) in New Guinea, language socialization takes place more often in multiparty interaction, where caregivers orient children to interaction with other members of the community:

> [I]f one defines language input as the language directed to the child then it is reasonable to say that for Kaluli children who have not yet begun to speak there is very little. However, this does not mean that the Kaluli children grow up in an impoverished verbal environment and do not learn how to speak. Quite the opposite is true. The verbal environment of the infant is rich and varied, and from the very beginning the infant is surrounded by adults and older children who spend a great deal of time talking to one another. Furthermore, as the infant develops and begins to crawl and engage in play activities and other independent actions, these actions are frequently referred to, described, and commented upon by

members of the household, especially older children, to each other. Thus the ongoing activities of the preverbal child are an important topic of talk among members of the household, and this talk about the here-and-now of the infant is available to the infant, though it is not talk addressed the infant. (pp. 291–292)

Ochs and Schieffelin report that in Kaluli society, when children begin to talk, their caregivers model what the children should say and instruct them to "say it like that" (p. 292). This research indicates that the child's tendency to interact with conspecifics and to become like them may be responded to in different ways. The study of how the interactional instinct is manifest in various societies becomes a research area for elaborating the theory.

But it must be noted that some aspects of child-caregiver interaction appear to be universal. Bryant and Barrett (2008) conducted research to explore the universality of speech generated by adults and directed to infants (infant-directed speech). They recorded the prosody of English-speaking mothers expressing various intentions as though they were speaking to their infants (prohibition, approval, comfort, and attention). They also recorded these mothers expressing the same intentions as they would to adults. The intonation patterns (without words or any kind of semantic reference) were then played to adults in a community of South American hunter-horticulturalists called the Shuar. The Shuar adults were able to distinguish infant-directed from adult-directed speech, and they were also able to identify the intentions expressed by the prosody.

The Pedagogical Stance

Gergely and Csibra (2006; see also Csibra and Gergely, 2005) have proposed that humans maintain a pedagogical stance. By this they mean that humans have an innate tendency to learn from and to teach conspecifics. In other words, humans look to one another as sources of information and see themselves as recipients of novel information. We have evolved a dedicated communicative system which inclines us and allows us to both impart and acquire novel cultural information from conspecifics "by actively seeking out, attending to, and being specially receptive to such communicative manifestations of knowledgeable others" (Gergely and Csibra, 2006, p. 9). They describe such knowledge transfer as taking place in "pedagogical interactions" (Csibra and Gergely, 2005, p. 249). In these interactions, the teacher must indicate his or her pedagogical intentions by using ostensive signals, such as eye contact, gaze shift, and pointing. Even infant learners must recognize that these signals index the manifestation of new cultural information that is important for them to learn. The infants respond with interest and attention, which allow them to identify the behavior that carries the new information and facilitates their acquisition of it.

It is clear that the interactional instinct is closely related to Gergely and Csibra's notion of pedagogical stance. A possible integration of the two perspectives might be that humans' interactional instinct enables them to attach, bond, and affiliate with conspecifics in order to become like them. The instinct also enables universal language acquisition, which enormously facilitates the pedagogy. Since humans have a very lengthy period of infancy, childhood, juvenility, and adolescence, during which their brains continue to develop, the pedagogical stance supports the socialization, enculturation, and education required for them to become members of the cultural group.

As evidence of adaptation for pedagogy in human infants, infants are prepared for instruction because they are born with tendencies for eye contact, contingent responsivity, and receptiveness to infant-directed speech. When newborns seek interaction with conspecifics, they are not just looking for faces; they are searching for teachers. Additionally, the infants' vocalizations elicit contingent vocalizations from caregiver conspecifics, and this interaction provides the infants with the information that conspecifics are attempting communication. Motherese signals that the communication is directed to the infant.

We might argue that eye contact, contingency, and motherese are components of the interactional instinct, which leads to language, which facilitates pedagogy.

Prodynorphin

All primates have a gene that produces a protein called prodynorphin. This protein serves as a building block for endorphins, opiates involved in the rewarding aspects of interpersonal interaction. There is a stretch of DNA on that gene that regulates the production of prodynorphin. Nonhuman primates have only one copy of this DNA regulation sequence, but humans have two to four copies. An analysis of 150 people around the world demonstrated that Europeans and East Africans have three copies, and people from China generally have two copies (Bower, 2005; Rockman et al., 2005). It is possible that because of the increased socialization demands on humans, we have evolved a more powerful opiate-producing system that may make interaction much more rewarding for us.

The Interactional Instinct in Other Animals

An interactional instinct seems to exist in other social animals. Our position is that all social animals have an interactional instinct commensurate with their socialization needs, but because humans have such prolonged infancy, childhood, juvenility, and adolescence, the socialization demands are extended. For this reason, the interactional instinct in humans may be much stronger and more elaborated than in other animals, even closely related primates.

Summary

Interactional instinct theory rejects the notion of autonomous grammar, and Williams syndrome and special cases of mental retardation do not provide a strong cases for the independence of grammatical abilities from general cognition. Interactional deficits in autism and the interactional hypertrophies in Williams syndrome are important arenas for gaining a fuller understanding of the interactional instinct. Finally, all animal species may have an interactional instinct commensurate with their socialization needs. However, mutations in the DNA regulatory mechanism for prodynorphin may have made interpersonal interaction especially rewarding for humans, and this reward may support the pedagogical interactions necessary for socializing, enculturating, and educating humans throughout their extended periods infancy, childhood, juvenility, and adolescence.

References

Abercrombie, E. D., Keefe, K. A., DiFrischia, D. S., and Zigmond, M. J. (1989). Differential effect of stress on in vivo dopamine release in striatum, nucleus accumbens, and medial frontal cortex. *Journal of Neurochemistry, 52*, 1655–1658.

Adamson, J., and Frick, J. (2003). The still-face: A history of shared experimental paradigm. *Infancy, 4*(4), 451–473.

Aggleton, J. (1992). *The Amygdala: Neurobiological Aspects of Emotion, Memory and Mental Dysfunction.* New York: Wiley-Liss.

Agren, G., Olsson, C., Uvnas-Moberg, K., and Lundeberg, T. (1997). Olfactory cues from an oxytocin-injected male rat can reduce energy loss in its cagemates. *NeuroReport, 8*, 2551–2555.

Aldridge, M., Stillman, R. D., and Bower, T. G. R. (2001). Newborn categorization of vowel like sounds. *Developmental Science, 4*, 220–232.

Allman, J. M. (1999). *Evolving Brain.* New York: Scientific American Library.

Als, H., and Brazelton, T. B. (1981). Assessment of the behavioral organization of a preterm and full-term infant. *Journal of the American Academy of Child Psychiatry, 20*, 239–263.

Als, H., Tronick, E., and Brazelton, T. B. (1980). Affective reciprocity and the development of autonomy: The study of a blind infant. *Journal of the American Academy of Child Psychiatry, 19*, 22–40.

Alsina, A. (2001). On the nonsemantic nature of argument structure. *Journal of Linguistics, 11*, 213–237.

Andersen, S. L., Thomson, A. T., Rutstein, M., Hostetter, J. C., and Teicher, M. H. (2000). Dopamine receptor pruning in prefrontal cortex during the periadolescent period in rats. *Synapse, 37*, 167–169.

Anderson, B., Vietze, P., and Dokecki, P. (1978). Interpersonal distance and vocal behavior in the mother-infant dyad. *Infant Behavior and Development, 1*, 381–391.

Atallah, H. E., Lopez-Paniagua, D., Rudy, J. W., and O'Reilly, R. C. (2007). Separate neural substrates for skill learning and performance in the ventral and dorsal striatum. *Nature Neuroscience, 10*, 126–131.

Avranel, E., and De Yong, N. (1991). Does object modeling elicit imitative-like gestures from young infants? *Journal of Experimental Child Psychology, 52*(1), 22–40.

Baird, G., Cass, H., and Slonims, V. (2003). Diagnosis of autism. *BMJ, 327*, 488–493.

Bakhtin, M. M. (1986). *Speech Genres and Other Late Essays.* Austin: University of Texas Press.

Bard, K. (1994). Evolutionary roots of intuitive parenting: Maternal competence in chimpanzees. *Early Development and Parenting, 3*, 19–28.

Bard, K. (1995). Parenting in primates. In M. Bornstein (Ed.), *Handbook of Parenting, Vol. 2* (pp. 27–58). Mahwah, NJ: Lawrence Erlbaum.

Bard, K. (1998). Social-experiential contributions to imitation and emotion in chimpanzees. In S. Braten (Ed.), *Intersubjective Communication and Emotion in Early Ontogeny* (pp. 208–227). Cambridge: Cambridge University Press.

Bard, K. (2003). Development of emotional expression in chimpanzees (Pan troglodytes). *Annual New York Academy of Sciences, 1000*, 88–90.

Bard, K., Platzman, K., Lester, B., and Suomi, S. (1992). Orientation to social and nonsocial stimuli in neonatal chimpanzees in humans. *Infant Behavior and Development, 15*, 43–56.

Barlow, H., and Mollon, J. D. (Eds.). (1982). *The Senses.* Cambridge: Cambridge University Press.

Batali, J. (1998). Computational simulations of the emergence of grammar. In J. R. Hurford, M. Studdert-Kennedy, and C. Knight (Eds.), *Approaches to the Evolution of Language* (pp. 405–426). Cambridge: Cambridge University Press.

Bates, E., Dale, P. S., and Thal, D. (1994). Individual differences and their implications for theories of language development. In P. Fletcher and B. MacWhinney (Eds.), *Handbook of Child Language* (pp.99–151). Oxford, UK: Basil Blackwell.

Bates, E., and Goodman, J. C. (1997). On the inseparability of grammar and the lexicon: Evidence from acquisition, aphasia, and real-time processing. *Language and Cognitive Processes, 12*, 507–586.

Bates, E., Thal, D., and Janowsky, J. (1992). Early language development and its neural correlates. In I. Rapin and S. Segalowitz (Eds.), *Handbook of Neuropsychology 7: Child Neuropsychology* (pp. 69–110). Amsterdam: Elsevier.

Bateson, M. C. (1979). The epigenesis of conversational interaction: A personal account of research development. In M. Bullowas (Ed.), *Before Speech: The Beginning of Human Communication* (pp. 63–77). London: Cambridge University Press.

Bavelas, J. B. (1999). Come the millennium. *Research on Language and Social Interaction, 32* (1/2), 5–10.

Bear, M. F., Connors, B. W., and Paradiso, M. A. (2006). *Neuroscience: Exploring the Brain:* Baltimore, MD: Lippincott Williams and Wilkins.

Becker, A. L. (1984). The linguistics of particularity: Interpreting superordination in a Javanese text. *Berkeley Linguistics Society, 10*, 425–436.

Beebe, B., Stern, D., and Jaffe, J. (1979). The kinesic rhythm of mother-infant interactions. In S. F. Aron and W. Siegman (Eds.), *Of Speech and Time* (pp. 23–34). Hillsdale, NJ: Lawrence Erlbaum.

Berger, P., and Luckmann, T. (1966). *The Social Construction of Reality: A Treatise in the Sociology of Knowledge.* New York: Doubleday.

Bickerton, D. (1981). *Roots of Language.* Ann Arbor, MI: Karoma.

Bickerton, D. (1984). The language bioprogram hypothesis. *Behavioral and Brain Sciences, 7*, 173–221.

Bickerton, D. (1990). *Language and Species.* Chicago: Chicago University Press.

Bie, P. (1980). Osmoreceptors, vasopressin, and control of renal water excretion. *Physiological Reviews, 60,* 961–1048.

Bielsky, I., Hu, S. B., Szegba, K. L., Westphal, H., and Young, L. (2004). Profound impairment in social recognition and reduction in anxiety-like behavior in vasopressin V1a receptor knockout mice. *Neuropsychopharmacology, 29,* 483–493.

Bielsky, I., and Young, L. (2004). Oxytocin, vaspressin, and social recognition in mammals. *Peptides 25*(9), 1565–1574.

Bijeljac-Babic, R., Bertocini, J., and Mehler, J. (1991). How do four-day-old infants categorize multisyllabic utterances? *Developmental Psychology, 29,* 711–721.

Bissiere, S., Humeau, Y., and Luthi, A. (2003). Dopamine gates LTP induction in lateral amygdala by suppressing feedforward inhibition. *Nature Neuroscience, 6,* 587–592.

Blass, E., Ganchrow, J. R., and Steiner, J. E. (1984). Classical conditioning in newborn humans 2–48 hours of age. *Infant Behavior and Development, 7,* 223–235.

Boukydis, C. F. Z. (1979). Adult response to infant cries. Unpublished doctoral dissertation. Pennsylvania State University, University Park.

Bower, B. (2005). DNA clues to our kind: Regulatory gene linked to human evolution. *Science News, 168*(22), 147.

Bower, T. G. (1977). *A Primer of Infant Development.* San Francisco: W. H. Freeman.

Bowlby, J. (1969). *Attachment and Loss, Vol. 1.* New York: Basic Books.

Brazelton, T., and Cramer, B. (1990). *The Earliest Relationship: Parents, Infants, and the Drama of Early Attachment.* Reading, PA: Addison-Wesley.

Brazelton, T., Koslowski, B., and Main, M. (1974). The origins of reciprocity: The early mother-infant interaction. In M. Lewis and L. Rosenblum (Eds.), *The Effect of the Infant on Its Caregiver* (pp. 49–76). New York: John Wiley.

Brazelton, T. B. (1981). Precursors for the development of emotions in early infancy. In H. Kellerman (Ed.), *Emotion, Theory, Research and Experience, Vol. 2* (pp. 33–55). New York: Academic Press.

Briggs, J., and Peat, F. D. (1989). *Turbulent Mirror.* New York: Harper and Row.

Bromberger, S. (2002). Chomsky's revolution. *New York Review of Books,* April 25.

Bryant, G. A., and Barrett, H. C. (2007). Recognizing intentions in infant-directed speech: Evidence for universals. *Psychological Science, 18*(8), 746–751.

Bryant, G. A., and Barrett, H. C. (2008). Vocal emotion recognition across disparate cultures. *Journal of Cognition and Culture, 8*(1–2), 135–148.

Buccino, G., Binkofski, F., Fink, G. R., Fadiga, L., Fogassi, L., Gallese, V., Seitz, R. J., Zilles, K., Rizzolatti, G., and Freund, H. J. (2001). Action observation activates premotor and parietal areas in a somatotropic manner: An fMRI study. *European Journal of Neuroscience, 13,* 400–404.

Buccino, G., Vogt, S., Ritzl, A., Fink, G. R., Zilles, K., Freund, H. J., and Rizzolatti, G. (2004). Neural circuits underlying imitation of hand actions: An event related fMRI study. *Neuron, 42,* 323–334.

Bybee, J. and Hopper, P. J. (2001). Introduction to frequency and the emergence of linguistic structure. In J. Bybee and P. J. Hopper (Eds.), *Frequency and the Emergence of Linguistic Structure* (p. 126). Amsterdam: John Benjamins.

Cairns, G., and Butterfield, E. C. (1975). Assessing infants' auditory functioning. In B. Friedlander et al. (Eds.), *Exceptional Infant, Vol. 2* (pp. 84–108). New York: Brunner/Mazel.

Calvin, W. H., and Bickerton, D. (2000). *Lingua ex Machina: Reconciling Darwin and Chomsky with the Human Brain.* Cambridge, MA: MIT Press.

Carden, G., and Stewart, W. (1988). Binding theory, bioprogram, and creolization: Evidence from Haitian Creole. *Journal of Pidgin and Creole Languages, 3,* 1–67.

Carpenter, G. C. (1973). Differential response to mother and stranger within the first month of life. *Bulletin of British Psychological Society, 26,* 138.

Carpenter, G. C., Tecce, J. J., Stechler, G., and Freidmann, S. (1970). Differential visual behavior to human and humanoid faces in early infancy. *Merrill-Palmer Quarterly, 16,* 91–108.

Carr, L., Iacoboni, M., Dubeau, M., Mazziotta, J., and Lenzi, G. (2003). Neural mechanisms of empathy in humans: A relay from neural systems for imitation to limbic areas. *Proceedings of the National Academy of Sciences, 100*(9), 5497–5502.

Carstairs-McCarthy, A. (1998). Synonymy avoidance, phonology and the origin of syntax. In J. R. Hurford, M. Studdert-Kennedy, and C. Knight (Eds.), *Approaches to the Evolution of Language* (pp. 279–296). Cambridge: Cambridge University Press.

Carter, R., and McCarthy, M. (2002). *Exploring Spoken English.* Cambridge: Cambridge University Press.

Carter, R., and McCarthy, M. (2004). Talking, creating: Interactional language, creativity, and context. *Applied Linguistics, 25*(1), 62–88.

Chafe, W. (1985). Linguistic differences produced by differences between speaking and writing. In D. R. Olsen, N. Torrance, and A. Hilyard (Eds.), *Literacy, Language, and Learning* (pp. 105–123). London: Cambridge University Press.

Chafe, W. (1987). Cognitive constraints on information flow. In R. Tomlin (Ed.), *Coherence and Grounding in Discourse* (pp. 21–51). Amsterdam: John Benjamins.

Chafe, W. (1994). *Discourse, Consciousness, and Time: The Flow and Displacement of Conscious Experience in Speaking and Writing.* Chicago: University of Chicago Press.

Chafe, W., and Tannen, D. (1987). The relation between written and spoken language. *Annual Review of Anthropology, 16,* 383–407.

Chapillon, P., Patin, V., Roy, V., Vincent, A., and Caston, J. (2002). Effects of pre- and postnatal stimulation on developmental, emotional, and cognitive aspects in rodents: A review. *Developmental Psychobiology, 41*(4), 373–387.

Charlesworth, W., and Kreutzer, M. A. (1973). Facial expressions of infants and children. In P. Ekman (Ed.), *Darwin and Facial Expressions* (pp. 91–168). New York: Academic Press.

Chipere, N. (1998). Real language users. Retrieved April 3, 2006, from http://cogprints.org/712/00/real.PDF.

Chomsky, N. (1957). *Syntactic Structures.* The Hague/Paris: Mouton.

Chomsky, N. (1975). *Reflections on Language.* New York: Pantheon.

Chomsky, N. (1991). Linguistics and cognitive science: Problems and mysteries. In A. Kasher (Ed.), *The Chomskyan Turn* (pp. 26–53). Cambridge, MA: Blackwell.

Chomsky, N. (2002). Chomsky's revolution: An exchange in response to Chomsky's revolution. *New York Review of Books,* April 25.

Chomsky, N., and Lasnik, H. (1993). The theory of principles and parameters. In J. Jacobs, A. von Stechow, W. Sternefeld, and T. Vannemann (Eds.), *Syntax: An International Handbook of Contemporary Research, Vol. 1* (pp. 506–569). Berlin: Walter de Gruyter.

Christophe, A., Gout, A., Peperkamp, S., and Morgan, J. (2003). Discovering words in the continuous speech stream: The role of prosody. *Journal of Phonetics, 31,* 585–598.

Christophe, A., Mehler, J., and Sebastian-Galles, N. (2001). Perception of prosodic boundary correlates by newborn infants. *Infancy, 2*(3), 385–394.

Clark, H. H., and Wilkes-Gibbs, D. (1986). Referring as a collaborative process. *Cognition, 22*(1), 1–39.

Cochin, S., Barthelemy, C., Roux, S., and Martineau, J. (1998). Perception of motion and qEEG activity in human adults. *Electroencephalography and Clinical Neurophysiology, 107*, 287–295.

Cochin, S., Barthelemy, C., Roux, S., and Martineau, J. (1999). Observation and execution of movement: similarities demonstrated by qualified electroencephalography. *European Journal of Neuroscience, 11*, 1839–1842.

Cohn, J., and Tronick, E. (1983). Three-month-old infants' reaction to simulated maternal depression. *Child Development, 54*, 185–193.

Comrie, B. (1992). Before complexity. In J. A. Hawkins and M. Gell-Mann (Eds.), *The Evolution of Human Languages.* Redwood City, CA: Addison-Wesley.

Condon, W. (1977). A primary phaze in the organization of infant responding. In H. R. Schaffer (Ed.), *Studies in Mother-Infant Interaction* (pp. 153–176). London: Academic Press.

Condon, W. S. (1980). Cultural microrhythms. In M. Davis (Ed.), *Interaction Rhythm: Proceedings of the First Annual Research Conference of the Institute for Nonverbal Communication Research, Teachers College, Columbia University, 1979* (pp. 53–76). New York: Human Science Press.

Condon, W. S., and Sander, L. W. (1974a). Neonate movement is synchronized with adult speech: Interactional participation and language acquisition. *Science, 183*, 99–101.

Condon, W. S., and Sander, L. W. (1974b). Synchrony demonstrated between movements of the neonate and adult speech. *Child Development, 45*, 456–462.

Conel, J. L. (1963). *The Postnatal Development of the Human Cerebral Cortex, Vols. 3–6.* Cambridge, MA: Harvard University Press.

Contini-Morava, E. (1995). Introduction: On linguistic sign theory. In E. Contini-Morava and B. S. Goldberg (Eds.), *Meaning as Explanation: Advances in Linguistic Sign Theory* (pp. 1–40). Berlin: Mouton de Gruyter.

Contini-Morava, E., Kirsner, R. S., and Rodriguez-Bachiller, B. (Eds.). (2004). *Cognitive and Communicative Approaches to Linguistic Analysis.* Amsterdam: John Benjamins.

Contini-Morava, E., and Tobin, Y. (Eds.) (2000). *Between Grammar and Lexicon.* Amsterdam: John Benjamins.

Conway, C., and Christiansen, M. (2002). Sequential learning through touch, vision, and audition. In *Proceedings of the 24th Annual Conference of the Cognitive Science Society* (pp. 220–225). Mahwah, NJ: Lawrence Erlbaum.

Coupland, J., and Gwyn, R. (Eds.). (2003). *Discourse, the Body, and Identity.* New York: Palgrave Macmillan.

Crown, C. L., Feldstein, S., Jasnow, M., Beebe, B., and Jaffe, J. (2002). The cross-modal coordination of interpersonal timing: Six-week-old infants' gaze with adults' vocal behavior. *Journal of Psycholinguistic Research, 31*(1), 1–23.

Csibra, G., and Gergely, G. (2005). Social learning and social cognition: The case for pedagogy. In M. H. Johnson and Y. Munakata (Eds.), *Processes of Change in Brain and Cognitive Development: Attention and Performance, XXI* (pp. 249–274). Oxford: Oxford University Press.

Csiffary, A., Ruttner, Z., Toth, Z., and Palkovits, M. (1992). Oxytocin nerve fibers innervate B-endorphin neurons in the arcuate nucleus of the rat hypothalamus. *Neuroendocrinology, 56,* 429–435.

Curtis, S. (1994). Language as a cognitive system: Its independence and selected vulnerability. In C. Otero (Ed.), *Noam Chomsky Critical Assessments, Vol. IV: From Artificial Intelligence to Theology: Chomsky's Impact on Contemporary Thought, Tome I.* London: Routledge.

Curtis, S., and deBode, S. (2003). How normal is grammatical development in the right hemisphere following hemispherectomy? The root infinitive stage and beyond. *Brain and Language, 86,* 193–206.

Dahlin, S., Hu, X.-T., Xue, C.-J., and Wolf, M. (1994). Lesions of prefrontal cortex or amygdala, but not fimbria fornix, prevent sensitization of amphetamine-stimulated horizontal locomotor activity. *Abstracts of the Society for Neuroscience, 20,* 1621.

Damasio, A. R. (1994). *Descartes' Error: Emotion, Reason, and the Human Brain.* New York: G. P. Putnam's Sons.

Dapretto, M., Davies, M., Pfeifer, J., Scott, A., Sigman, M., Bookheimer, S., and Iacoboni, M. (2006). Understanding emotions in others: Mirror neuron dysfunction in children with autism spectrum disorders. *National Review of Neurosciences, 9*(1), 28–30.

Deacon, T. W. (1997). *The Symbolic Species: The Co-evolution of Language and the Brain.* New York: W. W. Norton.

Deacon, T. W. (2003). Universal grammar and semiotic constraints. In M. H. Christiansen and S. Kirby (Eds.), *Language Evolution* (pp. 111–139). Oxford: Oxford University Press.

De Boer, B. (2000). Emergence of sound systems through self-organization. In C. Knight, M. Studdert-Kennedy, and J. R. Hurford (Eds.), *The Evolutionary Emergence of Language* (pp. 146–160). Cambridge: Cambridge University Press.

De Haan, M., Pascalis, O., and Johnson, M. (2002). Specialization of neural mechanisms underlying face recognition in human infants. *Journal of Cognitive Neuroscience, 14*(2), 199–209.

DeHaene, S. (1997). *The Number Sense: How the Mind Creates Mathematics.* Oxford: Oxford University Press.

Deigo, M. A., Field, T., and Hernandez-Reif, M. (2005). Vagal activity, gastric motility, and weight gain in massaged preterm neonates. *Journal of Pediatrics, 147*(1), 50–55.

Denenberg, V. H., Woodcock, J. M., and Rosenberg, K. M. (1968). Long-term effects of preweaning and postweaning free-environment experience on rats' problem-solving behavior. *Journal of Comparative and Physiological Psychology, 66,* 533–535.

Depue, R. A., and Morrone-Strupinsky, J. V. (2005). A neurobehavioral model of affiliative bonding: Implications for conceptualizing a human trait of affiliation. *Behavioral and Brain Sciences, 28*(3), 313–350.

De Ruiter, J. P., Mitterer, H., and Enfield, N. J. (2006). Projecting the end of a speaker's turn: A cognitive cornerstone of conversation. *Language, 82*(3), 515–535.

De Waal, F. (1989). *Peacemaking among Chimpanzees.* Cambridge, MA: Harvard University Press.

Diamond, M. C., Scheibel, A. B., Murphy, J. G. M., and Harvey, T. (1985). On the brain of a scientist: Albert Einstein. *Experimental Neurology, 98,* 198–204.

Dixon, J., Yogman, M. W., Tronick, E., Als, H., Adamson, L., and Brazelton, T. B. (1981). Early social interaction of parents and strangers. *Journal of the American Academy of Child Psychiatry, 20,* 32–52.

Donald, M. (1998). Mimesis and the executive suite: Missing links in language evolution. In J. R. Hurford, M. Studdert-Kennedy, and C. Knight (Eds.), *Approaches to the Evolution of Language* (pp. 44–67). Cambridge: Cambridge University Press.

Drew, P., and Heritage, J. (1992). Analyzing talk at work: An introduction. In P. Drew and J. Heritage (Eds.), *Talk at Work* (pp. 3–65). Cambridge: Cambridge University Press.

Dunbar, R. (1998). Theory of mind and the evolution of language. In J. R. Hurford, M. Studdert-Kennedy, and C. Knight (Eds.), *Approaches to the Evolution of Language* (pp. 92–110). Cambridge: Cambridge University Press.

Eckerman, C., Oehler, J., Medvin, M., and Hannan, T. (1994). Premature newborns as social partners before term age. *Infant Behavior and Development, 17*, 55–70.

Eggins, S., and Slade, D. (1997). *Analysing Casual Conversation*. London: Cassell.

Eimas, P. (1975). Auditory and phonetic coding of the cues for speech: Discrimination of the [r-l] distinction by young infants. *Perception and Psychophysics, 18*, 341–347.

Eimas, P., and Miller, J. L. (1980). Discrimination of information for manner of articulation by young infants. *Infant Behavior and Development, 3*, 367–375.

Eimas, P., Siqueland, E. R., Jusczyk, P., and Vigorito, J. (1971). Speech perception in infants. *Science, 171*, 303–306.

Eisenberg, R. (1975). *Auditory Competence in Early Life: The Roots of Communicative Behavior*. Baltimore, MD: University Park Press.

Eisenberger, N. I., and Lieberman, M. D. (2004). "Why it hurts to be left out": The neurocognitive overlap between physical and social pain. *Trends in Cognitive Science, 8*, 294–300.

Ellis, N. C. (2002). Frequency effects in language processing: A review with implications for theories of implicit and explicit language acquisition. *Studies in Second Language Acquisition, 24*, 143–188.

Elman, J., Bates, E., Johnson, M., Karmiloff-Smith, A., Parisi, D., and Plunkett, K. (1996). *Rethinking Innateness: A Connectionist Perspective on Development*. Cambridge, MA: MIT Press.

Elman, J. L. (1993). Learning and development in neural networks: The importance of starting small. *Cognition, 48*, 71–99.

Escorihuela, R. M., Tobena, A., and Fernandez-Teruel, A. (1994). Environmental enrichment reverses the detrimental action of early inconsistent stimulation and increases the beneficial effects of postnatal handling on shuttlebox learning in adult rats. *Behavioural Brain Research, 61*, 169–173.

Everett, D. L. (2005). Cultural constraints on grammar and cognition in Piraha: Another look at the *design features* of human language. *Current Anthropology, 46*(4), 621–646.

Everitt, B., and Robbins, T. (1992). Amygdala-ventral striatal interactions and reward related processes. In J. Aggleton (Ed.) *The Amygdala: Neurobiological Aspects of Emotion, Memory and Mental Dysfunction* (pp. 401–483). New York: Wiley-Liss.

Fabre-Nys, C., Ohkura, A., and Kendrick, K. M. (1997). Male faces and odours evoke differential patterns of neurochemical release in the mediobasal hypothalamus of the ewe during oestrus: An insight into sexual motivation? *European Journal of Neuroscience, 9*, 1666–1677.

Fadiga, L., Buccino, G., and Rizzolatti, G. (2002). Speech listening specifically modulates the excitability of tongue muscles: A TMS study. *European Journal of Neuroscience, 15*, 399–402.

Fadiga, L., Fogassi, L., Pavesi, G., and Rizzolatti, G. (1995). Motor facilitation during action observation: A magnetic stimulation study. *Journal of Neurophysiology, 73*, 2608–2611.

Fantz, R. L. (1963). Pattern vision in newborn infants. *Science, 140*, 296–297.

Farroni, T., Csibra, G., Simion, F., and Johnson, M. (2002). Eye contact detection in humans from birth. *Proceedings of the National Academy of Sciences, 99*, 9602–9605.

Farroni, T., Massaccesi, S., Pividori, D., and Johnson, M. (2004). Gaze following in newborns. *Infancy, 5*(1), 39–60.

Ferber, S. G., Kuint, J., Weller, A., Feldman, R., Dollberg, S., Arbel, E., et al. (2002). Massage therapy by mothers and trained professionals enhances weight gain in preterm infants. *Early Human Development, 67*, 37–45.

Ferguson, J., Aldag, M., Insel, T., and Young, L. (2001). Oxytocin in the medial amygdala is essential for social recognition in the mouse. *Journal of Neuroscience, 21*(20), 8278–8285.

Ferguson, J., Young, L. J., Hearn, E. F., Matzuk, M. M., Insel, T. R., and Winslow, J. T. (2000). Social amnesia in mice lacking the oxytocin gene. *Nature Genetics, 25*, 284–288.

Ferrari, P. F., Gallese, V., Rizzolatti, G., and Fogassi, L. (2003). Mirror neurons responding to the observation of ingestive and communicative mouth actions in the monkey ventral premotor cortex. *European Journal of Neuroscience, 17*, 1703–1714.

Field, T. (1984). Early interactions between infants and their postpartum depressed mothers. *Infant Behavior and Development, 7*, 517–522.

Field, T. (1985). Neonatal perception of people: Maturational and individual differences. In T. Field and N. Fox (Eds.), *Social Perception in Infants*. Norwood, NJ: Ablex.

Field, T. (2001). Massage therapy facilitates weight gain in preterm infants. *Current Directions in Psychological Science, 10*, 51–54.

Field, T., Woodson, R., Cohen, D., Greenberg, R., Garcia, R., and Collins, K. (1983). Discrimination and imitation of facial expressions by term and preterm neonates. *Infant Behavior and Development, 6*, 485–490.

Field, T., Woodson, R., Greenberg, R., and Cohen, D. (1982). Discrimination and imitation of facial expressions by neonates. *Science, 218*, 179–181.

Fisher, J., and Aslin, R. (2002). Statistical learning of new visual feature combinations by infants. *Proceedings of the National Academy of Sciences, 99*(24), 15822–15826.

Fitch, T., Houser, M., and Chomsky, N. (2005). The evolution of the language faculty: Clarifications and implications. *Cognition, 97*, 179–210.

Fleming, A. S., O'Day, D. H., and Kraemer, G. W. (1999). Neurobiology of mother-infant interactions: Experience and central nervous system plasticity across development and generations. *Neuroscience and Biobehavioral Reviews, 23*, 673–685.

Fodor, J. A., and Bever, T. (1965). The psychological reality of linguistic elements. *Journal of Verbal Learning and Verbal Behavior, 4*, 414–420.

Fodor, J. A., Bever, T., and Garrett, M. (1976). *The Psychology of Language*. New York: McGraw-Hill.

Fogassi, L., Ferrari, P. F., Gesierich, B., Rozzi, S., Chersi, F., and Rizzolatti, G. (2005). Parietal lobe: From action understanding to intention understanding. *Science, 308*, 662–667.

Fontaine, R. (1984). Imitative skills between birth and six months. *Infant Behavior and Development, 7*, 323–333.

Ford, C. E. (2004). Contingency and units in interaction. *Discourse Studies, 6*(1), 27–52.

Ford, C. E., and Fox, B. A. (1996). Interactional motivations for reference formulation: *He* had. *This* guy had, a beautiful, thirty-two Olds. In B. A. Fox (Ed.), *Studies in Anaphora* (pp. 145–168). Amsterdam: Benjamins.

Ford, C. E., Fox, B. A., and Thompson, S. A. (2002a). Constituency and the grammar of turn increments. In C. E. Ford, B. A. Fox, and S. A. Thompson (Eds.), *The Language of Turn and Sequence* (pp. 14–38). Oxford: Oxford University Press.

Ford, C. E., Fox, B. A., and Thompson, S. A. (2002b). Introduction. In C. E. Ford, B. A. Fox, and S. A. Thompson (Eds.), *The Language of Turn and Sequence* (pp. 3–13). Oxford: Oxford University Press.

Ford, C. E., and Thompson, S. (1996). Interactional units in conversation: Syntactic, intonational, and pragmatic resources for the management of turns. In E. Ochs, E. A. Schegloff, and S. A. Thompson (Eds.), *Interaction and Grammar* (pp. 134–184). Cambridge: Cambridge University Press.

Fox, B. (1999). Directions in research: Language and the body. *Research on Language and Social Interaction, 32*(1/2), 51–59.

Fox, B. A., Hayashi, M., and Jasperson, R. (1996). Resources and repair: A cross-linguistic study of syntax and repair. In E. Ochs, E. A. Schegloff, and S. A. Thompson (Eds.), *Interaction and Grammar* (pp. 185–237). Cambridge: Cambridge University Press.

Fox, B. A., Jurafsky, D., Michaelis, L. A. (Eds.). (1999). *Cognition and Function in Language*. Stanford, CA: Center for the Study of Language and Information.

Fox, B. A., and Thompson, S. A. (1990). On formulating reference: An interactional approach to relative clauses in English conversation. *Papers in Pragmatics, 4*(1/2), 183–196.

Fox, C., Merali, Z., and Harrison, C. (2006). Therapeutic and protective effect of environmental enrichment against psychogenic and neurogenic stress. *Behavioural Brain Research, 175*(1), 1–8.

Fraiberg, S. (1974). Blind infants and their mothers: An examination of the sign system. In L. R. M. Lewis (Ed.), *The Effects of the Infant on Its Caregiver* (pp. 215–232). New York: John Wiley.

Freedle, R., and Lewis, M. (1977). Prelinguistic conversation. In L. R. M. Lewis (Ed.), *Interaction, Conversation and the Development of Language, Vol. 5* (pp. 157–186). New York: John Wiley.

Friederici, A., and Wessels, J. M. I. (1993). Phonotactic knowledge of word boundaries and its use in infant speech-perception. *Perception and Psychophysics, 54*, 287–295.

Frijda, N. H. (1986). *The Emotions*. Cambridge: Cambridge University Press.

Gaffan, D. (1992). Amygdala and the memory of reward. In J. Aggleton (Ed.), *The Amygdala: Neurobiological Aspects of Emotion, Memory and Mental Dysfunction* (pp. 471–483). New York: Wiley-Liss.

Gallese, V. (2006). Intentional attunement: A neurophysiological perspective on social cognition and its disruption in autism. *Cognitive Brain Research, 1079*(1), 15–24.

Gardner, B., and Gardner, R. A. (1989). Prelinguistic development of children and chimpanzees. *Human Evolution, 4*, 433–460.

Gardner, R. C., and Lambert, W. E. (1972). *Attitudes and Motivation in Second-Language Learning*. Rowley, MA: Newbury House.

Gelbard, H. A., Teicher, M. H., Faedda, J. G., and Baldessarini, R. J. (1989). Postnatal development of dopamine D1 and D2 receptor sites in rat striatum. *Brain Research, 49*, 123–130.

Gell-Mann, M. (1995). What is complexity? *Complexity, 1*(1), 16–19.

Gergely, G., and Csibra, G. (2006). Sylvia's recipe: The role the imitation and pedagogy in the transmission of cultural knowledge. In N. J. Enfield and S. C. Levenson (Eds.), *Roots of Human Sociality: Culture, Cognition, and Human Interaction* (pp. 229–255). Oxford, UK: Berg.

Gianino, A., and Tronick, E. (1988). The mutual regulation model: The infant's self and interactive regulation coping and defense. In T. Field, P. McCabe, and N. Schneiderman (Eds.), *Stress and Coping* (pp. 47–68). Hillsdale, NJ: Lawrence Erlbaum.

Gingrich, B., Liu, Y., Cascio, C., Wang, Z., and Insel, T. R. (2000). Dopamine D2 receptors in the nucleus accumbens are important for social attachment in female prairie voles (*Microtus ochrogaster*). *Behavioral Neuroscience, 114*(1), 173–183.

Goffman, E. (1978/1984). Response cries. *Language, 54*(4), 787–815.

Gomez, G., and Gerken, L. (1999). Artificial grammar learning by 1-year-olds leads to specific and abstract knowledge. *Cognition, 70,* 109–135.

Goodwin, C. (1979). The interactive construction of a sentence in natural conversation. In G. Psathas (Ed.), *Everyday Language: Studies in Ethnomethodology* (pp. 97–121). New York: Irvington.

Goodwin, C. (1980). Restarts, pauses, and the achievement of a state of mutual gaze at turn-beginning. *Sociological Inquiry, 50*(3/4), 277–302.

Goodwin, C. (1986). Audience, diversity, participation and interpretation. *Text, 6*(3), 283–316.

Goodwin, C. (1996). Transparent vision. In E. Ochs, E. A. Schegloff, and S. A. Thompson (Eds.), *Interaction and Grammar* (pp. 370–404). Cambridge: Cambridge University Press.

Goodwin, C. (2000a). Action and embodiment within situated human interaction. *Journal of Pragmatics, 32,* 1489–1522.

Goodwin, C. (2000b). Practices of seeing: Visual analysis: An ethnomethodological approach. In T. van Leeuwen and C. Jewitt (Eds.). *Handbook of Visual Analysis* (pp. 157–182). London: Sage.

Goodwin, C. (2003a). The body in action. In J. Coupland and R. Gwyn (Eds.), *Discourse, the Body, and Identity* (pp. 19–42). New York: Palgrave Macmillan.

Goodwin, C. (Ed.). (2003b). *Conversation and Brain Damage.* London: Oxford University Press.

Goodwin, C., Goodwin, M. H., and Olsher, D. (2002). Producing sense with nonsense syllables: Turn and sequence in conversations with a man with severe aphasia. In C. E. Ford, B. Fox, and S. A. Thompson (Eds.), *The Language of Turn and Sequence* (pp. 56–80). Oxford: Oxford University Press.

Goren, C., Sarty, M., and Wu, P. (1975). Visual following and pattern discrimination of face-like stimuli by newborn infants. *Pediatrics, 56,* 544–549.

Greenfield, P. M. (1991). Language, tools and brain: The ontogeny and phylogeny of hierarchically organized sequential behavior. *Behavioral and Brain Sciences, 14*(4), 531–551.

Greenfield, P. M. (2006). Implications of mirror neurons for the ontogeny and phylogeny of cultural processes: The examples of tools and language. In M. A. Arbib (Ed.), *Action to Language via the Mirror Neuron System* (pp. 501–532). Cambridge: Cambridge University Press.

Greenfield, P. M., Maynard, A. E., Boehm, C., and Yut Schmidtling, E. (2000). Cultural apprenticeship and cultural change: Tool learning and imitation in chimpanzees and humans. In S. T. Parker, J. Langer, and M. L. McKinney (Eds.), *Biology, Brains, and Behavior: The Evolution of Human Development* (pp. 237–277). Santa Fe, NM: SAR Press.

Greenfield, P., and Savage-Rumbaugh, S. (1990). Grammatical combination in Pan paniscus: Process of learning and invention in the evolution and development of language. In S. Parker and K. Gibson (Eds.), *Language and Intelligence in Monkeys and Apes: Comparative Development Perspectives* (pp. 540–578). Cambridge: Cambridge University Press.

Greenough, M. T., and Volkmar, F. R. (1973). Pattern of dendritic branching in occipital cortex of rats reared in complex environments. *Experimental Neurobiology, 40*, 491–504.

Greenough, M. T., Whiters, G. S., and Wallace, C. S. (1990). Morphological changes in the nervous system arising from behavioral experience: What is the evidence that they are involved in learning and memory? In L. R. Squire and E. Lindenlaub (Eds.), *The Biology of Memory: Symposia Medica Hoechst 23* (pp. 159–185). Stuttgart and New York: Schattauder Verlag.

Greenspan, S. I., and Shanker, S. (2004). *The First Idea: How Symbols, Language, and Intelligence Evolved from Our Primate Ancestors to Modern Humans.* Cambridge, MA: Da Capo Press.

Grice, H. P. (1975). Logic and conversation. In P. Cole and L. L. Morgan (Eds.), *Syntax and Semantics, Vol. 3: Speech Acts* (pp. 41–58). New York: Academic Press.

Grimshaw, J. (1993). *Semantic Structure and Semantic Content.* New Brunswick, NJ: Rutgers University Press.

Groenewegen, H., Mulder, A. B., Beijer, A. V. J., Wright, C. I., Lopes da Silva, F., and Pennartz, C. M. A. (1999). Hippocampal and amygdaloid interactions in the nucleus accumbens. *Psychobiology, 27*(2), 149–164.

Groenewegen, H., Wright, C., Beijer, A., and Voorn, P. (1999). Convergence and segregation of ventral striatal inputs and outputs. In J. F. McGinty (Ed.), Advancing from the ventral striatum to the extended amygdale. *Annals of the New York Academy of Sciences, 877*, 49–63.

Gropen, J. (2000). Methods for studying the production of argument structure in children and adults. In L. Menn and N. B. Ratner (Eds.), *Methods for Studying Language Production* (pp. 95–114). Mahwah, NJ: Lawrence Erlbaum.

Guasti, M. T. (2002). *Language Acquisition: The Growth of Grammar.* Cambridge, MA: MIT Press.

Guiora, A. Z., Beit-Hallahmi, B., Brannon, R. C., Dull, C. T., and Scovel, T. (1972). The effects of experimentally induced changes in ego states on pronunciation ability in a second language: An exploratory study. *Comprehensive Psychiatry, 13*(5), 421–428.

Hadjikhani, N., Joseph, R., Snyder, J., and Tager-Flusberg, H. (2006). Anatomical differences in the mirror neuron system and social cognition network in autism. *Cerebral Cortex, 16*(9), 1276–1282.

Hale, K., and Keyser, S. J. (2002). *Prolegomenon to a theory of argument structure.* Cambridge, MA: MIT Press.

Halford, S. (1990). The complexity of oral syntax. In B. Halford and H. Pilch (Eds.), *Syntax Gesprochener Sprachen* (pp. 33–43). Tubingen, Germany: Gunter Narr.

Halliday, M. A. K. (1967). *Intonation and Grammar in British English.* The Hague: Mouton.

Halliday, M. A. K. (1973). *Exploration in the Functions of Language.* London: Edward Arnold.

Harlow, H. F. (1958). The nature of love. *American Psychologist, 13,* 573–685.

Harlow, H. F. (1959). *Love in infant monkeys.* San Francisco: W. H. Freeman.

Harlow, H., Dodsworth, R., and Harlow, M. (1965). Total isolation in monkeys. *Proceedings of the National Academy of Sciences, 54,* 90–97.

Harris, C. L., and Bates, E. A. (2002). Clausal backgrounding and pronominal reference: A functionalist approach to c-command. *Language and Cognitive Studies, 17*(3), 237–269.

Haviland, J. B. (1993). Anchoring, iconicity, and orientation in Guugu Yimidhirr pointing gestures. *Journal of Linguistic Anthropology, 3*(1), 3–45.

Hayashi, M. (1999). Where grammar and interaction meet: A study of co-participant completion in Japanese conversation. *Human Studies, 22,* 475–499.

Heimann, M. (1989). Neonatal imitation, gaze aversion, and mother-infant interaction. *Infant Behavior and Development, 12,* 495–505.

Heimann, M. (2002). Notes on individual difference and the assumed elusiveness of neonatal imitation. In A. Meltzoff and W. Prinz (Eds.), *The Imitative Mind: Development, Evolution, and Brain Bases* (pp. 74–84). Cambridge: Cambridge University Press.

Herbert, J. (1993). Peptides in the limbic system: Neurochemical codes for co-ordinated adaptive responses to behavioral and physiological demand. *Progress in Neurobiology, 41*(6), 723–791.

Heritage, J. (1984). A change-of-state token and aspects of its sequential placement. In J. Maxwell Atkinson and J. Heritage (Eds.), *Structures of Social Action* (pp. 299–345). Cambridge: Cambridge University Press.

Hindmarsh, J., and Heath, C. (2003). In J. Coupland and R. Gwyn (Eds.), *Discourse, the Body, and Identity* (pp. 43–69). New York: Palgrave Macmillan.

Hoey, M. (2004). Lexical priming and the properties of text. In L. Harmann, J. Morley, and A. Partington (Eds.), *Corpora and Discourse* (pp. 385–412). Bern: Peter Lang.

Hoffmeyer, J. (1996). *Signs of Meaning in the Universe.* Bloomington: Indiana University Press.

Hohne, E., and Jusczyk, P. (1994). Two-month-old infants' sensitivity to allophonic differences. *Perception and Psychophysics, 56,* 613–623.

Holland, J. H. (1975). *Adaptation in Natural and Artificial Systems.* Ann Arbor: University of Michigan Press.

Holland, J. H. (1995). *Hidden Order: How Adaptation Builds Complexity.* Cambridge, MA: Perseus Books.

Hollander, E., Bartz, J., Chaplin, W., Phillips, J., Soorya, L., Anagnostou, E., and Wasserman, S. (2006). Oxytocin increases retention of social cognition in autism. *Biological Psychiatry, 61*(4), 498–503.

Hollander, E., Novotny, S., Hanratty, M., Yaffe, R., DeCaria, C. M., Aronowitz, B. R., and Mosovich, S. (2003). Oxytocin infusion reduces repetitive behaviors in adults with autistic and Asperger's disorders. *Neuropsychopharmacology, 28,* 193–198.

Hopper, P. J. (1987). Emergent grammar. *Berkeley Linguistic Society, 13,* 139–157.

Hopper, P. J. (1988). Emergent grammar and the a priori grammar postulate. In D. Tannen (Ed.), *Linguistics in Context* (pp. 117–134). Norwood, NJ: Ablex.

Hopper, P. J. (1998). Emergent grammar. In M. Tomasello (Ed.), *The New Psychology of Language: Cognitive and Functional Approaches to Language Structure* (pp. 155–175). Mahwah, NJ: Lawrence Erlbaum.

Hopper, P. J., and Traugott, E. C. (1993). *Grammaticalization*. Cambridge: Cambridge University Press.

Hopper, R. (1999). Going public about social interaction. *Research on Language and Social Interaction, 32*(1/2), 77–84.

Houser, M., Chomsky, N., and Fitch, T. (2002). The language faculty: What is it, who has it, and how did it evolve? *Science, 298*, 1569–1579.

Huttenlocher, P. R. (1979). Synaptic density in human frontal cortex: Developmental changes and effects of aging. *Brain Research, 163*(2), 195–205.

Iacoboni, M., Koski, L., Brass, M., Bekkering, H., Woods, R., Dubeau, M., Mazziotta, J., and Rizzolatti, G. (2001). Reafferent copies of imitated actions in the right superior temporal cortex. *Proceedings of the National Academy of Sciences, 98*(24), 13995–13999.

Iacoboni, M., Molnar-Szakacs, I., Gallese, V., Buccino, G., Mazziotta, J. C., and Rizzolatti, G. (2005). Grasping the intentions of others with one's own mirror neuron system. *PLos Biology, 3*(3), 529–535.

Iacoboni, M., Woods, R., Brass, M., Bekkering, H., Mazziotta, J., and Rizzolatti, G. (1999). Cortical mechanisms of human imitation. *Science, 286*, 2526–2528.

Insel, T. R. (1997). A neurobiological basis of social attachment. *American Journal of Psychiatry, 154*(6), 726–733.

Insel, T. R., and Shapiro, L. E. (1992). Oxytocin receptor distribution reflects social organization in monogamous and polygamous voles. *Proceedings of the National Academy of Sciences USA, 89*, 5981–5985.

Insel, T. R., and Winslow, J. T. (1998). Serotonin and neuropeptides in affiliative behaviors. *Biological Psychiatry, 44*, 207–219.

Itoh, K., and Izumi, A. (2005). Affiliative bonding as a dynamical process: A view from ethology. *Behavioral and Brain Sciences, 28*(3), 355–356.

Izard, C. (1978). Emotions and motivations: An evolutionary-developmental perspective. In H. Howe (Ed.), *Nebraska Symposium of Motivation, Vol. 26* (pp. 163–199). Lincoln: University of Nebraska Press.

Jackendoff, R. (1990). *Semantic Structures*. Cambridge, MA: MIT Press.

Jackendoff, R., and Pinker, S. (2005). The nature of language faculty and its implications for evolution of language (reply to Fitch, Houser, and Chomsky). *Cognition, 97*, 211–225.

Jaffe, J., Beebe, B., Feldstein, S., Crown, C., and Jasnow, M. (2001). *Rhythms of Dialogue in Infancy: Coordinated Timing in Development, Vol. 66*. Boston: Blackwell.

Janssen, T. (2007). A speaker/hearer-based grammar: The case of possessives and compounds. In M. Hannay and G. J. Steen (Eds.), *Structural-Functional Studies in English Grammar: In Honour of Lachlan Mackenzie* (pp. 353–387). Amsterdam: Benjamins.

Janus, C., Koperwas, J. S., Janus, M., and Roder, J. (1995). Rearing environment and radial maze exploration in mice. *Behavioural Processes, 34*, 129–140.

Jefferson, G. (1973). A case of precision timing in ordinary conversation: Overlapped tag-positioned address terms in closing sequences. *Semiotica, 9*, 47–96.

Jefferson, G. (1974). Error correction as an interactional resource. *Language Socialization, 2*, 181–199.

Jefferson, G. (1983). Notes on some orderliness of overlap onset. *Tilburg Papers in Language and Literacy, 28*, 1–28.

Jefferson, G. (1985). An exercise in the transcription and analysis of laughter. In T. A. van Dijk (Ed.), *Handbook of Discourse Analysis, Vol. 3* (pp. 25–34). London: Academic Press.

Jefferson, G. (1996). On the poetics of ordinary talk. *Text and Performance Quarterly, 16*(1), 1–61.

Joaquin, A. (2005). How we do dialogic interaction: Some possible biological and ontogenetic precursors for resonance. Unpublished master's thesis, University of California, Los Angeles.

Johnson, E., and Jusczyk, P. (2001). Word segmentation by 8-month-olds: When speech cues count more than statistics. *Journal of Memory and Language, 44*, 548–567.

Johnson, J. S., and Newport, E. L. (1989). Critical period effects in second language learning: The influence of maturational state on the acquisition of English as a second language. *Cognitive Psychology, 21*, 60–99.

Johnson, M., Dziurawiec, S., Ellis, H., and Morton, J. (1991). Newborn's preferential tracking of face-like stimuli and its subsequent decline. *Cognition, 40*, 1–19.

Johnson, S. (2001). *Emergence*. New York: Scribner.

Jones, N. E. (2006). The use of deictic and cohesive markers in narratives by children with Williams syndrome. Unpublished doctoral dissertation, University of California, Los Angeles.

Jones, S. (1996). Imitation or exploration? Young infants' matching of adults' oral gestures. *Child Development, 67*, 1952–1969.

Jurmain, R., Nelson, H., Kilgore, L., and Trevathan, W. (2000). *Introduction to Physical Anthropology*, 8th ed. Belmont, CA: Wadsworth/Thomson Learning.

Jusczyk, P. (1997). *The Discovery of Spoken Language*. Cambridge, MA: MIT Press.

Jusczyk, P. (2001). Learning a language: What infants know about it, and what we don't know about that. In E. Dupoux (Ed.), *Language, Brain, and Cognitive Development: Essays in Honor of Jacques Mehler*. Cambridge, MA: MIT Press.

Kalin, N. H., Shelton, S. E., and Lynn, D. E. (1995). Opiate systems in mother and infant primates coordinate intimate contact during reunion. *Psychoneuroendocrinology, 20*, 735–742.

Kalivas, P. (1995). Interactions between dopamine and excitatory amino acids in behavioral sensitization to psychostimulants. *Drug and Alcohol Dependence, 37*, 95–100.

Kalivas, P. W., and Stewart, J. (1991). Dopamine transmission in the initiation and expression of drug- and stress-induced sensitization of motor activity. *Brain Research Reviews, 16*(3), 223–244.

Karmiloff-Smith, A., Tyler, L., Voice, K., Sims, K., Udwin, O., Howlin, P., and Davies, M. (1998). Linguistic dissociations in Williams syndrome: Evaluating receptive syntax in on-line and off-line tasks. *Neuropsychologia, 36*(4), 343–351.

Karp, H. (2004). The "fourth trimester": A framework and strategy for understanding and resolving colic. *Contemporary Pediatrics, 21*(2), 94–114.

Kawamura, S. (1959). The process of sub-culture propagation among Japanese macaques. *Primates, 2*, 43–60.

Kegl, J. A., Senghas, A., and Coppola, M. (1999). Creation through contact: Sign language emergence and sign language change in Nicaragua. In M. DeGraff (Ed.), *Language Creation and Language Change: Creolization, Diachrony, and Development*. Cambridge, MA: MIT Press.

Kelso, J. A. S. (1995). *Dynamic Patterns: The Self-organization of Brain and Behavior*. Cambridge, MA: MIT Press.

Kempermann, G., Kuhn, H. G., and Gage, F. H. (1997). More hippocampal neurons in adult mice living in an enriched environment. *Nature, 386*, 493–495.

Kendon, A. (1970). Movement coordination in social interaction: Some examples described. *Acta Psychologica, 32*, 100–125.

Kendrick, K. M., Da Costa, A. P. A., Broad, K. D., Ohkura, S., Guevara, R., Levy, F., et al. (1997). Neural control of maternal behaviour and olfactory recognition of offspring. *Brain Research Bulletin, 44*(4), 383–395.

Kendrick, K. M., Levy, F. and Keverne, E. B. (1992). Changes in the sensory processing of olfactory signals induced by birth in sheep. *Science, 256*, 833–836.

Keverne, E. B. (1996). Psychopharmacology of maternal behaviour. *Journal of Psychopharmacology, 10*(1), 16–22.

Keysers, C., Kohler, E., Umilta, M. A., Nanetti, L., Fogassi, L., and Gallese, V. (2003). Audiovisual mirror neurons and action recognition. *Experimental Brain Research, 153*(4), 628–636.

Kinney, H. C., Brody, B. A., Kloman, A. S., and Gilles, F. H. (1988). Sequence of central nervous system myelination in human infancy, II: Patterns of myelination in autopsied infants. *Journal of Neuropathology and Experimental Neurology 47*(3), 217–234.

Kirby, S. (1998). Fitness and the selective adaptation of language. In J. R. Hurford, M. Studdert-Kennedy, and C. Knight (Eds.), *Approaches to the Evolution of Language* (pp. 359–383). Cambridge: Cambridge University Press.

Kita, S. (Ed.). (2003). *Pointing: Where Language, Culture and Cognition Meet.* Hillsdale, NJ: Lawrence Erlbaum.

Knowlton, B. J., Mangels, J. A., and Squire, L. R. (1996). A neostriatal habit learning system in humans. *Science, 273*, 1399–1402.

Koepke, J., Hamm, M., Legerstee, M., and Russell, M. (1983). Neonatal imitation: Two failures to replicate. *Infant Behavior and Development, 6*, 97–102.

Kohler, E., Keysers, C., Umilta, M. A., Fogassi, L., Gallese, V., and Rizzolatti, G. (2002). Hearing sounds, understanding actions: Action representation in mirror neurons. *Science, 297*, 846–848.

Koob, G. (1992). Drugs of abuse: Anatomy, pharmacology, and function of reward pathways. *Trends in Pharmacological Science, 13*, 177–198.

Krause, M., and Penke, M. (2004). Regular and irregular inflectional morphology in German Williams syndrome. In S. Bartke and J. Siegmüller (Eds.), *Williams Syndrome across Languages* (pp. 245–270). Philadelphia: John Benjamins.

Kugiumutzakis, G. (1998). Neonatal imitation in the intersubjective companion space. In S. Braten (Ed.), *Intersubjective Communication and Emotion in Early Ontogeny* (pp. 63–88). Cambridge: Cambridge University Press.

Kugiumutzakis, G. (1999). Genesis and development of early infant mimesis to facial and vocal models. In G. B. J. Nadel (Ed.), *Imitation in Infancy* (pp. 36–59), Cambridge: Cambridge University Press.

Kuhl, P. (2000). A new view of language acquisition. *Proceedings of the National Academy of Sciences, 97*(22), 11850–11857.

Kuhl, P. (2004). Early language acquisition: Cracking the speech code. *Nature, 5*, 831–843.

Kuhl, P., Andruski, J., Chistovich, I., Chistovich, L., Kozhevnikova, E., Ryskina, V., Stolyarova, E., Sundberg, U., and Lacerda, F. (1997). Cross-language analysis of phonetic units in language addressed to infants. *Science, 277*, 684–686.

Kuhl, P., and Miller, J. (1978). Speech perception by the chinchilla: Identification functions for synthetic VOT stimuli. *Journal of the Acoustical Society of America, 63*(3), 905–917.

Ladefoged, P., and Broadbent, D. (1960). Perception of sequence in auditory events. *Quarterly Journal of Experimental Psychology, 12*, 162–170.

Langacker, R. W. (1977). Syntactic reanalysis. In C. N. Li (Ed.), *Mechanisms of Syntactic Change* (pp. 57–139). Austin, TX, and London: University of Austin Press.

Langacker, R. W. (1987). *Foundations in Cognitive Grammar, Vol. 1: Theoretical Prerequisites.* Stanford, CA: Stanford University Press.

Langacker, R. W. (1991). *Foundations in Cognitive Grammar, Vol. 2: Descriptive Application.* Stanford, CA: Stanford University Press.

Langacker, R. W. (2002). *Concept, Image and Symbol: The Cognitive Basis of Grammar.* Berlin: Mouton de Gruyter.

Langellier, K. M., and Peterson, E. E. (2004). *Storytelling in Daily Life: Performing Narrative.* Philadelphia: Temple University Press.

Larsen-Freeman, D. (1997). Chaos/complexity science and second language acquisition. *Applied Linguistics, 18*(2), 141–165.

Le Doux, J. E. (1986). The neurobiology of emotion. In J. E. Le Doux and W. Hirst (Eds.), *Mind and Brain: Dialogues in Cognitive Neuroscience* (pp. 301–354). New York: Cambridge University Press.

Lee, N. (2003). Emergence of language as complex adaptive systems. Unpublished doctoral dissertation, University of California, Los Angeles.

Lee, N., and Schumann, J. H. (2005). The interactional instinct: The evolution and acquisition of language. Paper presented at the Congress of the International Association for Applied Linguistics, Madison, WI.

Leechman, D., and Hall, R. A. (1980). American Indian pidgin English: Attestations and grammatical peculiarities. In J. Dillard (Ed.), *Perspectives on American English.* The Hague: Mouton de Gruyter.

Legerstee, M. (1991). The role of person and object in eliciting early imitation. *Journal of Experimental Child Psychology, 51*, 424–433.

Legerstee, M., Pomerleau, A., Malcuir, G., and Feider, H. (1987). The development of infants' responses to people and a doll: Implications for research in communication. *Infant Behavior and Development, 10*, 81–95.

Lenneberg, E. H. (1967). *Biological Foundations of Language.* New York: Wiley.

Lerner, G. H. (1996). On the "semi-permeable" character of grammatical units in conversation: Conditional entry into the turn space of another speaker. In E. Ochs, E. A. Schegloff, and S. A. Thompson (Eds.), *Interaction and Grammar* (pp. 238–276). Cambridge: Cambridge University Press.

Lerner, G. H. (2002). Turn-sharing: The choral co-production of talk in interaction. In C. Ford, B. A. Fox, and S. A. Thompson (Eds.), *The Language of Turn in Sequence* (pp. 225–256). Oxford: Oxford University Press.

Lester, B., Hoffman, J., and Brazelton, B. (1985). The rhythmic structure of mother-infant interaction in term and preterm infants. *Child Development, 56*(1), 15–27.

Levinson, S. (2006). Cognition at the heart of human interaction. *Discourse Studies, 8*(1), 85–93.

Levy, F., Kendrick, K., Keverne, E., Piketty, V. and Poindron, P. (1992). Intracerebral oxytocin is important for the onset of maternal behavior in inexperienced ewes delivered under peridural anesthesia. *Behavioral Neuroscience, 106*, 427–432.

Lewica, M., and Haviland, J. (1983). Ten-week-old infants' reactions to mother's emotional expressions. Paper presented at the biennial meeting of the Society for Research in Child Development, Detroit.

Lewis, M., and Freedle, R. O. (1972). Mother-infant dyad: The cradle of meaning. Paper presented at the Symposium on Language and Thought: Communication and Affect, March, Erindale College, University of Toronto.

Li, S., Cullen, W. K., Anwyl, R., and Rowan, M. J. (2003). Dopamine-dependent facilitation of LTP induction in hippocampal CA1 by exposure to spatial novelty. *Nature Neuroscience, 6*, 526–531.

Liberman, A. M., and Mattingly, I. G. (1985). The motor theory of speech perception revised. *Cognition, 21*, 1–36.

Lieberman, P. (2000). *Human Language and Our Reptilian Brain.* Cambridge, MA: Harvard University Press.

Lightfoot, D. (1989). The child's trigger experience. *Behavioral and Brain Sciences, 12*, 321–375.

Liu, H., Kuhl, P., and Tsao, F. (2003). An association between mother's speech clarity and infants' speech discrimination skills. *Developmental Science, 6*(3), F1–F10.

Locke, J. H. (1998). Social sound making as precursor of spoken language. In J. A. Hurford, M. Studdert-Kennedy, and C. Knight (Eds.), *Approaches to the Evolution of Language* (pp. 190–201). Cambridge, MA: Cambridge University Press.

Locke, J. L. (1986). The linguistics significance of babbling. In B. Lindblom and R. Zetterstrom (Eds.), *Precursors of Early Speech* (pp. 143–162). Stockholm: M. Stockton Press.

Locke, J. L., and Bogin, B. (2006). Language and life history: A new perspective on the development and evolution of human language. *Behavioral and Brain Sciences, 29*(3), 259–280.

Louilot, A., LeMoal, M., and Simon, H. (1986). Differential reactivity of dopaminergic neurons in the nucleus accumbens in response to different behavioral situations. An in vivo voltammetric study in free moving rats. *Brain Research, 397*, 395–400.

Luciana, M. (2001). Dopamine-opiate modulations of reward seeking behavior: Implications for the functional assessment of prefrontal development. In C. A. Nelson and M. Luciana (Eds.), *Handbook of Developmental Cognitive Neuroscience* (pp. 647–662). Cambridge, MA: MIT Press.

MacFarlane, A. (1975). Olfaction in the development of social preferences in the human neonate. In R. Porter and M. O'Connor (Eds.), *Parent-Infant Interaction* (pp. 103–117). Amsterdam: Elsevier.

MacIntyre, P. D., Dornyei, A., Clement, R., and Noels, K. A. (1998). Conceptualizing willingness to communicate in L2: A situation model of L2 confidence and affiliation. *Modern Language Journal, 82*(4), 545–562.

MacNeilage, P. F., and Davis, B. L. (2000). Evolution of speech: The relation between ontogeny and phylogeny. In C. Knight, M. Studdert-Kennedy, and J. R. Hurford (Eds.), *The Evolutionary Emergence of Language* (pp. 146–160). Cambridge: Cambridge University Press.

Maestripieri, D., Ross, S., and Megna, N. (2002). Mother-infant interactions in Western lowland gorillas (*Gorilla gorilla* gorilla): Spatial relationships, communication, and opportunities for social learning. *Journal of Comparative Psychology, 116*(3), 219–227.

Makin, J., and Porter, R. (1989). Attractiveness of lactating females' breast odors to neonates. *Child Development, 60*(4), 803–810.

Malatesta, C., and Izard, C. E. (1984). The ontogenesis of human social signals: From biological imperative to symbol utilization. In N. Fox and R. J. Davidson (Eds.), *The Psychobiology of Affective Development* (pp. 161–206). Hillsdale, NJ: Lawrence Erlbaum.

Malenka, R., and Nicoll, R. (1999). Long-term potentiation: A decade of progress? *Science, 285,* 1870–1874.

Malinowski, R. (1923). The problem of meaning in primitive languages. In C. K. Ogden and I. A. Richards (Eds.), *The Meaning of Meaning.* London: Routledge and Kegan Paul.

Maratos, O. (1973). The origin and development of imitation in early infancy. Unpublished doctoral dissertation, Geneva University, Geneva.

Marcus, G., Vijaya, S., Bandi Rao, S., and Vishton, P. M. (1999). Rule learning by seven-month-old-infants. *Science, 283,* 77–80.

Maurer, D. (1985). Infants' perception of facedness. In T. Field and N. Fox (Eds.), *Social Perception in Infancy* (pp. 73–100). Norwood, NJ: Ablex.

Maurer, D., and Barrera, M. (1981). Infants' perception of natural and distorted arrangements of a schematic face. *Child Development, 52,* 196–202.

McCarthy, M. (1998). *Spoken Language and Applied Linguistics.* Cambridge: Cambridge University Press.

McDougall, W. (1908). *An Introduction to Social Psychology.* London: Methuen.

McIntosh, D., Reichmann-Decker, A., Winkielman, P., and Wilbarger, J. (2006). When the social mirror breaks: Deficits in automatic, but not voluntary, mimicry of emotional facial expressions in autism. *Developmental Science, 9*(3), 295–302.

McKenzie, B., and Over, R. (1983). Young infants fail to imitate facial and manual gestures. *Infant Behavior and Development, 6,* 85–95.

McWhorter, J. (2001). *The Power of Babel: A Natural History of Language.* New York: Times Books.

Mehler, J., and Christophe, A. (1995). Maturation and learning of language in the first year of life. In M. S. Gazzaniga (Ed.), *The Cognitive Neurosciences: A Handbook for the Field* (pp. 943–954). Cambridge, MA: MIT Press.

Mehler, J., Jusczyk, P., Lambertz, G., Halsted, N., Bertoncini, J., and Amiel-Tison, C. (1988). A precursor of language acquisition in young infants. *Cognition, 29,* 143–178.

Meltzoff, A. (1998). Infant intersubjectivity: Broadening the dialogue to include imitation, identity and intention. In S. Braten (Ed.), *Intersubjective Communication and Emotion in Early Ontogeny* (pp. 47–62). Cambridge: Cambridge University Press.

Meltzoff, A., and Moore, K. (1977). Imitation of facial and manual gestures by human neonates. *Science, 198,* 75–78.

Meltzoff, A., and Moore, K. (1983). Newborn infants imitate adult facial gestures. *Child Development, 54,* 702–709.

Meltzoff, A., and Moore, K. (1989). Imitation in newborn infants: Exploring the range of gestures imitated and the underlying mechanisms. *Developmental Psychology, 25*(6), 954–962.

Meltzoff, A., and Moore, K. (1992). Early imitation within a functional framework: The importance of person identity, movement, and development. *Infant Behavior and Development, 15,* 479–505.

Meltzoff, A., and Moore, K. (1994). Imitation, memory, and the representation of persons. *Infant Behavior and Development, 17,* 83–99.

Meltzoff, A., and Moore, K. (1997). Explaining facial imitation: A theoretical model. *Early Development and Parenting, 6*, 179–192.

Meyer-Lindenberg, A., Mervis, C. B., and Berman, F. B. (2006). Neural mechanisms in Williams syndrome: A unique window to genetic influences on cognition and behavior. *Nature Reviews Neuroscience, 7*, 380–393.

Mikesell, L. (2004a). Examining argument structure in conversation: A matter of indexical grounding. Unpublished master's thesis, University of California, Los Angeles.

Mikesell, L. (2004b). The indexical nature of argument structure: Its implications for what evolved. Paper presented at Language Learning Roundtable, November, Language Evolution: What Evolved? University of California, Los Angeles.

Mikesell, L. (2005). Opposing forces of reported speech employed to accomplish a unitary goal. Unpublished manuscript, University of California, Los Angeles.

Miller, J. (2000). *The Mating Mind.* New York: Doubleday.

Miller, J. (2002). Questions about constructions. *Journal of Child Language, 29*, 470–474.

Miller, J., and Weinert, R. (1998). *Spontaneous Spoken Language: Syntax and Discourse.* Oxford, UK: Clarendon Press.

Modahl, C., Green, L., Fein, D., Morris, M., Waterhouse, L., Feinstein, C., and Levin, H. (1998). Plasma oxytocin levels in autistic children. *Biological Psychiatry, 43*(4), 270–277.

Moon, C., Cooper, R. P., and Fifer, W. P. (1993). Two-day-olds prefer their native language. *Infant Behavior and Development, 16*, 495–500.

Morgensen, J. (1991). Influences of the rearing conditions on functional properties of the rats prefrontal system. *Behavioral Brain Research, 42*, 135–142.

Morse, P. (1972). The discrimination of speech and nonspeech stimuli in early speech. *Experimental Child Psychology, 13*, 477–492.

Mottonen, R., Jarvelainen, J., Sams, M., and Hari, R. (2004). Viewing speech modulates activity in the left SI mouth cortex. *NeuroImage, 24*, 731–737.

Moynihan, M. (1970). The control, suppression, decay, disappearance and replacement of displays. *Journal of Theoretical Biology, 29*, 85–112.

Mrzljak, L., Uylings, H. B. M., Van Eden, C. G., and Judas, M. (1990). Neuronal development n human prefrontal cortex in prenatal and postnatal stages. *Progress in Brain Research, 85*, 185–222.

Mufwene, S. S. (2001). *The Ecology of Language Evolution.* Cambridge: Cambridge University Press.

Muhlhausler, P. (1986). *Pidgin and Creole Linguistics.* Oxford, UK: Blackwell.

Muhlhausler, P. (1997). *Pidgin and Creole Linguistics.* London: University of Westminster Press.

Murray, L., and Trevarthen, C. (1985). Emotional regulations of interactions between two-month-olds and their mothers. In N. F. Tiffany Field (Ed.), *Social Perception in Infants* (pp. 101–125). Norwood, NJ: Ablex.

Myowa-Yamakoshi, M., Tomonaga, M., Tanaka, M., and Matsuzawa, T. (2004). Imitation in neonatal chimpanzees (Pan troglodytes). *Developmental Science, 7*(4), 437–442.

Nadel, J., Guerini, C., Peze, A., and Rivet, C. (1999). The evolving nature of imitation as a format for communication. In J. Nadel and G. Butterworth (Eds.), *Imitation in Infancy* (pp. 209–234). Cambridge: Cambridge University Press.

Nadel, J., Prepin, K., and Okanda, M. (2005). Experiencing contingency and agency: First step toward self-understanding in making a mind? *Interaction Studies, 6*(3), 447–462.

Napoli, D. J. (1996). *Linguistics.* Oxford: Oxford University Press.

Nazzi, T., Bertoncini, J., and Mehler, J. (1998). Language discrimination by newborns: Toward an understanding of the role of rhythm. *Journal of Perception and Performance, 24*(3), 756–766.

Newmeyer, F. J. (2003). Grammar is grammar and usage is usage. *Language, 79*(4), 682–707.

Nishitani, N., and Hari, R. (2000). Temporal dynamics of cortical representation for action. Paper presented at the Proceedings of the National Academy of Sciences.

Oberman, L., Hubbard, E., McCleery, J., Altschuler, E., Ramachandran, V., and Pineda, J. (2005). EEG evidence for mirror neuron dysfunction in autism spectrum disorders. *Cognitive Brain Research, 24*, 190–198.

Ochs, E., and Schieffelin, B. B. (1986). Language acquisition and socialization: Three developmental stories and their implications. In R. Shweder and R. Levine (Eds.), *Culture Theory: Essays on Mind, Self and Emotion* (pp. 276–320). New York: Cambridge University Press.

O'Grady, W. (2005). *Syntactic Carpentry: An Emergentist Approach to Syntax.* Mahwah, NJ: Lawrence Erlbaum.

Ong, W. J. (2002). *Orality and Literacy.* New York: Routledge.

Ortony, A., Clore, G. L., and Collins, A. (1988). *The Cognitive Structure of Emotions.* New York: Cambridge University Press.

Ostrowski, N. L. (1998). Oxytocin receptor mRNA expression in rat brain: Implications for behavioral integration and reproductive success. *Psychoneuroendocrinology, 23*(8), 989–1004.

Pagel, M. (2000). The history, rate and pattern of world linguistic evolution. In C. Knight, M. Studert-Kennedy, and J. Hurford (Eds.), *The Evolutionary Emergence of Language* (pp. 391–416). New York: Cambridge University Press.

Papousek, H., and Papousek, M. (1987). Intuitive parenting: A didactic counterpart to the infant's precocity in integrative capacities. In J. Osofsky (Ed.), *Handbook of Infant Development, Vol. 2* (pp. 669–720). New York: John Wiley.

Pawlby, S. (1977). Imitative interaction. In H. R. Schaffer (Ed.), *Studies in Mother-Infant Interaction* (pp. 203–226). London: Academic Press.

Pessiglione, M., Seymour, B., Flandin, G., Dolan, R., and Frith, C. D. (2006). Dopamine-dependent prediction errors underpin reward-seeking behavior in humans. *Nature, 442*, 1042–1045.

Pike, K. L. (1945). *The Intonation of American English.* Ann Arbor: University of Michigan Press.

Pinker, S. (1994). *The Language Instinct.* New York: Morrow.

Pinker, S. (1999). The language mavens. In R. S. Wheeler (Ed.), *The Working of Language: From Prescriptions to Perspectives* (pp. 3–14). Westport, CT: Praeger.

Pinker, S. (2000). *The Language Instinct: How the Mind Creates Language.* New York: Perennial Classics.

Pinker, S. (2002). "Words and rules": An exchange. *New York Review of Books,* June 27.

Pinker, S., and Jackendoff, R. (2005). The faculty of language: What's special about it? *Cognition, 95*, 201–236.

Pintar, J. E., and Scott, R. E. M. (1993). Ontogeny of mammalian opioid systems. In A. Herz (Ed.), *Opioids I: Handbook of Experimental Pharmacology, Vol. 104* (pp. 711–727). New York: Springer-Verlag.

Plooij, F. (1984). *The Behavioral Development of Free Living Chimpanzee Babies and Infants.* Norwood, NJ: Ablex.

Poldrack, R. A., Clark, J., Pare-Blagoev, E. J., Shohamy, D., Creso Moyano, J., Myers, C., and Gluck, M. A. (2001). Interactive memory systems in the human brain. *Nature, 414,* 546–550.

Poldrack, R., and Packard, M. G. (2003). Competition among multiple memory systems: Converging evidence from animal and human brain studies. *Neuropsychologia, 41,* 245–251.

Pomerantz, A. (1984). In J. M. Atkinson and J. Heritage (Eds.), *Structures of Social Action* (pp. 57–101). New York: Cambridge University Press.

Popik, P., and Van Ree, J. M. (1992). Long term facilitation of social recognition in rats by vasopressin related peptides: A structure-activity study. *Life Sciences, 50,* 567–572.

Porges, S. W. (2001). The polyvagal theory: Phylogenetic substrates of a social nervous system. *International Journal of Psychophysiology, 42*(2), 123–146.

Porges, S. W. (2003). Social engagement and attachment: A phylogenetic perspective. *Annals of the New York Academy of Science, 1008,* 31–47.

Prigogine, I. (1988). Origins of complexity. In A. C. Fabian (Ed.), *Origins: The Darwin College Lectures* (pp. 69–88). Cambridge: Cambridge University Press.

Pulvermuller, F. (2002). *The Neuroscience of Language: On Brain Circuits of Words and Serial Order.* Cambridge: Cambridge University Press.

Ramus, F. (2001). Perception of linguistic rhythms by newborn infants. Unpublished manuscript, Laboratoire de Sciences Cognitives et Psycholinguistique (EHESS/CNRS), Paris, France.

Ramus, F. (2002). Language discrimination by newborns. *Annual Review of Language Acquisition, 2,* 85–115.

Ramus, F., Hauser, M., Miller, C., Morris, D., and Mehler, J. (2000). Language discrimination by human newborns and by cotton-top tamarin monkeys. *Science, 288,* 349–351.

Redgrave, R., Prescott, T. J., and Gurney, K. (1999). Is the short-latency dopamine response too short to signal reward error? *Trends in Neuroscience, 22*(4), 146–151.

Reid, W., Otheguy, R., and Stern, N. (Eds.). (2002). *Signal, Meaning, and Message: Perspectives on Sign-Based Linguistics.* Amsterdam: John Benjamins.

Reissland, N. (1988). Neonatal imitation in the first hour of life: Observations in rural Nepal. *Developmental Psychology, 24*(4), 464–469.

Rijt-Plooij, H. V. D., and Plooij, F. X. (1987). Growing independence, conflict, and learning in mother-infant relations in free-ranging chimpanzees. *Behavior, 101,* 191–221.

Rizzolatti, G. (2005). The mirror neuron system and imitation. In S. Hurley and N. Chater (Eds.), *Perspectives on Imitation from Neuroscience to Social Science.* Cambridge, MA: MIT Press.

Rizzolatti, G., and Craighero, L. (2004). The mirror neuron system. *Annual Review of Neuroscience, 27,* 167–192.

Robins, R. H. (1971). Malinowski, Firth, and the "context of situation." In E. Ardener (Ed.), *Social Anthropology and Language* (pp. 33–46). London: Tavistock.

Rockman, M. V., Hahn, M. W., Soranzo, N., Zimprich, F., Goldstein, D. B., and Wray, G. A. (2005). Ancient and recent positive selection transformed opioid cis regulation in humans. *PLos Biology, 3,* 2208–2219.

Romaine, S. (1988). *Pidgin and Creole Languages.* London: Longman.

Romaine, S. (1992). The evolution of linguistic complexity in pidgin and creole languages. In J. A. Hawkins and M. Gell-Mann (Eds.), *The Evolution of Human Languages.* Redwood City, CA: Addison-Wesley.

Rosenzweig, M. R., Bennett, E. L., and Diamond, M. C. (1972). Cerebral effects of differential experience in hypophysectomized rats. *Journal of Comparative and Physiological Psychology, 79*, 56–66.

Ross-Hagebaum, S., and Koops, C. (2006). Structural integration and discourse function of English WH-clefts. Paper presented at the Penn Linguistics Colloquium, February, Philadelphia.

Sacks, H. (1972). An initial investigation of the usability of conversational data for doing sociology. In D. N. Sudnow (Ed.), *Studies in Social Interaction* (pp. 31–74). New York: Free Press.

Sacks, H., and Schegloff, E. A. (1979). Two preferences in the organization of reference to persons in conversation and their interaction. In G. Psathas (Ed.), *Everyday Language: Studies in Ethnomethodology* (pp. 15–21). New York: Irvington.

Sacks, H., Schegloff, E. A., and Jefferson, G. (1974). A simplest systematics for the organization of turn-taking for conversation. *Language, 50*(4), 696–735.

Saffran, J. (2001). Words in a sea of sounds: The output of infant statistical learning. *Cognition, 81*, 149–169.

Saffran, J., Aslin, R., and Newport, E. (1996). Statistical learning by 8-month-old infants. *Science, 274*, 1926–1928.

Saffran, J., and Thiessen, E. (2003). Pattern induction by infant language learners. *Developmental Psychology, 39*(3), 484–494.

Sampson, G. (1997). *Educating Eve: The Language Instinct Debate*. London: Cassell Wellington House.

Sampson, G. (2005). *The "Language Instinct" Debate*. New York: Continuum.

Santi, A., Servos, P., Vatikiotis-Bateson, E., Kuratate, T., and Munhall, K. (2003). Perceiving biological motion: Dissociating visible speech from walking. *Journal of Cognitive Neuroscience, 15*(6), 800–809.

Sarnat, H. B. (2003). Function of the corticospinal and corticobulbar tracts in the human newborn. *Journal of Pediatric Neurology, 1*(1), 3–8.

Savage-Rumbaugh, E., Rumbaugh, D. M., and Boysen, S. T. (1978). Symbolic communication between two chimpanzees (Pan troglodytes). *Science, 201*, 641–644.

Schachter, J. (1988). Second language acquisition and its relationship to universal grammar. *Applied Linguistics, 9*, 219–235.

Schegloff, E. A. (1979). The relevance of repair to syntax for conversation. In T. Givon (Ed.), *Syntax and Semantics, Vol. 12: Discourse and Syntax* (pp. 261–286). New York: Academic Press.

Schegloff, E. A. (1982). Discourse as an interactional achievement: Some uses of "uh huh" and other things that come between sentences. In D. Tannen (Ed.), *Analyzing Discourse: Text and Talk* (pp. 71–93). Washington, DC: Georgetown University Press.

Schegloff, E. A. (1987). Recycled turn beginnings: A precise repair mechanism in conversation's turn-taking organisation. In G. Button and J. R. E. Lee (Eds.), *Talk and Social Organization* (pp. 70–85). Clevedon, UK: Multilingual Matters.

Schegloff, E. A. (1992). Repair after next turn: The last structurally provided defense of intersubjectivity in conversation. *American Journal of Sociology, 97*(5), 1295–1345.

Schegloff, E. A. (1996a). Issues of relevance for discourse analysis: Contingency in action, interaction and co-participant context. In E. H. Hovy and D. R. Scott (Eds.), *Computational and Conversational Discourse: Burning Issues—An Interdisciplinary Account* (pp. 3–35). Berlin: Springer-Verlag.

Schegloff, E. A. (1996b). Some practices for referring to persons in talk-in-interaction: A partial sketch of a systematics. In B. A. Fox (Ed.), *Studies in Anaphora* (pp. 437–485). Amsterdam: John Benjamins.

Schegloff, E. A. (1996c). Turn organization: One intersection of grammar and interaction. In E. Ochs, E. A. Schegloff, and S. A. Thompson (Eds.), *Interaction and Grammar* (pp. 52–133). Cambridge: Cambridge University Press.

Schegloff, E. A. (1997). Practices and actions: Boundary cases of other-initiated repair. *Discourse Processes, 23*, 499–545.

Schegloff, E. A. (1998). Body torque. *Social Research, 65*(3), 535–596.

Schegloff, E. A. (2000a). On turns possible completion, more or less: Increments and trail-offs. Paper presented at the EuroConference on Interactional Linguistics, Spa, Belgium.

Schegloff, E. A. (2000b). Overlapping talk and the organization of turn-taking for conversation. *Language in Society, 29*, 1–63.

Schegloff, E. A. (2002). Overwrought sentences: "Complex sentences" in a different sense. In J. L. Bybee and M. Noonan (Eds.), *Complex Sentences in Grammar and Discourse: Essays in Honor of Sandra A. Thompson* (pp. 322–336). Amsterdam: John Benjamins.

Schegloff, E. A. (2007). *Sequence Organization in Interaction: A Primer in Conversation Analysis, Vol. 1.* Cambridge: Cambridge University Press.

Scherer, K. R. (1984). Emotion as a multi-component process: A model and some cross-cultural data. In P. Shaver (Ed.), *Review of Personality and Social Psychology: Vol. 5. Emotions, Relationships and Health* (pp. 37–63). Beverly Hills, CA: Sage.

Scherer, K. R. (1988). Criteria for emotion-antecedent appraisal: A review. In V. Hamilton, G. H. Bower, and N. H. Frijda (Eds.), *Cognitive Perspectives on Emotion and Motivation* (pp. 89–126). Dordrecht, Netherlands: Kluwer.

Schober, M. F., and Clark, H. H. (1989). Understanding by addressees and overhearers. *Cognitive Psychology, 21*, 211–232.

Schore, A. N. (1994). *Affect Regulation and the Origin of the Self: The Neurobiology of Emotional Development.* Hillsdale, NJ: Lawrence Erlbaum.

Schore, A. (2000). Healthy childhood and the development of the human brain. Paper presented at Healthy Children for the 21st Century, University of California at Los Angeles School of Medicine.

Schultz, W. (1997). Dopamine neurons and their role in reward mechanisms. *Current Opinion in Neurobiology, 7*, 191–197.

Schultz, W. (2001). Reward signaling by dopamine neurons. *Neuroscientist, 7*(4), 293–302.

Schultz, W. (2002). Getting formal with dopamine and reward. *Neuron, 36,* 241–263.

Schultz, W., Dayan, P., and Montague, P. R. (1997). A neural substrate of prediction and reward. *Science, 275*(5306), 1593.

Schultz, W., Romo, R., Ljungberg, T., Mirenowicz, J., Hollerman, J. R., and Dickenson, A. (1995). Reward related signals carried by dopamine neurons. In J. C. Houk, J. L. Davis, and D. G. Beiser (Eds.), *Models of Information Processing in the Basal Ganglia* (pp. 233–248). Cambridge, MA: MIT Press.

Schumann, J. H. (1976). Second language acquisition: The pidginization hypothesis. *Language Learning, 26*(2), 391–408.

Schumann, J. H. (1978). The acculturation model for second language acquisition. In R. C. Gingras (Ed.), *Second Language Acquisition and Foreign Language Learning* (pp. 27–50). Washington, DC: Center for Applied Linguistics.

Schumann, J. H. (1997). *The Neurobiology of Affect in Language.* Malden, MA: Blackwell.

Schumann, J. H. (2001). Learning as foraging. In Z. Dornyei and R. Schmidt (Eds.), *Motivation and Second Language Acquisition* (pp.21–28). Honolulu: University of Hawai'i Second Language Teaching and Curriculum Center.

Schumann, J. H. (2004). The neurobiology of aptitude. In J. H. Schumann et al., *The Neurobiology of Learning: Perspectives from Second Language Acquisition* (pp. 6–22). Mahwah, NJ: Lawrence Erlbaum.

Schumann, J. H., Crowell, S. E., Jones, N. E., Lee, N., Schuchert, S. A., and Wood, L. A. (2004). *The Neurobiology of Learning: Perspectives from Second Language Acquisition.* Mahwah, NJ: Lawrence Erlbaum.

Schumann, J. H., Favareau, D., Goodwin, C., Lee, N., Mikesell, L., Tao, H., Veronique, D., and Wray, A. (2006). Language evolution: What evolved? *Marges Linguistiques, 11*, 167–199.

Schumann, J. H., and Wood, L.A. (2004). The neurobiology of motivation. In J. H. Schumann et al., *The Neurobiology of Learning: Perspectives from Second Language Acquisition* (pp. 23–42). Mahwah, NJ: Lawrence Erlbaum.

Searle, J. (1972). A special supplement: Chomsky's revolution in linguistics. *New York Review of Books*, June 29.

Searle, J. (2002). End of the revolution. *New York Review of Books,* February 28.

Sebba, M. (1997). *Contact Languages: Pidgins and Creoles.* New York: St. Martin's Press.

Seeman, P., Bzowej, N. H., Guan, H. C., Bergeron, C., Becker, L. E., Reynolds, G. P., Bird, E. D., Riederer, P., Jellinger, K., Watanabe, S., and Tourtellowe, W. W. (1987). Human brain dopamine receptors in children and aging adults. *Synapse, 1*, 399–404.

Senghas, A. (1995a). Children's contribution to the birth of Nicaraguan Sign Language. Unpublished doctoral dissertation, MIT, Cambridge, MA.

Senghas, A. (1995b). Conventionalization in the first generation: A community acquires a language. *Journal of Contemporary Legal Issues, 6*, 501–519.

Senghas, A. (1995c). The development of Nicaraguan Sign Language via the language acquisition process. *Proceedings of the Boston University Conference on Language Development, 19*, 543–552.

Senghas, A. (2000). The development of early spatial morphology in Nicaraguan Sign Language. *Proceedings of the Boston University Conference on Language Development, 24*, 696–707.

Senghas, A., and Coppola, M. (2001). Children creating language: How Nicaraguan Sign Language acquired a spatial grammar. *Psychological Science, 12*(4), 323–328.

Senghas, A., Coppola, M., Newport, E. L., and Supalla, T. (1997). Argument structure in Nicaraguan Sign Language: The emergence of grammatical devices. *Proceedings of the Boston University Conference on Language Development, 21*, 550–561.

Sherman, S. M., and Spear, P. D. (1982). Organization of visual pathways in normal and visually deprived cats. *Physiological Review, 62*, 738–855.

Shohamy, D., Myers, C. E., Grossman, S., Sage, J., Gluck, M., and Poldrack, R. A. (2004). Cortico-striatal contributions to feedback-based learning: converging data from neuroimaging and neuropsychology. *Brain, 127*(4), 851–859.

Smith, N. (1999). *Chomsky: Ideas and Ideals.* Cambridge: Cambridge University Press.

Spanagel, R., and Weiss, F. (1999). The dopamine hypothesis of reward: Past and current status. *Trends in Neurosciences, 22*(11), 521–527.

Spitz, R. A. (1949). The role of ecological factors in emotional development in infancy. *Child Development, 20*(3), 145–155.

Steels, L. (1998). Synthesizing the origins of language and meaning using coevolution, self-organization and level formation. In J. R. Hurford, M. Studdert-Kennedy, and C. Knight (Eds.), *Approaches to the Evolution of Language* (pp. 384–404). Cambridge: Cambridge University Press.

Steiner, J. (1979). Human facial expressions in response to taste and smell stimulation. In H. Reese and L. P. Lipsitt (Eds.), *Advances in Child Development and Behavior, Vol. 13* (pp. 257–295). New York: Academic Press.

Stephens, D. W., and Krebs, J. R. (1986). *Foraging Theory.* Princeton, NJ: Princeton University Press.

Stern, D. (2002). *The First Relationship.* Cambridge, MA: Harvard University Press.

Stevenson, M., Ver Hoeve, J., Roach, M., and Leavitt, L. (1986). The beginning of conversation: Early patterns of mother-infant vocal responsiveness. *Infant Behavior and Development, 9,* 423–440.

Sundara, M., Namasivayam, A. K., and Chen, R. (2001). Observation-execution matching system for speech: A magnetic stimulation study. *NeuroReport, 12,* 1341–1344.

Swainson, R., Rogers, R. D., Sahakian, B. J., Summers, B. A., Polkey, C. E., and Robbins, T. W. (2000). Probabilistic learning and reversal deficits in patients with Parkinson's disease of frontal or temporal lobe lesions: Possible adverse effects of dopaminergic medication. *Neuropsychologia, 38,* 596–612.

Talmy, L. (2000). *Toward a Cognitive Semantics.* Cambridge, MA: MIT Press.

Tanaka, Y., and Arayama, T. (1969). Fetal responses to acoustic stimuli. *Practica Oto-Rhino-Laryngologica, 31,* 269–273.

Tannen, D. (Ed.). (1982). *Spoken and Written Language: Exploring Orality and Literacy.* Norwood, NJ: Ablex.

Tao, H. (2001). Discovering the usual with corpora: The case of remember. In R. Simpson and J. Swales (Eds.), *Corpus Linguistics in North America: Selections from the 1999 Symposium* (pp. 116–144). Ann Arbor: University of Michigan Press.

Tao, H. (2003). A usage-based approach to argument structure: "Remember" and "forget" in spoken English. *International Journal of Corpus Linguistics, 8*(1), 75–95.

Tao, H. (2007). A corpus-based investigation of *absolutely* and related phenomena in spoken English. *Journal of English Linguistics, 35*(1), 5–29.

Tao, H., and McCarthy, M. J. (2001). Understanding non-restrictive *which*-clauses in spoken English, which is not an easy thing. *Language Sciences, 23,* 651–677.

Tao, H., and Meyer, C. F. (2006). Gapped coordinations in English: Form, usage, and implications for linguistics theory. *Corpus Linguistics and Linguistic Theory, 2*(2), 129–163.

Tarone, E., and Bigelow, M. (2005). Impact of literacy on oral language processing: Implications for second language acquisition research. *Annual Review of Applied Linguistics, 25,* 77–97.

Teicher, M. H., Andersen, S. L., and Hostetter, J. C., Jr. (1995). Evidence for dopamine receptor pruning between adolescence and adulthood in striatum but not nucleus accumbens. *Brain Research, 89,* 167–172.

Tettamanti, M., Buccino, G., Saccuman, M. C., Gallese, V., Danna, M., Scifo, P., Fazio, F., Rizzolatti, G., Cappa, S., and Perani, D. (2005). Listening to action-related sentences activates fronto-parietal motor circuits. *Journal of Cognitive Neuroscience, 17,* 273–281.

Thomason, S. G., and Kaufman, T. (1988). *Language Contact, Creolization, and Genetic Linguistics.* Berkeley: University of California Press.

Thompson, R., Gupta, S., Miller, K., Mills, S., and Orr, S. (2004). The effects of vasopressin in human facial responses related to social communication. *Psychoneuroendocrinology, 29*, 35–48.

Thompson, S. A. (2002). "Object complements" and conversation: Towards a realistic account. *Studies in Language, 26*(1), 125–164.

Thompson, S. A., and Hopper, P. J. (2001). Transitivity, clause structure, and argument structure: Evidence from conversation. In J. Bybee and P. J. Hopper (Eds.), *Frequency and the Emergence of Linguistic Structure* (pp. 27–60). Amsterdam: John Benjamins.

Tomasello, M. (1999). *The Cultural Origins of Human Cognition.* Cambridge, MA: Harvard University Press.

Tomasello, M. (2002). The emergence of grammar in early child language. In T. Givon and B. F. Malle (Eds.), *The Evolution of Language out of Pre-language* (pp. 309–328). Amsterdam: John Benjamins.

Tomasello, M. (2003). *Constructing a Language: A Usage-Based Theory of Language Acquisition.* Cambridge, MA: Harvard University Press.

Tomasello, M., Call, J., and Hare, B. (1998). Five primate species follow the visual gaze of conspecifics. *Animal Behavior, 55*(4), 1063–1069.

Tomasello, M., Carpenter, M., Call, J., Behne, T., and Moll, H. (2005). Understanding and sharing intention: The origins of cultural cognition. *Behavioral and Brain Sciences, 28*, 675–691.

Tomasello, M., and Kruger, A. C. (1992). Joint attention on actions: Acquiring verbs in ostensive and non-ostensive contexts. *Journal of Child Language, 19*(2), 311–333.

Tomizawa, K., Iga, N., Lu, Y.-F., Moriwaki, A., Matsushita, M., Li, S.-T., Miyamoto, O., Itano, T., and Matsui, H. (2003). Oxytocin improves long-lasting spatial memory during motherhood through MAP kinase cascade. *Nature Neuroscience, 6*, 384–390.

Traugott, E. C. (2008). Grammaticalization, constructions and the incremental development of language: Suggestions from the development of degree modifiers in English. In R. Eckardt, G. Jaeger, and T. Veenstra (Eds.), *Variation, Selection, Development— Probing the Evolutionary Model of Language Change* (pp. 219–250). Berlin/New York: Mouton de Gruyter.

Trehub, S. (1973). Infants' sensitivity to vowel and tonal contrasts. *Developmental Psychology, 9*, 91–96.

Trehub, S., Trainor, L. J., and Unyk, A. M. (1993). Music and speech processing in the first year of life. *Advances in Child Development and Behaviour, 24*, 1–35.

Trevarthen, C. (1974). Conversations with a two-month-old. *New Scientist, 62*, 230–235.

Trevarthen, C. (1977). Descriptive analyses of infant communicative behavior. In H. R. Schaffer (Ed.), *Studies in Mother-Infant Interaction* (pp. 227–270). London: Academic Press.

Trevarthen, C. (1979). Communication and cooperation in early infancy: A description of primary intersubjectivity. In M. M. Bulowa (Ed.), *Before Speech: The Beginning of Interpersonal Communication* (pp. 321–347). New York: Cambridge University Press.

Tronick, E. (1989). Emotions and emotional communication in infants. *American Psychologist, 44*(2), 112–119.

Tronick, E., Als, H., and Adamson, L. (1979). Structure of early face-to-face communicative interactions. In M. Bullowa (Ed.), *Before Speech* (pp. 349–370). Cambridge: Cambridge University Press.

Tronick, E., Als, H., Adamson, L., Wise, S., and Brazelton, T. B. (1978). The infant's response to entrapment between contradictory messages in face-to-face interaction. *Journal of Child Psychiatry, 17*, 1–13.

Tsao, F., Liu, H., and Kuhl, P. (2004). Speech perception in infancy predicts language development in the second year of life: A longitudinal study. *Child Development, 75*(4), 1067–1084.

Ullstadius, E. (1998). Neonatal imitation in a mother-infant setting. *Early Development and Parenting, 7*, 1–8.

Umilta, M. A., Kohler, E., Gallese, V., Fogassi, L., Fadiga, L., Keysers, C., and Rizzolatti, G. (2001). "I know what you are doing": A neurophysiological study. *Neuron, 32*, 91–101.

Uylings, H. B., Kuypers, K., Diamond, M. C., and Veltman, W. A. (1978). Effects of differential environments on plasticity of dendrites of cortical pyramidal neurons in adult rats. *Experimental Neurology, 62*, 658–677.

Van Rees, S., and de Leeuw, R. (1987). *Born Too Early: The Kangaroo Method with Premature Babies.* Video. Stiching Lichaamstaal, Scheyvenhofweg 12, 6093, PR Heythuysen, The Netherlands.

Vinter, A. (1986). The role of movement in eliciting early imitations. *Child Development, 57*, 66–71.

Wainwright, P. E., Levesque, S., Krempulec, L., Bulman-Fleming, B., and McCutcheon, D. (1993). Effects of environmental enrichment on cortical depth and Morris-maze performance in B6D2F2 mice exposed prenatally to ethanol. *Neurotoxicology and Teratology, 15*, 11–20.

Waldrop, M. M. (1992). *Complexity.* New York: Touchstone.

Waterhouse, L., Fein, D., and Modahl, C. (1996). Neurofunctional mechanisms in autism. *Psychological Review, 103*(3), 457–489.

Watkins, K. E., Strafella, A. P., and Paus, T. (2002). Seeing and hearing speech excites the motor system involved in speech production. *Neuropsychologia, 41*, 989–994.

Weber, B., and Deacon, T. (2000). Thermodynamic cycles, developmental systems, and emergence. *Cybernetics and Human Knowing, 7*, 21–43.

Weisel, T. (1982). Postnatal development of the visual cortex and the influence of the environment. *Nature, 299*, 583–592.

White, L. (1987). Markedness and second language acquisition: The question of transfer. *Studies in Second Language Acquisition, 9*, 261–285.

Wicker, B., Keysers, C., Plailly, J., Royer, J., Gallese, V., and Rizzolatti, G. (2003). Both of us disgusted in My Insula: The common neural basis of seeing and feeling disgust. *Neuron, 40*, 655–664.

Williams, J., Waiter, G., Gilchrist, A., Perrett, D., Murray, A., and Whiten, A. (2006). Neural mechanisms of imitation and "mirror neuron" functioning in autism spectrum disorder. *Neuropsychologia, 44*, 610–621.

Wilson, S., Saygun, A. P., Sereno, M. I., and Iacoboni, M. (2004). Listening to speech activates motor areas involved in speech production. *Nature Neuroscience, 7*, 701–702.

Wise, R. A., and Rompre, P. P. (1989). Brain dopamine and reward. *Annual Review of Psychology, 40*, 191–225.

Witelson, S. F., Kigar, D. L., and Harvey, T. (1999). The exceptional brain of Albert Einstein. *Lancet, 353*, 2149–2153.

Wong, A. Y.-L. (2005). Searching for the neurobiology of language: An examination of the neuronal constructs of Calvin, Fuster, and Pulvermuller. Unpublished master's thesis, University of California, Los Angeles.

Wurm, S. A. (1977). The nature of New Guinea pidgin. In S. A. Wurm (Ed.), *New Guinea Areas Languages and Language Study, Vol. 3: Pacific Linguistics*, Series C, no. 40. Canberra: Australian National University, Research School of Pacific Studies.

Young, L. J., Nilsen, R., Waymire, K., MacGregor, G., and Insel, T. R. (1999). Increased affiliative response to vasopressin in mice expressing the V1a receptor from a monogamous vole. *Nature, 400*, 766–768.

Index

acculturation model, second-language
  acquisition, 170–172
acquisition. *See also* language
  acquisition; primary-language
  acquisition (PLA); second-language
  acquisition (SLA)
  interactional instinct, 5–7,
    108, 167
  language, 3, 108–109
  language, by autistics, 145–146
  second-language, 9–10
adrenocorticotropic hormone (ACTH),
  141–142
affiliation
  affiliative-memory system, 159, 160
  appetitive rewards, 155, 156, 159
  basolateral amygdala, 159, 161
  beginning at birth, 154–155
  beta-endorphins, 156
  consummatory rewards, 155,
    156, 159
  dopamine, 157–159
  extended amygdala, 159, 161
  infant-mother behaviors, 155
  motivation for interaction, 129–131
  neurobiology, 155–165
  neuropeptides, 163–164
  opiate system, 155–156, 157
  rewards, 156–165

  role in primary-language acquisition,
    167–170
age factor, Nicaraguan sign language, 42
aggregation, complex adaptive system
  (CAS), 19–21, 52–53
agreements per verb, Nicaraguan sign
  language, 40–41
allophones, infants, 132
alpha rhythm, mirror neurons, 135
amygdala
  basolateral and extended, 159, 160, 161
  mirror-neuron network, 141–142
  stimulus appraisal, 174–175
animals, interactional instinct, 192
ant colonies
  complex adaptive systems, 4
  queen ant, 22
anthropological veto, interactional
  instinct, 190–191
appetitive rewards, behaviors, 155, 156,
  159
appraisal system
  human brain, 5, 6
  neural mechanism, 7
  value, 129
arguments per verb, Nicaraguan sign
  language, 40
argument structure, conversation,
  89–94, 96

Aspects of the Theory of Syntax, 11
attachment
    affiliative relationships, 9
    infants, 124–126
    motivation for interaction, 129–131
attention, selective, of infants, 112–113,
    115
attitude, second-language acquisition,
    170, 171
autism
    causes, 144
    language acquisition, 145–146
    mirror neurons, 144–145
    symptoms, 143–144
autistics, interactional instinct in,
    143–146
autonomous grammar
    mental retardation, 188–190
    Williams syndrome, 187–188

basolateral amygdala, affiliation, 159,
    160, 161
Batali's simulation, language
    emergence, 30–31
bed nucleus of stria terminalis (BNST),
    neurobiology, 156, 157, 159
behavior-bond feedback loop, language
    acquisition, 167, 168
behaviors
    emotional perception and expression,
        122–124
    gesture imitation, 117, 118
    human specificity, 124–126
    imitation, 116–120
    infant-initiatedness, 120–122
    interpersonal organization,
        128–129
    neonatal imitation, 116, 117
    organization of interpersonal
        interaction, 126–128
    premature baby imitation, 119
    still-face response pattern, 122, 123
Bernard convection, 15
beta-endorphins
    intimate contact, 130
    neurobiology, 156
beta rhythm, mirror neurons, 135
biological adaptations
    adult and infant prespeech, 112, 114

facial expressions, 111–112
gestures, 111–112, 113
interactions, 109–110
selective attention, 112–113, 115
sensory abilities, 110–111
vocalizations, 111–112
biological basis, language, 55–58
bioprogram, 46
body proper, stimulus appraisal,
    175–176
bonding, neuropeptides, 130–131
bottom-up
    indirect control and emergence, 25–26
    local interactions, pattern match, and,
        control, 50–52
brain stem, body proper via, and
    hypothalamus, 175–176
building blocks, multistrata of, 21

caregivers. *See also* infant-caregiver
        interaction
    instinct, 133–134
chaos
    classical dynamics and new science,
        16–17
    discovery of, 12–17
    end of determinism, 12–13
    nonlinearity, 16
    pattern emergence, 13–16
children
    language learning, 7–8
    Williams syndrome, 187–188
chimpanzees
    communication, 146–147
    divergence of hominid and, 20
    emotional expressions, 147–148
    interaction and pattern-finding, 148
"Chomsky's Revolution," innatism, 11
circular causality, feedback and, 26–27
classical dynamics
    assumptions, 12
    and new science, 16–17
clauses, conversation, 94–96
Clausius, entropy, 13
climax, story telling, 84–85
coactive episodes, mother-infant
        interaction, 127
cognitive developments, primary-
        language acquisition, 168–169

cognitive grammar (CG), linguistics, 56–57n.2
cohesiveness, second-language acquisition, 170, 171
Columbia school (CS), linguistics, 56–57n.2
communication
    infant gestures in, 112, 113
    interaction, 97–98
    language acquisition, 3
    mother-infant interaction, 126–128
    neuropeptides, 130–131
    vasopressin and social, 144
communicative intention reading, primary-language acquisition, 168–169
competence
    sentence, 63
    speakers of language, 101–105
complements, object, in conversation, 86–89
complement-taking predicates (CTPs), 87–89
complex adaptive systems (CASs)
    aggregation, 19–21, 52–53
    bottom-up and indirect control, 25–26
    CASs and emergentism, 17–28, 29
    feedback and circular causality, 26–27
    flow, 24–25
    internal model and pattern match, 23–24
    language, 4
    language as, 8
    local and random interactions, 21–23
    local interactions, pattern match, and bottom-up control, 50–52
    lock-in, 27–28
    multistrata of building blocks, 21, 53–54
    tagging, 23
    term, 17–18
    theory, 8
complexity theory
    complex adaptive systems, 4
    origin of grammar, 12
computer networks, learning, 47
constituency, conversational analysis, 76–79
constructions

gapping, in writing, 60
    pseudo-cleft, 79–81
    sentences, 60, 98
    two-part, 74–76
consummatory rewards, behaviors, 155, 156, 159
context
    role in language, 65–67
    sentences, 66
continuers, two-part construction, 79
conversation
    argument and clause structures in, 89–94
    complement-taking predicates (CTPs), 87–89
    context in, 66
    habitat for language, 57
    language form, 58
    object complements in, 86–89
    relative clauses in, 94–96
conversation analysis (CA)
    anticipatory completion, 74–76
    contribution to linguistic notions, 76–79
    grammar of verbs, 81–85
    motivation of word selection, 81–85
    pitch, 72–73
    pseudo-cleft constructions, 79–81
    research area, 68–69
    turn-constructional unit (TCU), 70–74
    two-part constructions, 74–76
    understanding grammar in wild, 69–85, 85–86
coping potential, stimulus appraisal, 173
cortical development, infants, 151–152
corticospinal system, infants, 154
creativity, language, 81n.32
creoles. See also language emergence; pidgins
    aggregation, 52–53
    emergence, 32
    predictability, 49–50
    process of creolization, 37
    rise among adults, 37–38
    term, 36, 37
cultural artifact, language as, 4–5
cultural shock, second-language acquisition, 171, 172

dendritic arborization, infants, 151–152
determinism, end of, 12–13
deterministic predictability, versus stochastic, 49–54
developmental psychologists, interaction of infants, 109
discourse analysts
    examining language in natural habitat, 97–100
    participation framework, 81–85
    theory of action, 100
discovery of chaos, end of determinism, 12–13
disfluencies, linguistics, 101–104
dopamine (DA)
    DA-glutamate interactions, 162
    genetic variation, 179
    intimate contact, 130
    neurobiology of affiliation, 157–160, 162–163
    ontogenetic changes, 181–185
    stimulus appraisal, 178

ego permeability, second-language acquisition, 171, 172
emergence. See also language emergence
    Nicaraguan sign language, 38–42
emergentism
    complex adaptive systems and, 17–28
    phenomenon example, 18
emotional perception
    infant's sensitivity, 122–124
    interpersonal organization, 128–129
emotions, understanding and perceiving, 140–142
enclosure, second-language acquisition, 170, 171
entropy, measure of disorder, 13
equilibrium state, chaos and patterns, 14
evolution, understanding language, 55–57, 60, 105–107
experience-dependent variation, language learning, 179–180
expressions
    emotional perception of infants, 122–124
    infant-caregiver, 133–134
    nonhuman primates, 147–148

extended amygdala, affiliation, 159, 160, 161
eye gaze, interaction, 99

faces, infant response, 126
face-to-face discourse
    interaction, 65
    repetition, 98
facial expressions
    infant-caregiver, 133
    infants, 111–112
    infants imitating, 117, 118
    mother-infant interaction, 128
feedback
    behavior-bond, loop, 167, 168
    positive, in language behavior, 26–27
flow, network of, to complex adaptive system, 24–25
French, development from Latin, 53

gapping constructions, writing, 60
gaze, infant-caregiver, 133–134
generative linguistics, assumption, 46–47
genetic assimilation, language, 4–5
genetics, universal grammar (UG), 3
genetic variation, behavior, 179
gestures, infants, 111–112, 113
goal significance, stimulus appraisal, 173
gonadal steroids, role in behaviors, 162–163
grammar. See also universal grammar (UG)
    anticipatory completion, 74–76
    argument and clause structures in conversation, 89–94
    CA (conversation analysis), 69–85, 85–86
    competence, 101–105
    complexity theory and origin of, 12
    contribution of CA to understanding constituency, 76–79
    contributions of usage-based approaches, 96–97
    evolutionary or neurobiological terms, 55–58, 105–107
    innatism, 11
    motivation of word selection, 81–85

object complements in conversation, 86–89
organization of language, 57–58
orientations of bodies and gestures, 100
patterns, 8–9, 44
pseudo-cleft constructions, 79–81
relative clauses in conversation, 94–96
social nature of, 79–85
structure of language, 68–69
turn-constructional unit (TCU), 70–74
two-part constructions, 74–76
usage-based approaches to understanding, 86–96
verbs, 81–85
grammar pattern, language change, 44
grammaticalization
historical linguistics and, 42–46
tendency of language change, 44–45
grooming method, language as, 20

Hawaiian pidgin, 33–34
high-amplitude sucking technique (HAS), infants, 131
historical linguistics
and grammaticalization, 42–46
predictability, 50
history, Nicaraguan sign language, 39–40
homeostatic value, human brain, 6
hominid communities
linguistic structures, 20
local and random interactions, 22
human brain, functions, 5–6
human cortex, dendritic arborization, 151–152
human evolution, language organization, 20–21
human infants. See also infants
behavior with language, 9
human instinct, language, 63–64
humans
comparisons to nonhuman primates, 148–149
matching patterns, 24
prodynorphin, 192
human specificity
interpersonal organization, 128–129
motivation of instinct, 124–126

hypothalamus, body proper via brain stem and, 175–176

imitation
definition, 116
infant facial, 116, 117
interpersonal organization, 128–129
mirror-neuron network, 137–139
mouth openings and tongue protrusions, 117, 118
neonatal, 117–119
organ identification, 119–120
role-reversal, 169
incorrect usage, language, 63–64
indirect control, principle of emergence, 25–26
infant-caregiver interaction
affiliative behavior, 155, 164–165
biological adaptations, 109–115
comparing infant and adult prespeech, 112, 114
facial expressions, 111–112, 133
gaze, 133–134
gestures, 111–112, 113
selective attention, 112–113, 115
sensory abilities, 110–111
vocalizations, 111–112, 154
infant-directed speech (IDS), 134
infants
affiliation, 154–155
behavior with language, 9
cortical development, 151–152
developmental abilities, 108–109
emotional perception and expression, 122–124
environmental enrichment, 152–153
initiating interaction, 120–122, 128–129
learning strategies, 47, 131–133
mother-infant interaction, 126–128
motivation of interaction, 124–126
organ identification, 119–120
pattern perception, 131–133
pedagogy in human, 191–192
statistical learning, 131–133
sustenance, 153–154
vocalization and contact with mother, 129–130
voluntary control, 154

inflections, Nicaraguan sign language, 40–41
initiation, interpersonal interaction, 120–122, 128–129
innatism, theory, 11
insula, mirror-neuron network, 141–142
intentions, role of mirror neurons in understanding, 135–137
interaction
  basis of using language, 64
  casual conversation or talk–in, 59–60
  communication, 98–99
  face-to-face discourse, 65
  infants initiating, 120–122
  mother-infant, 126–128
  performance errors, 101–104
  resources and constraints, 99–100
  understanding organization, 126–128
interactional instinct
  animals, 192
  anthropological veto, 190–191
  autistics, 143–146
  drive, 108
  language acquisition, 5–7
  neurobiology for, 151
  nonhuman primates, 146–149
  pedagogical stance, 191–192
  social affiliation model, 9
interactions, mother-infant nonhuman primates, 147–148
internal model, pattern match, 23–24
interpersonal communication, language, 64
interpersonal interaction, understanding organization, 126–128

jargon, transition to pidgin, 36
joint attention, primary-language acquisition, 168
journalistic writing, gapping construction, 60

keyboard layout, lock-in principle, 27–28
kinesic patterns, mother-infant interaction, 127
Kirby's simulation, language emergence, 30

language
  audio and visual technology, 8
  as complex adaptive system (CAS), 19n.2
  conversation and writing, 58
  cultural artifact, 4–5
  different kinds of, 61–65
  evolutionary or neurobiological terms, 55–58, 105–107
  grammatical organization, 57–58
  grooming method, 20
  human instinct and incorrect usage, 63–64
  mechanism of, acquisition, 5–7
  natural habitat, 97–100
  nature of human mind, 55
  pattern-finding capacities, 5
  patterns, 8–9
  phenomenon, 31
  role of context, 65–67
  second-language acquisition (SLA), 9–10
  speech and conversation, 57
  syntax, 58–60
language acquisition. See also primary-language acquisition (PLA); second-language acquisition (SLA)
  autistics, 145–146
  interactional instinct, 3, 108–109
  ontogenetic changes, 181–185
  role of affiliation in primary, 167–170
language change
  motivation for, 45–46
  trends, 43–45
language creativity, 81n.32
language emergence. See also creoles; pidgins
  aggregation, 52–53
  Batali's simulation, 30–31
  experiments supporting, 30–31
  historical linguistics and grammaticalization, 42–46
  Kirby's simulation, 30
  local interactions, pattern match, and bottom-up control, 50–52
  motivation for language change, 45–46
  multistrata, 53–54
  Nicaraguan sign language (NSL), 38–42

open systems and far-from-
    equilibrium state, 48–49
pidgins and creoles, 32–38
predictability, 49–54
Steels's robotics, 31
traditional and new interpretations,
    46–54
trends of language change, 43–45
word order in NSL, 41–42
language shock, second-language
    acquisition, 171–172
language use
    interpersonal communication and
        social action, 64–65
    literate individuals, 62–63
Latin, French from, 53
learning, strategies for infants, 47,
    131–133
Lenguaje de Signos Nicaraguense (LSN).
    See also Nicaraguan sign language
    (NSL)
    sign language, 39–40
lexical words, language change, 44
limbic system, mirror-neuron network,
    141–142
linguistic complexity, language change,
    43–45
linguistics
    errors or disfluencies, 101–104
    schools of, 56–57n.2
    universal grammar (UG), 55–56
literature individuals, language use,
    62–63
local interactions
    complex adaptive system and
        emergence, 21–23
    pattern match and bottom-up control,
        50–52
lock-in, complex adaptive system, 27–28

macaque monkey brain, mirror neurons,
    134–135
mechanism
    language acquisition, 5–7
    language learning with maturation,
        7–10
    tagging as CAS mechanism, 23
memory
    affiliative, 160

stimulus appraisal, 176
mental retardation, 188–190
mirror neurons
    amygdala and insula, 141–142
    autistics, 144–145
    humans, 135
    imitation, 137–139
    new class of premotor neurons,
        134–135
    rhythms, 135
    speech perception, 139–140
    stimulus-appraisal system, 141–142
    symbol formation, 142–143
    understanding and perceiving
        emotions, 140–142
    understanding intentions and
        prediction, 135–137
morphology, language change, 43
mothers. See also infant-caregiver
    interaction; infants
    infants initiating interaction, 120–122
    infant vocalization to contact,
        129–130
    mother-infant interaction, 126–128
    nonhuman primates and
        development, 147
    still-face studies, 122–124
motivation
    attachment and affiliation, 129–131
    language change, 45–46
    second-language acquisition, 171, 172
    word selection, 81–85
motor-evoked potentials (MEPs), speech
    perception, 139–140
motor systems, human brain, 5, 6
motor theory, speech perception, 139–140
multiplier effect, network of flows, 25
multistrata, complex adaptive system
    and emergence, 21, 53–54
mu rhythm, mirror neurons, 135
mutual gaze, transactions, 130
myelination, infants, 151–152

natural habitat, language in, 97–100
near-equilibrium state, chaos and
    patterns, 14
need significance, stimulus appraisal, 173
network of flows, complex adaptive
    system, 24–25

neurobiology
    affiliation, 155–165
    appraisal to activity, 178–179
    interactional instinct and language,
        6–7, 8
    neuropeptides, 163–164
    second-language acquisition,
        180–181
    stimulus appraisal, 174–176
    understanding language, 55–57, 60,
        105–107
neurons. *See* mirror neurons
neuropeptides
    neurobiology of affiliation, 163–164
    social bonding and communication,
        130–131
new science, classical dynamics and, 16–17
Newtonian view of world, challenge, 13
Newton's dynamics, end of
        determinism, 12–13
Nicaraguan sign language (NSL)
    age factor, 42
    aggregation, 53
    emergence, 38–42
    history, 39–40
    inflections and agreement per verb,
        40–41
    number of arguments per verb, 40
    studies and findings, 40–42
    word order, 41–42
non-coactive episodes, mother-infant
        interaction, 127
non-equilibrium state
    chaos and patterns, 14
    languages, open systems, and
        far-from-equilibrium, 48–54
nonhuman primates. *See* chimpanzees
    comparison to humans, 148–149
    interactional instinct, 146–149
    prodynorphin, 192
nonlinearity, 16
nonlinguistic resources, language, 100
nonrestrictive relative clauses (NRRC),
        conversation, 94–96
novelty, stimulus appraisal, 173
nucleus accumbens shell (NAS)
    dopamine receptors, 181, 183
    neurobiology, 156, 157, 159, 161–163
    stimulus appraisal, 178

object complements, conversation, 86–89
ontogenetic changes
    dopamine, 181–185
    language learning, 181–185
    opiate level, 185
open systems, complex adaptive
        systems (CAS), 48–54
opiate system
    affiliation, 155–156, 157
    genetic variation, 179
    ontogenetic changes, 185
    oxytocin, 164
oral cultures, natural habitat, 97
oral language, writing versus, 61–62
oral literature, term, 61–62
orbitofrontal cortex, stimulus appraisal,
        175
organ identification, infants, 119–120
oxytocin
    autistic children, 144
    genetic variation, 179
    intimate contact, 130
    neurobiology of affiliation, 163–164
    social bonding and communication,
        130–131

participation frameworks, discourse,
        81–85
pattern emergence, chaos and, 13–16
pattern-finding capacities, language, 5
pattern of integration, second-language
        acquisition, 170–171
pattern perception, learning strategy,
        131–133
patterns
    humans and chimpanzees, 148
    internal model and pattern match, 23–24
    language and grammatical, 8–9
    local interactions, pattern match, and
        bottom-up control, 50–52
pedagogical stance, interactional
        instinct, 191–192
performance
    language, 101–105
    sentence, 63
performance errors, linguistics, 101–104
phonotactics, infants, 132
pidgins. *See also* creoles; language
        emergence

aggregation, 52–53
dynamic changes of, 35–37
emergence, 32
Hawaiian, 33–34
jargon, 36
Lenguaje de Signos Nicaraguense
(LSN), 39
predictability, 49–50
Russenorsk, 32–33
structure, 32–35
term, 35, 37
pitch, conversation analysis, 72–73
pleasantness, stimulus appraisal, 173
positive feedback, and circular
causality, 26–27
predictability, deterministic versus
stochastic, 49–54
prediction, role of mirror neurons in
understanding, 135–137
premotor neurons. See also mirror
neurons
new class in macaque monkey brains,
134–135
prespeech, comparing adults and
infants, 112, 114
Prigogine
chaos and patterns, 14–15
language emergence, 49
primary-language acquisition (PLA). See
also language acquisition; second-
language acquisition (SLA)
behavior-bond feedback loop, 167, 168
cognitive developments, 168–169
communicative intention reading,
168–169
joint attention, 168
role-reversal imitation, 169
sociocognitive development, 169–170
prodynorphin, human and nonhuman
primates, 192
pseudo-cleft constructions, social nature
of grammar, 79–81
psychological integration
second-language acquisition, 171–172
stimulus appraisals underlying
variables, 172–174

quantum mechanics, 13
QWERTY keyboard layout, lock-in
principle, 27–28

random interactions, complex adaptive
system and emergence, 21–23
recycling effect, network of flows, 25
repetition, face-to-face interaction, 98
rewards
affiliative, 155, 156, 159
consummatory, 155, 156, 159
dopamine response, 158
rhythms, mirror neurons, 135
robotics, language emergence, 31
role-reversal imitation, primary-
language acquisition, 169
Russenorsk, pidgin, 32–33

sanitized syntax, context, 67
second-language acquisition (SLA). See
also language acquisition; primary-
language acquisition (PLA)
acculturation model, 170–172
amygdala, 174–175
body proper via brain stem and
hypothalamus, 175–176
coping potential, 173
experience-dependent variation,
179–180
genetic variation, 179
goal/need significance, 173
initiating and reassessing goals in,
176–179
learning as foraging, 176–177
neurobiological account of stimulus
appraisal, 174–176
neurobiology differences, 179–181
neurobiology of appraisal to activity,
178–179
novelty and pleasantness, 173
older learners, 8
orbitofrontal cortex, 175
process, 9–10
role of memory, 176
self/norm compatibility,
173–174
stimulus appraisals underlying
psychological variables, 172–174
variables for psychological
integration, 171–172
variables for social integration,
170–171
second law of thermodynamics, 13,
15–16

selective attention, infants, 112–113, 115
self/norm compatibility, stimulus appraisal, 173–174
self-organization, pattern emergence, 15–16
semiotic fields, understanding and communicating, 98
sensory abilities, infants, 110–111
sensory systems, human brain, 5–6
sentences
  context, 66
  hierarchical structure, 58–59
sex hormones, role in behaviors, 162–163
sign language. *See* Nicaraguan sign language (NSL)
silences, conversation analysis, 73n.25
simulations, language emergence, 30–31
social action, language, 64
social affiliation
  infants, 124–126
  interactional instinct, 9
social bonding, neuropeptides, 130–131
social engagement system, 165
social integration, second-language acquisition, 17–171
sociocognitive development, primary-language development, 169–170
sociostatic value, human brain, 6–7
sounds, language change, 43–44
specificity, human, of infants, 124–126
speech
  habitat for language, 57
  infant-directed, 134
  verbal conversation, 61
speech perception, mirror neurons, 139–140
statistical learning, caregiver-infant, 131–133
Steels's robotics, language emergence, 31
still-face studies, emotional perception of infants, 122–124
stimulus appraisals
  amygdala, 174–175
  body proper via brain stem and hypothalamus, 175–176
  mirror-neuron network, 141–142

neurobiology, 174–176
orbitofrontal cortex, 175
role of memory, 176
second-language acquisition (SLA), 176–177
underlying psychological variables, 172–174
stochastic predictability, deterministic versus, 49–54
story, climax, 84–85
superior temporal sulcus (STS), cortical network for imitation, 138–139
survival, affiliative behavior, 151–155
symbol formation, mirror-neuron network, 142–143
Syntactic Structures, Chomsky, 27
syntax
  formal properties, 58–60, 84
  sanitized, 67

tagging, complex adaptive system (CAS) mechanism, 23
talk-in-interaction
  social life, 105
  term, 65
terminal overlap, conversation analysis, 72–73
thermodynamics, second law of, 13, 15–16
top-down influence, circular causality, 26–27
transcriptions, mothers' response to infants, 129–130
trends, language change, 43–45
turn-constructional unit (TCU), conversation analysis, 70–74
two-part constructions, grammar, 74–76

uncertainty principle, Heisenberg's, 13
unfacelike, infant response, 124–125
universal grammar (UG). *See also* grammar
  acquisition and Williams syndrome, 189–190
  generative linguistics, 3
  innatist idea, 27–28
  theme of linguistic paradigms, 55–56
usage, incorrect, of language, 63–64
usage-based approach to grammar

argument and clause structures in
    conversation, 89–94
complement-taking predicates (CTPs),
    87–89
object complements in conversation,
    86–89
relative clauses in conversation,
    94–96
understanding grammar in wild,
    96–97
usages of words and phrases, language
    change, 44

value types, appraisal system, 129
vasopressin
    genetic variation, 179
    neurobiology of affiliation, 163–164
    social bonding and communication,
        130–131
    social communication, 144
ventral tegmental area (VTA)
    dopamine projections from,
        181–182

neurobiology of affiliation, 158–160,
    162–163
stimulus appraisal, 178
verbs, grammar, 81–85
vocalizations
    infant, for contact with mother,
        129–130
    infants, 111–112, 154
    mother-infant interaction, 128
voice-onset time (VOT), infants, 131
voluntary control, infants, 154

Williams syndrome, 187–188
word order, Nicaraguan sign language,
    41–42
word searches, pseudo-cleft
    constructions, 80–81
word selection, social nature of
    grammar, 81–85
writing
    gapping constructions, 60
    language form, 58
    oral language versus, 61–62